THE WRIGHT BROTHERS

A Biography by
Fred C. Kelly

DOVER PUBLICATIONS, INC.
New York

Published in Canada by General Publishing Company, Ltd., 30 Lesmill
Road, Don Mills, Toronto, Ontario.
Published in the United Kingdom by Constable and Company, Ltd., 10
Orange Street, London WC2H 7EG.

This Dover edition, first published in 1989, is an unabridged, unaltered
republication of the work first published by Harcourt, Brace and
Company, New York, 1943, under the title *The Wright Brothers: A Biography
Authorized by Orville Wright.*

Manufactured in the United States of America
Dover Publications, Inc., 31 East 2nd Street, Mineola, N.Y. 11501

Library of Congress Cataloging-in-Publication Data

Kelly, Fred C. (Fred Charters), 1882–1959.
    The Wright brothers : a biography / by Fred C. Kelly. — Dover ed.
        p.   cm.
    Reprint. Originally published: New York : Harcourt, Brace, c1943.
    Includes index.
    ISBN 0-486-26056-9
    1. Wright, Orville, 1871–1948. 2. Wright, Wilbur,   1867–1912.
3. Aeronautics—United States—Biography. I. Title.
TL540.W7K4 1989
629.13′0092—dc20
    [B]   89-7757
                                                                          CIP

TO

The Brave Flyers of the United Nations
Fighting All over the World for Humanity
and Decency Against the Forces of Barbarism,

This Book Is Dedicated

AUTHOR'S PREFACE

THE aim in this book has been to satisfy the curiosity of the average, non-technical reader regarding the work of the Wright Brothers, and to do so as simply as possible. No attempt has been made to go into minute technical details. Nor does the book cover the scientific researches and numerous inventions by Orville Wright since the death of his brother.

To give credit to everyone who has been gracious with help in the preparation of what I have written would require so long a list, with risk of names being unintentionally omitted, that I shall not attempt it.

But one name naturally and obviously comes first and foremost—that of Orville Wright himself. He has read my manuscript and given generously of his time in verifying the accuracy of various statements and in correcting inaccuracies which otherwise would have appeared.

Next in importance to that of Orville Wright has been the help received from his secretary, Miss Mabel Beck, whose memory and knowledge of Mr. Wright's voluminous files enabled her quickly to produce documentary evidence to make certain of accuracy.

FRED C. KELLY

Peninsula, Ohio

CONTENTS

Author's Preface   vii
Prologue   3
I. BOYHOOD   5
II. BACKGROUND   19
III. PRINTING—AND BICYCLES   29
IV. FIRST THOUGHTS OF FLIGHT   45
V. GLIDING AT KITTY HAWK   58
VI. FIRST POWER FLIGHT   84
VII. AFTER THE EVENT   112
VIII. EXPERIMENTS OF 1904-'05   120
IX. IT STILL WASN'T "NEWS"   139
X. U. S. ARMY NOT INTERESTED   147
XI. EUROPE DISCOVERS THE WRIGHTS   166
XII. THE WRIGHTS IN EUROPE   194
XIII. A DEAL WITH THE U. S.   207
XIV. END OF DISBELIEF   226
XV. WHEN WILBUR WRIGHT WON FRANCE   233
XVI. FURTHER ADVENTURES IN 1909   254
XVII. IN AVIATION BUSINESS   268
XVIII. PATENT SUITS   287
XIX. WHY THE WRIGHT PLANE WAS EXILED   300
Index   335

LIST OF ILLUSTRATIONS

THE FIRST CAMP AT KITTY HAWK 52

THE 1902 GLIDER 53

INSIDE THE 1902 CAMP 84

FROM ORVILLE WRIGHT'S DIARY 85

FIRST FLIGHT 116

THE FIRST POWER PLANE 117

THE HUFFMAN PASTURE 148

THE WRIGHT PATENT 149

THE U. S. ARMY TEST 180

AT FORT MYER 181

THE WRIGHT PLANE IN FRANCE 212

THE WRIGHTS AND WILBUR'S FRENCH PUPILS 213

THE OLD AND THE NEW IN TRANSPORTATION 244

DEMONSTRATION AT PAU 245

TWO ACES AND KING 276

THE WRIGHT HOME AND SHOP 277

THE WRIGHT BROTHERS

PROLOGUE

IN a corner of the Pullman smoking compartment, by the window, the man who had been explaining the whole economic system mentioned inventors as an example of the fortunate relationship between desire for money and scientific progress.

"Take the Wright brothers," he said. "Would they have worked all those years trying to fly just for their health?"

Another passenger ventured to ask: "Don't people sometimes become curious about a problem and work to see what they can find out?"

The man by the window chuckled tolerantly as he replied: "Do you think those Wright brothers would have kept on pouring money into their experiments and risking their lives if they hadn't hoped to get rich at it? No, sir! It was the chance to make a fortune that kept them going." Most of the other passengers in the compartment nodded in agreement.

Not long afterward, one of those who had overheard that conversation was in Dayton, Ohio, and inquired of his friend Orville Wright: "Do you think the expectation of profit is the main incentive to inventors?"

Orville Wright didn't think so. He doubted if Alexander Graham Bell expected to make much out of the telephone. And it seemed to him unlikely that Edison started out with the idea of making money. Certainly, he said, Steinmetz had little interest in financial reward. All Steinmetz asked of life was the opportunity to spend as much time as possible in the laboratory working at problems that interested him.

"And the Wright brothers?"

If they had been interested in invention with the idea of making money, said Orville Wright, looking amused, they "most assuredly would have tried something in which the chances for success were brighter."

I

BOYHOOD

FROM earliest years both Wilbur and Orville Wright were motivated by what Thorstein Veblen called the "instinct of workmanship." Their father, the Reverend Milton Wright, used to encourage them in this and never chided them for spending on their hobbies what little money they might have. But he did urge them to try to earn enough to meet the costs of whatever projects they were carrying on. "All the money anyone needs," he used to say, "is just enough to prevent one from being a burden on others."

Both brothers were fascinated by mechanics almost from the time they were conscious of interest in anything. The childhood events most vivid in the recollections of Orville Wright have had to do with mechanical devices of one kind or another. One of the high spots was the day he attained the age of five, because he received for a birthday gift a gyroscopic top that would maintain its balance and spin while resting on the edge of a knife-blade.

Shortly after that fifth birthday, and partly because of his inborn enthusiasm over mechanics, Orville began an association with another boy that had an important influence on his life. His mother started him to kindergarten. The school was within a short walking distance of the Wright home and Orville set out after breakfast each morning with just enough time to reach the classroom if he didn't loiter. His mother bade him return home promptly after he was dismissed and he always arrived punctually at the time expected. When asked how he was getting along, he cheerfully said all was going well, but did not go into details. At the end of a month his mother went to visit the kindergarten to learn just how Orvie was doing.

"I hope the child has been behaving himself," said the mother to the teacher.

The teacher stared at her in astonishment. "Why," said she, "you know, since the first few days I haven't *seen* him. I supposed you had decided to keep him at home."

It turned out that Orville had almost immediately lost interest in kindergarten and instead had regularly gone to a house two doors from his own, on Hawthorne Street, to join a playmate, Edwin Henry Sines. With an eye on the clock to adjust himself to the kindergarten hours, he had stayed there and played with young Sines until about a minute before he was due at home.

Orville's father and mother were not too severe when this little irregularity was discovered, because the boys had not been engaged in any mischief. On the contrary, their play had been of a sort that might properly be called "constructive." The thing that had occupied them most was an old sewing-machine belonging to Sines' mother. They "oiled" it by dropping water from a feather into the oil-holes!

Both Orville and Wilbur followed their father's advice and earned whatever money they spent. One source of income was from wiping dishes in the evening, for which their mother paid a flat rate of one cent. Sometimes she employed them to make minor household repairs. Orville seemed to find more outlets for money than did Wilbur, who was more saving, and from time to time he borrowed from Wilbur—but he kept his credit good by sticking to an arrangement they always made that the next money earned should be applied on the debt.

One of Orville's early money-making ventures was the collecting of old bones in near-by alleys, vacant lots, or neighbors' yards, and selling them to a fertilizer factory. He and another boy first did this as a means for raising funds with which to buy candy for use while fishing. They accumulated a weight of bones that it seemed to them must represent a small fortune—and were somewhat shocked when the buyer paid them only three cents.

At first, Orville's associates in his projects were boys of his own age rather than Wilbur, who was more than four years older and moved in a different group; but a day came when the brothers began to share curiosity over a mechanical phenomenon. In June, 1878, when Orville was seven years old and Wilbur eleven, the Wright family left Dayton, because the work of the father, who had been made a Bishop of the United Brethren church, was shifted to Cedar Rapids, Iowa. And it was in a house on Adams Street, in Cedar Rapids, not long after their arrival there, that an event occurred which was to have much influence on the lives of

Wilbur and Orville—as well as to have its effect on the whole human race.

Bishop Wright had returned from a short trip on church business bringing with him a little present for his two younger sons.

"Look here, boys," he said to Wilbur and Orville, holding out his hands with something hidden between them. Then he tossed the gift toward them. But instead of falling at once to the floor or into their hands, as they expected, it went to the ceiling where it fluttered briefly before it fell. It was a flying-machine, a helicopter, the invention of a Frenchman, Alphonse Pénaud. Made of cork, bamboo, and thin paper, the device weighed so little that twisted rubber bands provided all the power needed to send it aloft for a few seconds. As the brothers were to learn later, Pénaud, an invalid during most of his short life, had not only invented, as early as 1871, various kinds of toy flying-machines—both the helicopter type and others that flew horizontally—but was the originator of the use of rubber bands for motive power. Simple as was this helicopter—they called it the "bat"— Wilbur and Orville felt great admiration for its ingenuity. Though it soon went the way of all fragile toys, the impression it left on their minds never faded.

Not long afterward Wilbur tried to build an improvement on that toy helicopter. If so small a device could fly, why not make a bigger one that could fly longer and higher? Orville was still too young to contribute much to the actual building of larger models, but he was keenly interested as Wilbur made several, each larger than the one preceding. To the brothers' astonishment, they discovered that the bigger the machine, the less it would fly; and if it was much bigger than the original toy, it wouldn't fly at all. They did not yet understand that a machine of only twice the linear dimensions of another would require eight times the power.

Orville, meanwhile, had distinguished himself in another way, by organizing an army. His grade at school was dismissed one Friday afternoon, though the rest of the school was in session, and it occurred to Orville that it might be amusing to march by, throw gravel on the windows, and taunt those who were still at their lessons. Supported by his friend, Bert Shaffer, he proposed to a dozen other boys in the class that they form themselves into an army, and act not as individuals but as an organization. For having thought of the idea, Orville, who had been doing some reading about Napoleon, would be the General, but there would be Colonels and Captains as well. In fact, they used up all the military titles they knew. Lacking guns, they would have to carry wooden clubs, and these they got by removing some loose pickets from the school fence. All went well until the school janitor began to chase them, evidently intending to capture them. One of the boys made him pause by throwing a rock in his direction as he was crawling through a hole in the fence. After escaping into a distant alley, all in the army assumed they would probably be in plenty of trouble when they returned to school Monday morning.

"We'll be all right," said Orville, feeling bound, as

their commanding General, to try to uphold the army's morale, "if we stick together. They can't fire us all."

He mounted a box lying in the alley and outlined what they should do. The teacher would doubtless single out only two or three of them that had been recognized by the janitor and ask them to stay after school. But if the teacher asked one of them to stand up, they must all stand up; or, if she asked one to stay after school, all must stay, and show their solidarity. "All for one, and one for all," he quoted.

When they were back in school at the next session, the teacher said nothing to indicate that retribution was in the making; but when the class was dismissed at the end of the afternoon, she asked Orville to "remain." True to their pact, all the rest of the army stayed in their seats—or, rather, all except one under-sized lad. A few minutes later, the teacher asked Orville to come to her desk. As he stepped forward, all the others started to do likewise. "The rest of you sit down," commanded the teacher, and then added: "I don't know why you're here at all." Her tone was such that all meekly sat down.

When Orville reached her desk, she said: "You were speaking of a song you could bring for the exercises next Friday"—and went on to talk, pleasantly enough, of Orville's part in a forthcoming school entertainment.

She didn't even seem to know about the daring behavior of the army in the school yard. Probably the janitor, embarrassed over his failure to capture the culprits, had not reported them.

While in Cedar Rapids, Orville showed enterprise in another direction. He had enough intellectual curiosity to study lessons that the teacher had not yet assigned. When a little more than eight years old he told his father that he was tired of the Second Reader they were still studying at school and wished he had a Third Reader.

One morning, not long after that, at the middle of the school year, the principal came to the room Orville was in and announced that any pupils who showed enough proficiency in reading might be promoted at once, without waiting until the end of the year, and begin the Third Reader. The more promising members of the class, selected by the teacher, then stood toeing a chalk mark, up front, as was commonly done, and took turns at reading. In his alarm lest he might not do himself full justice, Orville, someone told him later, held his book upside down. That did not prevent him from reading accurately, as he knew the book by heart, and he was promoted.

"I'm now in the Third Reader class," he proudly announced when he reached home that noon.

"Well, that's a strange thing," said his father. "Just this morning I bought the Third Reader you asked for. But," he added, "you won't be able to use it today, because you're going to miss school this afternoon. I have arranged for you and Wilbur to go to the photographer's and have your pictures taken."

Orville's picture thus commemorated what had seemed to him an important event in his life.

After three years in Cedar Rapids, the Wright family, in June 1881, moved to Richmond, Indiana, partly that Mrs. Wright, who was not in robust health, might have the companionship of her sister who lived there. It was in Richmond that Orville took up the building and flying of kites. Though it interested him, Wilbur did not then take much part in this kite-flying sport, because he feared it might be considered too juvenile for a boy of his size. Orville came to be considered an expert at kite-making and sold kites to playmates as a convenient means of getting spending money. He made the framework of his kites as thin as possible, to reduce weight. Indeed, they were so thin that they would often bend in the wind and the kite formed an arc. But it did not then occur to Orville that this curvature of the kite's surface had any relation to its good flying qualities.

Though he had turned his kite-making to profit, Orville's best source of revenue in Richmond was a job of folding papers, a church publication. For additional spending money he entered the junk business. He would go after school or on Saturdays to pick up scraps of metal thrown out by a chain factory, and hauled this in his "express" wagon to a junk dealer's yard.

One of his projects was the building of a small wooden lathe. It was too small to be quite satisfactory, and Wilbur offered to help him build a larger lathe, seven or eight feet long. This was the first "big" mechanical job he and Wilbur worked on together.

The lathe was considered a great success, especially by neighbor boys who thought it a privilege to work the foot-treadle that provided the motive power. But Wilbur felt that it should be improved. He had noticed that bicycles were being equipped with ball-bearings to give easy running quality and he said the lathe ought to have ball-bearings. He looked about the barn for material that could be adapted and took some metal rings from an old set of harness. When two of these were held tightly side by side they formed the outer track for the ball-bearings; but, instead of steel balls, marbles were used—the common kind, made of clay, that we used to call "commies." Within this circle of marble bearings would rest the shaft of the lathe. The idea seemed so sound that the brothers' friends were much impressed. Many were on hand in the upper floor of the barn awaiting eagerly the final tinkering before the ball-bearing "patent" could be demonstrated. As soon as the lathe was put into operation, there was a terrible noise and then it seemed as if the barn itself was beginning to sway and shake. It was evident that the marbles in the bearing had not been strong enough to withstand the stress; but why should the barn become so agitated? Orville went downstairs to find out if there could be any other cause.

When he reached the outside he saw his sister Katharine held against the side of the house by an invisible force. A small cyclone was taking place! All the boys upstairs had been too absorbed to notice such minor phenomena as weather.

Some of the enterprises Orville got into at Richmond were not of a mechanical nature; and Wilbur, if sharing in them at all, appeared only in the background, or as a consultant, for he was at an age when a boy gave thought to his dignity. Orville had noticed that many boys chewed small hunks of tar. It seemed to him that if the tar could be flavored with sugar to make it more palatable, and small pieces were wrapped in tissue paper, a market for the product might be found. He and his friend, Harry Morrow, began a series of experiments in the Wright back yard, and they seemed well on their way to having a saleable article. But as they kept testing their samples, both became ill—some kind of stomach disorder, accompanied by nausea—and abandoned their plans. Wilbur, though not a partner in all this, was much interested and for years afterwards used to refer to "that chawin' gum corporation."

If Orville was "into" more different things at this time than his brother, it was mainly because Wilbur's great passion was for reading. And what he read, he absorbed. It wasn't long until he himself began to show a gift for writing. Because of that, Wilbur played an important part in one of Orville's early business ventures— though behind the scenes.

One of Orville's friends was a boy living next door named Gansey Johnston, whose father made a hobby of taxidermy. They often played in the Johnston barn where the father had a collection of stuffed birds and animals. One day Orville's imagination was much stirred. He saw possibilities for putting those birds and animals to good use—especially when he noted that there was even a huge black bear and a grizzly. It was obvious to him that he and the Johnston boy should form a partnership and he asked Gansey how he would feel about such an arrangement.

"Partnership to do what?" asked the boy.

Why, said Orville, to give a circus!

Though he had never thought of giving a circus, the Johnston lad caught the idea and soon was enthusiastic.

They then decided to take in Orville's friend, Harry Morrow, as a third partner. Their show would be known as The Great W. J. & M. Circus.

As the date for the big show approached, sixteen-year-old Wilbur Wright, who had been taking great interest in the preparations, asked Orville what he had done about advance notices in the newspapers. Orville had to admit that he had done nothing.

Wilbur appeared to be shocked that no one had taken steps fully to prepare the public mind for the coming event, and offered to write a suitable reading notice about the street parade. This, he said, should be placed in the Richmond *Evening Item*. He had absorbed the method of expression used in circus bills and his forecast of the parade was a masterpiece. There was nothing amateurish about the way he introduced such words as "mammoth," "colossal," and "stupendous," nor about his use of impressively large figures—"thousands of strange birds from all parts of the world" that would positively be in the menagerie. It was announced that the proprietors of the big show would personally lead the parade on "iron horses"; and that Davy Crockett would positively appear with a grizzly bear. At the end of the notice, in professional manner, was the exact route of the parade, that the populace might not miss the great free exhibition of wonders. The notice also gave the prices of admission to the big show—three cents for children under three years; others, five cents. Wilbur gave the piece of publicity to Orville to take to the *Item* office.

There was a little box just inside a door to a stairway

leading to the editorial rooms, and the boys knew it was intended for news items. But they walked up and down the street in front of the newspaper office for a long time before they had the courage to enter the stairway. What if someone should *see* them! Finally, when they thought no one was looking, one of them ran up to the box and in desperate haste deposited their piece of publicity. Then both ran up the street at a speed that could have attracted attention.

The editor of the *Item* evidently had a good news sense and recognized the mysterious "press release" as a local item worth printing. He had no way of knowing who "W. J. & M." were, but felt sure the account of that forthcoming parade had plenty of reader interest. It came about, therefore, that Wilbur's advance notice had a prominent position in the *Item* of September 10, 1883, under a heading that asked: "What Are the Boys Up To?"

Though some of Wilbur's figures about the number of rare birds and wild animals may have been a bit overdrawn, to conform to circus bill standards, he had not exaggerated the amazing nature of the parade. Two of the proprietors, Wright and Johnston, actually appeared at the head of the parade on their "iron horses." These were high-wheel bicycles, one of them having wooden spokes. The third associate proprietor of the big show, Harry Morrow, was unavoidably absent, because his parents had gone on a vacation trip to Michigan, and had insisted, much against his wishes, on taking him with them.

A principal "parade wagon" was the running gear of

an old buggy, with no body but only a few planks to make a platform on which were some of the "thousands of rare birds," and also the great, frightful grizzly bear held in leash by Davy Crockett. Though no horses were hitched to this "wagon," plenty of boys had volunteered their services as "slaves" to pull it through the streets. At the last minute, "Corky" Johnston, nine-year-old brother of one of the proprietors, got into a fight with the circus bosses, and they felt compelled to deny him the privilege of participating in the parade. This created a problem, for he had been cast for the role of Davy Crockett, wearing his father's hunting togs, including high boots. The circus chiefs got around that, the best they could, by assigning the Davy Crockett part to Corky's younger brother, Griswold, not yet five years old. He was almost overwhelmed by the hunting suit; but in the rush of getting the parade started he was the best Davy Crockett available.

Wilbur's advance notice was more successful than he had hoped for. It had aroused so much curiosity that when the parade reached that part of the announced line of march in the business section, the streets were lined with people—almost as many, in fact, as if the circus had been Barnum's.

Messrs. W. & J., astounded by the unexpected attention the parade was attracting, began to feel much too conspicuous. They hastily decided that their route must be changed, and the parade turned up an alley!

So many customers came that not all who clamored for admission to the Johnston barn could be accommodated, and it was decided to repeat the show. But while those who got into the barn were viewing the "menagerie," the boy who had been denied the privilege of appearing as Davy Crockett saw an opportunity to get his revenge. He got up on the barn roof and addressed the multitude, telling them they might as well disperse and seek their homes, because, he said, there would be no other performance.

The crowd took him at his word.

Orville Wright had previously organized another circus, in partnership with a neighbor boy named Miller, who had a Shetland pony. For this show the admission was only one cent. Though the gross receipts were not vast, the show was a great success, partly in consequence of the profound impression it had made on the Miller boy's father. At the close of the performance, he announced that the show people would be guests of honor at a reception, to which the spectators also were cordially invited. Lemonade, ice cream, and cake were served in lavish quantities, and every boy felt that, taking the afternoon as a whole, he had had his money's worth.

But of all the enterprises in which the Wright brothers showed their initiative in Richmond, the Great W. J. & M. Circus probably caused the most talk. People thought the boy who had organized that show would doubtless amount to something. Many ventured the opinion, too, that the youngster, whoever he was, who had prepared that notice for the newspaper about the parade, would surely be "heard from."

II

BACKGROUND

CERTAIN traits that were to show in Wilbur and Orville Wright—the pioneering urge, the gift for original thinking, and mechanical aptitude—were all in their ancestry.

Take, for example, their grandfather, John G. Koerner. Native of a German village, near Schleiz, he became so bitterly opposed to German militarism and autocracy that he determined to migrate to the United States. He sailed from Bremen to Baltimore early in 1818 and went to live in Virginia. Besides gaining recognition in the United States for his mechanical ability and for the superior quality of farm wagons and carriages he manufactured, he became known, too, as a person who did his own thinking. He did not accept all that he heard or read. Indeed, he seems to have been a "character." It was his habit to read newspapers aloud to his family, and when, as invariably happened, he came to something that interested him because of approval, disapproval, or for any other reason, he would interpolate comment without changing his tone or rate of utterance. It was impossible for a listener to tell just how much that he seemed to be reading was actually in the paper and which ideas were his own. One by one, members of his family would study the paper afterward

to see if various surprising statements were really there.
No matter how commonplace a newspaper article may
have been, it was never colorless as he read it.

His wife, the former Catherine Fry, American born,
also came of pioneer ancestry, from the German language section of Switzerland. Their daughter, Susan
Catherine Koerner, was born April 30, 1831, when they
lived at Hillsboro, Loudoun County, Virginia, but the
family moved to Union County, Indiana, shortly after
that—at a time when there was still pioneering life in
the Hoosier country. The Koerner farm became a
rather impressive one for those times. There were
finally a dozen or fourteen buildings, including the carriage shop, all conspicuous for their workmanlike construction and orderliness. John Koerner lived to the age
of eighty-six.

Perhaps the most interesting pioneer of all in the
Wright brothers' ancestry was Catharine [1] (Benham)
Van Cleve, the first white woman to set foot in Dayton.
Her husband, John Van Cleve, whom she had married
in New Jersey, was a descendant of a Van Cleve who
had come from Holland to Long Island before 1650.
When he proposed, a few years after their marriage,
that they should settle in the almost unexplored virgin
forest region of Ohio, she liked the adventurous idea.
They migrated to Cincinnati—then called Losantiville—
in 1790. Within two years after their arrival, John
Van Cleve was killed by Indians. His widow married
Samuel Thompson and, in April, 1796, they decided to
try their luck at a settlement about to be established,

---

[1] Note that the two families spelled the same name differently.

fifty miles to the north. The place had just been named in honor of Jonathan Dayton, a Revolutionary soldier. Three groups of people arranged to make the trip at about the same time. So unsettled was the country, and so nearly non-existent were the wagon trails, that the party which included Catharine Van Cleve Thompson preferred to travel in a flat-bottomed boat on the Miami River. The others went by land. Though the boat trip took about ten days, that group was the first to arrive. Among those in the boat were some of the Van Cleve children; another of them was in one of the overland parties. A Van Cleve son, Benjamin, became the first postmaster at Dayton, the first school teacher, and also the first county clerk. His marriage at Dayton in August, 1800, to Mary Whitten, was the first recorded in Montgomery County.

Margaret Van Cleve, a sister of Benjamin, had stayed in Cincinnati, because she was about to be married—to George Reeder, later an innkeeper. They had a daughter, Catharine, who became the wife of Dan Wright (not named Daniel, but plain Dan, as was also his father), who had come to Centerville, Ohio, near Dayton, in 1811. It was of this union that Milton Wright, father of Wilbur and Orville, was born—in a log cabin in Rush County, Indiana, November 17, 1828.

Dan Wright's ancestry could be traced back to one John Wright, known to have bought Kelvedon Hall, in Essex County, England, in 1538. A less remote ancestor, Samuel Wright, had migrated to America in 1636, and settled at Springfield, Mass.

At the time of his marriage, Dan Wright was employed in a distillery. But he evidently did not feel comfortable over his occupation and quit the distillery job to devote his whole attention to farming. Moreover, he "got religion" and would no longer even sell his corn to distillers. Perhaps it was because of the strong religious feeling of Dan Wright that his son, Milton, at the age of eighteen, had joined the United Brethren church.

Milton Wright attended a small college in near-by Hartsville, Indiana, and at the age of twenty-two he received from the United Brethren church his certificate entitling him to preach. But he did not at once actively enter the ministry. The pioneer urge was in him and he went to the Willamette Valley, in Oregon, where for two years he was a teacher in a small college conducted under the auspices of the church. It was three or four years after finishing his course at Hartsville that he met the young woman, a student there, who was to become his wife. Mutual friends had spoken to him of Susan Catherine Koerner, of how charming, how "smart" she was, and when he found an opportunity to be introduced to her, he was by no means disinclined to make her acquaintance. They were married on November 24, 1859, a week after his thirty-first birthday.

During the first few years after their marriage, the Milton Wrights lived at several different places in Indiana. Their first child, Reuchlin, was born in March, 1861, on a farm [1] near Fairmount; and Lorin, the second son, a year and a half later, in Fayette County, at the home of his grandparents. When Wilbur was born, April 16, 1867, the family was living on a small farm

[1] Owned years afterward by Orville Wright.

the father had bought near the village of Millville, eight miles east of New Castle. Wilbur was named for Wilbur Fiske, a churchman whom the father admired; but his name did not include the Fiske. None of the Wright children ever had a middle name.

For a year, the Rev. Milton Wright was minister of a church at Hartsville, and also taught in the college he had attended there. Then, in June, 1869, he became editor of the *Religious Telescope*, a United Brethren weekly, at Dayton, the home of those pioneer ancestors.

A year or more after their arrival for their first stay in Dayton, the Wright family bought, while it was still under construction, a modest seven-room house at 7 Hawthorne Street. This was on the West Side, across the Miami river, and about a mile from the main business section. Here Orville Wright—named for Orville Dewey, a Unitarian minister—was born on August 19, 1871; and his sister, Katharine, three years later to the day.

During the family's absence in Cedar Rapids and Richmond, the Hawthorne Street house was rented, but the Wright family was once again to live there, for in June, 1884, the Rev. Milton Wright's work brought him from Richmond back to Dayton. When, sixteen months later, the tenant's lease expired and they were settled again at 7 Hawthorne Street, all the family felt that they were where they "belonged."

The family's return to Dayton was a few days before Wilbur would have been graduated from high school at Richmond. With the final year of the course so nearly completed, he would have received his diploma if he had been present with his class on commencement day. But Wilbur did not consider the mere diploma itself important enough to justify a trip back to Richmond, even though the distance was less than fifty miles. His decision was a subject for family talks and all agreed that Wilbur should do as he thought best. The father felt, as did the others, that receiving a diploma was ceremonial and less important than the actual education gained.

Wilbur decided to take a special course at the high school in Dayton the next year. He wished especially to continue the study of Greek, and to learn trigonometry.

Orville had been in the sixth grade at Richmond, but a week or two before the end of the year he got into a bit of mischief that caused his teacher, Miss Bond, to dismiss him. She said he could not return to school until either his father or mother came with him to guarantee that his deportment would improve. But his father was away from home at the time, and his mother was too busy packing for the move to Dayton to take time for consultation with that teacher. Orville simply stayed out of school for the rest of the year.

When he entered school in Dayton the next September, with no certificate to show that he had completed the sixth grade, it looked as if he might have to be in that grade for another year. But Orville was so violent and uncompromising in his protests that the school authorities said he might try the seventh grade until they could see how well he got along. At the end of the year he passed into the eighth grade with the highest mark in arithmetic in the city.

When Orville entered the eighth grade, Miss Jennings, who taught grammar, evidently thought she detected something mischievous about him and assigned him to a front seat in her class.

The next year, the same teacher had been promoted to the high school, as a teacher of algebra, and again she put Orville up in front where she could keep an eye on him. Orville's front seats became a subject for family jests.

Later on in his high school course, Orville was demonstrating a problem in geometry on the blackboard, when his teacher, Miss Wilson, pointed out that though he had the correct answer, he evidently had not followed the textbook.

"I got it out of another book—Wentworth's geometry," Orville explained. And he added: "I get a lot of good stuff from Wentworth."

Instead of complimenting him on having enough interest in the subject to consult another source, the teacher chided him for referring to what she called "a beautiful science" as "stuff."

Orville had no compunction about telling at meal time of such episodes. He knew he wouldn't be scolded. It was simply good conversational material and would provoke sympathetic laughter.

The family was interested, too, in the inventiveness of the boys. Lorin had once invented an improvement on a hay-baling machine. Wilbur had designed and built a practical device for folding paper. This was while he had the contract for folding the entire weekly issue of an eight-page church paper. He had found the hand work tedious and got up a machine that could be worked by a foot-treadle.

For a long time the mechanical ability that had aroused the most family admiration, though, was in the mother. Susan Koerner Wright was more than ordinarily resourceful in adapting household tools or utensils to unexpected uses. She was clever at designing clothes, too; and once she had built a sled for the two older boys. As her family used to say, she "could mend anything."

The mother, however, was not long to be spared to her family. On July 4, 1889, or less than four years after the return to Hawthorne Street, she died. During the latter years of her life, Wilbur was much with his mother, and devoted himself almost constantly to her care, for he too at that time was an invalid, unable to engage in much outdoor activity.

Wilbur's illness was in consequence of an accident. While playing a game of shinny, on skates, he was hit in the face with a shinny club. The blow knocked out all his upper front teeth. He began to suffer from a heart disorder from which he did not completely recover for several years.

After the death of the mother, and the departure of the two older brothers to establish homes of their own, the other members of the Wright family were all the more drawn together. Whatever one of them was doing interested all. And all—especially Wilbur—did much reading.

Two groups of books were in the home, one in Bishop Wright's study upstairs, and another, used by the family, downstairs in the living room. Nearly all the books in the father's library were "very serious," but Wilbur often dipped into them, though the father made no effort to direct or control anyone's reading. Downstairs, however, were the books that both Wilbur and Orville liked best. These included a set of Washington Irving's works, both Grimm's and Andersen's fairy tales, Plutarch's *Lives*, a set of the *Spectator*, a set of Addison's essays, Boswell's *Life of Johnson*, a set of Sir Walter Scott, Gibbon's *Decline and Fall of the Roman Empire*, Green's history of England, Guizot's *France*, an incomplete set of Nathaniel Hawthorne, and a set in which was Marey's *Animal Mechanism*. Here also were a set of the *Encyclopaedia Britannica* and *Chambers' Encyclopedia*. The *Britannica* was an edition of the late 70's and the *Chambers' Encyclopedia* was an earlier edition. Though Wilbur was the great reader, Orville was not far behind him. He was fascinated by scientific articles in the encyclopedia almost from the time he learned to read.

Wilbur and Orville from time to time contributed to the family comfort in a substantial way. They built a spacious front porch, and all the lathe work for the posts they did themselves. Then they remodeled the interior of the house, changing the arrangement of the rooms. Other members of the family felt as much pride in such handiwork as if they had done it themselves.

More than their sturdy, intelligent, pioneer ancestry, it was probably the kind of home they lived in that had most to do with what the younger brothers were later to achieve. Orville expressed that with deep conviction many years afterward. A friend of his had re-marked to him: "Even though what you accomplished was without the idea of making money, the fact remains that the Wright brothers will always be favorite exam-ples of how American lads with no special advantages can get ahead."

"But," said Orville seriously, "that isn't true. Because, you see, we *did* have special advantages."

"What special advantages do you mean?"

"Simply that we were lucky enough to grow up in a home environment where there was always much en-couragement to children to pursue intellectual interests; to investigate whatever aroused curiosity. In a different kind of environment our curiosity might have been nipped long before it could have borne fruit."

III

PRINTING—AND BICYCLES

AT the age of twelve, while living in Richmond, Indiana, Orville Wright became interested in wood engravings. His curiosity had been stirred by seeing some woodcuts by Timothy Cole and T. Johnson in the *Century* magazine. Wondering how the cuts were made he began to search the encyclopedia and one or two other books that told a little about the technique used. He then decided that he might be able to make some woodcuts himself if he had a suitable tool—and he went ahead to fashion such a tool from the spring of an old pocketknife. (The next Christmas, Wilbur gave him a set of engraving tools.)

After trying his hand at his first few woodcuts, Orville naturally wished to make prints from them, and for this purpose he used a press his father had for copying letters. Today seldom seen, the old-fashioned letterpress consisted of two horizontal metal plates that could be forced close together by turning a little circular handle at the top of a threaded rod attached to the upper plate. One's letter was moistened and placed next to a thin tissue sheet in a record book which went between the plates of the press. Under pressure, a copy of the letter was transferred to the tissue. Such a press was a fascinating device for a boy to play with. Indeed, Orville had used it for other purposes than that for which it was intended. It had also served him as a vise. And now it worked fairly well for making proofs from his woodcuts.

It was at about this time that the Wright family returned to Dayton from Richmond, and Orville renewed close relations with his old chum, Ed Sines. To his delight he found that young Sines was already interested in printing. He had a small press, obtained by trading a file, covering more than a year, of a boys' magazine called *Golden Days*. This press was little more than a toy, capable of printing only one narrow line at a time, and the boys were never able to make much use of it. But, nevertheless, they immediately formed the printing firm of Sines & Wright.

At the beginning of the partnership of Sines & Wright, their printing establishment was in a corner of the Sines kitchen. Ed's mother summed up the situation there when one day she noticed an envelope addressed to "Messrs. Sines & Wright," from a type foundry. "It must be for you," she said to the partners, "for you certainly *are* a pair of messers."

Interested as they were in printing, Ed Sines and Orville had time for other hobbies. One of these was a telegraph line they rigged up between their homes. For years Wilbur Wright referred to it as "the first wireless telegraph," because the boys used to shout the messages back and forth to verify whatever they clicked out on the keys.

It soon became evident that Orville had printers' ink in his blood. This printing hobby was more than a passing fancy. His father was impressed by the boy's persistence in trying to use inadequate equipment. The father knew that two of his older sons, Wilbur and Lorin, had recently had a chance to trade a boat they had made, now seldom used, for a small printing press. If they would make that trade, he suggested, and donate the press to Orville, then he would buy for the youngster twenty-five pounds of brevier type. This deal was made. The new press would print anything up to 3 by 4½ inches.

As the Sines kitchen was not quite the ideal location for their printing plant, Orville arranged for quarters in a "summer kitchen," not often used, at the Wright home.

It now occurred to Messrs. Sines & Wright that it might be a good idea to print a newspaper for the benefit of their eighth grade classmates. They called it *The Midget*. Because of the limited capacity of their press, the paper was necessarily small, two narrow columns wide and four and one-half inches long. Most of the items in it were put directly into type, as they thought of them, and not from previously prepared copy. They found that the four pages they had planned entailed a surprising amount of work and to reduce this they put nothing on page three except "Sines & Wright," twice, diagonally across the page, in script type. After they had printed about one hundred copies for distribution, Orville's father saw one of these and immediately placed a ban on the whole issue. He insisted that the boys had not done themselves justice in slighting that third page.

Readers of the paper, he said, might get the impression that the publishers were lazy or shiftless.

In a way, this suppression of the issue came almost as a relief, for the publishers had begun to feel misgivings about one somewhat daring item they had taken the liberty of printing. It was about their teacher, Miss Jennings, who was a strict disciplinarian. The item read: "Next week we propose to publish one of Miss Jennings' famous lectures before the pupils of the Intermediate School on the Inherent Wickedness of School Children."

Maybe, they reflected, it was just as well that *The Midget* was not to be distributed. Miss Jennings might take the item as good clean fun, but, on the other hand, she might raise a rumpus.

Before long the partners had an opportunity to buy a quantity of display type for $2, and then they began trying to establish themselves in the job-printing business. They set up their headquarters in the Wright barn, though on cold days they were likely to do their typesetting on a table in the Wright dining-room. Neighborhood storekeepers gave them a few orders for printing, and the firm began to take on airs. They employed Forrest Whitfield, a neighbor boy, as printer's devil. He commanded a weekly wage of fifteen cents.

All was going well until one day they received an order from a man who wished to pay for his printing not in money but in popcorn. He assured them that this popcorn, on the cob, was worth more than the $2 the printing would have cost. But before deciding if they should accept the popcorn in payment, the partners prudently went to a grocer to get an estimate of its value. Sure enough, it was worth $2, and the grocer offered to buy it from them at that price.

Now Orville saw greater opportunities opening before them. With a liquid capital of $2, they could buy more type, do a greater variety of printing, and thus have more fun. But Ed Sines thought there was such a thing as over-extension of plant and equipment. Why not just divide their popcorn and *eat* it? Each was so uncompromising in his convictions that there was only one thing to do: one must buy out the other and they would dissolve the partnership. Inasmuch as Orville already owned the press they were using and most of the type, it seemed logical that he should be the buyer. By paying his share of the popcorn he was able to take over his partner's interest without much cash outlay. Thenceforth, when they worked together, as from time to time they continued to do, Ed Sines was no longer co-proprietor but an employee.

At about this time, something set Orville to thinking of how interesting it would be to print circus bills. He wished some of his friends would organize a circus. Then he could do their printing. The idea seemed worth promoting. He went to the Truxell boys, and Fred LaRue, neighbors up the street, and convinced them that they had just the kind of abilities to organize and present a wonderful circus—one that would make a great hit with all the kids. The result of this talk was The Great Truxell Bros. & LaRue Show. Orville refused to accept any payment for printing the handbills and tickets of admission to the big show. The fun of doing it was all the reward he wanted.

Mrs. Wright had cleared out an upstairs room for Orville's printing activities and that was his base for some time. He began to feel the need for a larger printing press and he determined to build one. The bed for the new press was an old gravestone he got from a marble dealer.

This press would print a sheet eleven by sixteen inches. Orville could now undertake larger printing projects. One order required more type than he had on hand. But that didn't stop him. After he had used up all his type, with the job only half done, he recalled having heard of stereotype plates. He looked up in an encyclopedia a description of how such plates were cast from the impression of the original type in wet cardboard. And he contrived to make such a plate from the type already set. Then he redistributed that type for use in setting the rest of the job.

Ambitious to be a really good printer, Orville took employment during two summer vacations with a printing establishment in Dayton, and worked there sixty hours a week. But he felt that the most fun and satisfaction in connection with printing had been from building his own press. Along in the spring of 1888, when he was nearly seventeen years old, he started to build another press, bigger than any he had used before. He didn't know exactly what he would do with it, but that question did not yet give him much concern. He would have the fun of building it. In the family woodshed was a pile of fire-wood cut in four-foot lengths.

From these he made much of the framework, though he had to buy at a lumber yard a few longer pieces. From near-by junk yards he collected odds and ends of iron or steel that could be used. A difficult problem was to find a means of forcing the type against the printing surface, always with the same pressure, just enough and not too much. Orville searched the Wright barn and tool-shed for something that could be adapted, but without success until his eye happened to alight on the old family buggy. The buggy had a folding top, held firmly in place, when raised, by steel bars hinged in the middle. They were designed to force the top just so far and no farther. Exactly what he needed!

The job turned out to be much more difficult than Orville had expected, and Wilbur Wright, observing his kid brother at a tough job, offered to help him build the press. Some of the suggestions Wilbur made for moving parts of that press were peculiar in that they seemed to violate all mechanical rules and could not possibly be expected to work. Yet they did. Some time later, a well-dressed stranger entered the shop where Orville, merrily whistling, was feeding paper into his press, and asked if he might look at that "home-made printing outfit." He had heard about it while visiting in Dayton. What at once astonished Orville and two or three boys in the shop was that the visitor, with complete disregard for his good clothes, lay right down flat on his back on the floor to study the press in operation. After he had observed it for several minutes, he got up, brushed himself off, and remarked: "It works all right, but I still don't understand *why* it works." Before leaving he laid his card on a table. He was the foreman of the pressroom of a newspaper in Denver.

Now that he had his new press, Orville wished he could put it to some purpose to make full use of the greatly increased printing capacity. The press was big enough and fast enough to print a newspaper. Why not start a neighborhood weekly? He had hardly more than thought of this before he decided to do so. It was probably the first time a paper was ever started just to use a press.

Orville now rented a room on West Third Street, near Broadway. The first issue of the paper—four three-column pages—appeared on March 1, 1889. In his salutatory, Orville said: "This week we issue the first number of the *West Side News*, a paper to be published in the interests of the people and business institutions of the West Side. Whatever tends to their advancement, moral, mental, and financial, will receive our closest attention."

There were seventeen advertisements. A leading feature was a story about Abraham Lincoln and General Sherman, from the *Youth's Companion;* and there was an article about Benjamin Franklin. The range of the publisher's reading was indicated by a number of short paragraphs on foreign affairs, and about the approaching inauguration of President-elect Benjamin Harrison. Altogether it was a creditable job. No boyish "boners" or typographical errors were to be found.

All copies of the first issue were distributed free, as samples, but the paper was soon a fairly profitable enterprise. After the first few numbers, it was enlarged from three columns wide to four columns. Ed Sines devoted himself to rounding up advertisements and news items. From time to time Wilbur Wright helped to fill space by writing humorous essays, and after a few weeks his name was added to the paper's masthead as "editor," along with Orville's as publisher.

Another contributor to the *West Side News* was a young Negro lad, a friend of Orville since grammar grades, Paul Laurence Dunbar, whose poetry afterward made him famous. Dunbar, in 1890, started a paper, *The Tattler*, for Negro readers, and Orville did the printing.

By the time the *West Side News* had been running a year, Orville had completed his course in high school. He thought the final year, devoted in the regular course largely to review, would hardly justify the time. Instead, having it in mind that he might decide to go to college and would need additional credits for college entrance requirements, he was a special student in Latin during that fourth year, attending high school an hour or two a day. The two elder Wright brothers had attended college in Iowa and Indiana, and later their sister Katharine took a degree at Oberlin, but both Wilbur and Orville gave up the idea of going to college, and neither ever received a diploma from high school. It may be added, however, that Orville in later years never agreed with those who suggested that "college might have ruined the Wright brothers." More than once he said they doubtless could have done their scientific work more easily if they had had the advantage of college education.

Having decided, partly because of interest in the job at hand, not to go to college, Orville, in April, 1890, with Wilbur as partner, converted the *West Side News* from a weekly to a four-page, five-column daily, called *The Evening Item*.

This venture, though it showed no loss, was never profitable. At that time the perfecting-press was coming into use and Dayton newspapers were issuing big, thick editions that proved to be increasingly keen competition for a small neighborhood sheet. After about four months the paper was suspended. But, as late as 1894, Orville and Wilbur published for a time a little two-column weekly called *Snapshots*, devoted to vigorous comments on current local events. After the first issue or two these were usually written by Wilbur.

Both Orville and Wilbur now became absorbed in one more new interest. Orville had owned in Richmond an old high wheel bicycle for which he had paid $3—borrowed from Wilbur. Now, a new European type of bicycle with wheels about the same size, and called a "safety," had begun to be popular. In 1892, Orville bought one of these, a Columbia. It had pneumatic tires and cost $160. Six months later, Wilbur got a bicycle. His was an Eagle and he was able to get it at an auction for $80.

Orville promptly became interested in track-racing and began to enter his name in various local racing events. Wilbur, though he had been a great athlete—a wonderful fancy skater and the best performer in Dayton on a horizontal bar—never went in for racing, because not yet completely recovered from the effects of his skating accident.

Within a few weeks or months from the time they bought their bicycles, these Wright brothers decided to go into the bicycle business—to sell certain well-known makes. Then they soon found that they would have to add a repair shop. Their first sales room was at 1005 West Third Street. They rented it in December, 1892, to be ready for business when the bicycle season began in the early spring of 1893. For a while Orville divided his time between the bicycle shop and the job printing business across the street in which Ed Sines was still employed. (Sines continued to work there until 1898 when an accident to a lame knee forced him to seek another kind of work, and a few months later the shop was sold.)

The brothers soon had to move their bicycle business to larger quarters, at 1034 West Third Street. They were successful both in selling new machines and general repairing. Among the bicycles they sold at one time or another were the Coventry Cross, Halladay-Temple, Warwick, Reading, Smalley, Envoy and Fleetwing.

By 1895 increased business had caused them to move once more, to 22 South Williams Street, and soon they began to manufacture bicycles. The first "custom made" model was called the Van Cleve—after their pioneer ancestors. A later and lower-priced model was the St. Clair; and finally they made a still lower-priced machine called the Wright Special. It sold for as low as $18. Before they were through with the business they had put out under their own brand several hundred bicycles. Many of these were built in the last building the brothers occupied, a remodeled dwelling house at 1127 West Third Street—the building afterward preserved as a museum at Henry Ford's Greenfield Village in Dearborn, Michigan.

Much of their work when building new bicycles was done in winter, when selling was slack, in rooms upstairs over the shop, and from time to time the brothers were interrupted by the necessity of going down to attend to wants of customers. Sometimes they went down to meet a caller who wished only to borrow their air-pump to inflate a tire. They had no pressure-tank but kept a large hand-pump on the wall near the front door. To avoid needless trips downstairs, the Wrights contrived mechanical means by which they could tell if a caller's wants required their attention. They took an old two-tone bell, intended to be fastened to a bicycle handlebar, and attached it to the wall in their upstairs work-rooms. By means of wires and other mechanism, the opening of the downstairs door yanked the thumb-lever on the bell in one direction, producing one tone; and shutting the door pulled the little lever in an opposite direction to cause the other tone. The hook on which the air-pump hung was also connected by a wire and a spring to a pointer upstairs. Thus it was possible to have secret knowledge upstairs if the caller might be a real customer or if he "only wanted air." If he promptly helped himself to the pump, there probably was no need for anyone to go down. Then when the pointer showed that the pump was back on the hook and the bell signaled the closing of the door, on the caller's departure, the brothers could feel sure they had not missed a sale of any kind by sticking to their work.

Throughout the time they were repairing, selling,

and building bicycles, the Wrights continued to make various experiments, just for the fun of it. They made in 1893 what was doubtless the first pair of "balloon" tires ever installed on a vehicle. It was necessary to build a special "front fork" and widen the frame at the rear to make room for the over-sized pneumatics.

Orville even found time during this period for experiments having nothing to do with bicycles. Along about 1895, he made a new kind of calculating machine for multiplying as well as for adding. He worked also on a typewriter more simplified than any in existence.

Occasionally the brothers took in trade an old high wheel. They had two of these, about the same size, that they couldn't sell for much, and the only way to get any benefit from them was to use them in a new way for sport. Why not, they asked themselves, convert them into a tandem? No one had ever heard of two high wheels operated as a unit, and though riding such an outfit might be dangerous, it also would be exciting. They put a swivel in the steel tube connecting the two wheels to prevent it from twisting and breaking. Then they began to practice, to learn the special technique the man on the rear seat had to know. It was a little different from any a bicyclist had needed before—a little like that of a man steering the rear end of a long fire truck. Though it looked fairly easy, only one person besides the Wrights ever succeeded in staying mounted. Indeed, riding even on the front seat was perilous enough. One afternoon Orville took the rear seat with a boy named Tom Thorne in front. As they tried to steer around a hole in the muddy street, the handle-bar caught the leg of the lad in front, which prevented his turning far enough.

Of course there was a spill. Orville from the rear seat managed to land on his feet, but Tom Thorne, with one leg pinioned, was hurled headfirst to the street. When he came up for air none of his features was to be seen, so thoroughly was he plastered with mud. He looked so frightful that none of the boys who saw the mishap showed any amusement. They were afraid he had ruined his face. But Orville at once realized that the soft mud had prevented any injury and his young friend's appearance struck him as the funniest thing he had ever seen. For some moments he was doubled up with mirth, unable to control himself, while the other rider, not exactly indignant but unable to enter into the hilarity, stood trying to gouge the mud out of his eyes with his thumbs. It happened that Tom Thorne had an intimate acquaintance with a family living near by and he went there, accompanied by Orville, to ask permission to wash up; but the girl who opened the door, though a lifelong friend, was unwilling to believe the strange-looking creature was anyone she knew. Tom asked her to call her mother. The mother had known him almost from the day of his birth, but she showed no sign of recognition now. She did finally identify him by his voice, however, and told him he might wash at the pump. He was able to remove some of the larger chunks of mud. Then he and Orville took the machine back to the shop. The episode was not one of the Wright triumphs. But neighbors who heard about it smiled and wondered:

What will those Wright boys be doing next?

As boys and girls of high school age were potential customers for bicycles, Wilbur Wright thought there should be an effective way to stir their interest in the makes of bicycles sold by the Wright Cycle Co. and he hit on a plan that showed him to have latent genius as an advertising man. He got a copy of a high school examination paper and had printed what appeared to be a set of examination questions—using the same kind of paper and the same typography. Then he arranged with one or two students to distribute these sheets at the high schools. At first glance a student would think he had got hold of an advance copy of an examination paper. But all the questions related to bicycles on sale by the Wrights!

A chum of the Wrights, Cordy Ruse, in 1896 had built the first horseless buggy ever run over the streets of Dayton. The Wrights and others used to sit and talk with him about some of his problems. They had many jokes about the difficulties of hitting upon a suitable ignition system, a workable differential, and other seeming insurmountables. Another problem, caused by the vibration of a horseless carriage, had impressed Wilbur most of all.

One day when the Wrights and several others were chatting with Cordy Ruse, Wilbur suddenly slapped his thigh and said:

"I've just thought of a wonderful invention! I'll have it patented. It's simple enough. All there is to it is a bed sheet to be fastened beneath an automobile to catch all the bolts, nuts, and other parts that'll keep dropping off."

Orville thought that, crude as horseless carriages were, they were probably the coming thing, and that eventually they might even hurt the bicycle trade. In 1897 he suggested to Wilbur that perhaps they might well give thought to the idea of going into the business of building automobiles.

No, insisted Wilbur, shaking his head, they would never be practical.

"To try to build one that would be any account," declared Wilbur, "you'd be tackling the impossible. Why, it would be easier to build a flying-machine!"

IV

FIRST THOUGHTS OF FLIGHT

EVER since the Wright brothers had played with their Pénaud toy helicopter in Cedar Rapids, Iowa, their interest in whatever they chanced to read about flying-machines was probably greater than if the seed had not been planted in childhood.

Along in the early 1890's, both Wilbur and Orville were likely to read any article they saw on a scientific subject, and to talk about it. Occasionally an article in a magazine that came to the Wright home dealt with attempts of man to fly. As time went on, such articles interested the brothers more and more. In 1895, both were impressed—perhaps more than they then realized—by a brief item they had come upon about the glider experiments, in Germany, by Otto Lilienthal. He had been gliding through the air, down the side of a hill, on a machine he had built. That, the brothers thought, must be the king of sports, to go soaring through the air on a gliding machine. They wished they knew more about Lilienthal and his work. All the reports they could find about him were meager enough; but what little they did learn increased their enthusiasm. Lilienthal, "the father of gliding flights," was to have a tremendous influence on them.

Their interest in anything relating to Lilienthal was

still strong in the summer of the next year, 1896, when Orville was taken ill—typhoid fever. Then, at a time when Orville was still delirious from the fever, Wilbur read that Lilienthal had been killed in a crash of his glider.

After Orville was well enough to hear about Lilienthal's fatal accident, both he and Wilbur felt a greater eagerness than ever to learn more about what Lilienthal had accomplished, as well as of what had been tried by others, toward human flight. Books dealing with attempts of man to fly appeared to be scarce, but the brothers got whatever was available in the Dayton library, besides looking up articles on the subject in the encyclopedia. All they read, however, during the next two or three years did not satisfy their craving for a better understanding of the whole problem of flight.

Knowing that the Smithsonian Institution, at Washington, was interested in the subject of human flight, they decided to send a letter to the Smithsonian asking for suggestions as to reading material. The reply, received early in June, 1899, suggested: Octave Chanute's *Progress in Flying Machines;* Professor Langley's *Experiments in Aerodynamics;* and the *Aeronautical Annuals* of 1895, 1896, and 1897, edited by James Means, which contained reprints of accounts of various experiments, clear back to the time of Leonardo da Vinci. Besides this list of suggested reading, the Smithsonian sent also some pamphlets, reprints of material extracted from their own annual reports, among which were Mouillard's *Empire of the Air,* Langley's *Story of Experiments in Mechanical Flight,* and a paper by Lilienthal on *The Problem of Flying and Practical Experiments in Soaring.*

This reading material arrived from Washington at a time when Katharine Wright had just returned from Oberlin College, accompanied by a young woman classmate. She had assumed that her brothers would help to entertain this guest, but, to her vexation, Wilbur and Orville had become too absorbed in their reading to have much time for girls.

It was now evident to the brothers that though the previous ten years had been a period of unusual activity, the results had not been encouraging. Maxim, after spending one hundred thousand dollars, had abandoned his work; the Ader machine, built at the expense of the French government, had been a failure; Lilienthal in Germany, and Pilcher, a marine engineer, in England, had been killed while trying to glide; Octave Chanute, too, after making some experiments in gliding, had quit.

Since Lilienthal had already aroused the brothers' admiration, they were especially interested in what he had done. With hundreds of short flights, he had had more flying practice than anyone else, even though he had been in the air a total of only five hours in five years. Lilienthal became the Wrights' hero. They decided that he, by his experiments, had made more advance in the flying art than had anyone else up to that time—an opinion, it may be added, that they never changed.

Their reading now gave the Wrights a good idea of how earlier experimenters had attempted to solve the problem of equilibrium. Some experimenters had placed the center of gravity far below the wings, on the theory that the weight would seek to remain at the lowest point. But it had been proved that the wings would then oscillate about the center of gravity in a manner destructive to stability. Others had arranged the wings in the shape of a broad V, to form a dihedral angle, with the center low and the wing tips elevated. This, too, tended to make the machine oscillate from side to side except in calm air. Pénaud, in his models propelled by rubber bands, had used wings that formed a dihedral angle, and a rear stabilizer set with its forward edge lower than the rear edge. This produced inherent stability in both lateral and longitudinal directions. Lilienthal, Chanute, and some of the others had used the Pénaud system in their gliders, but in addition to that system they counted on shifting the weight of their bodies to help maintain equilibrium.

All this reading, while adding to their store of knowledge, also gave the Wrights much misinformation. One wrong idea they got was that men already knew how to design wings and propellers of such efficiency that motors then available could easily sustain the machine in the air; another, that the greatest problem was to maintain equilibrium. They also were misled into thinking that fore and aft control of a flying machine would be much more difficult than lateral control.

That neither Lilienthal nor any other experimenter had ever tried any more adequate method to insure lateral balance struck Orville as surprising. Why, he asked himself, wouldn't it be possible for the operator to vary the inclination of sections of the wings at the tips and thus obtain force for restoring balance from the difference in the lifts of the two opposite wing tips? That seems today an obvious enough idea, but no one had ever done anything about it before. Orville had hit on a fundamental principle. (Indeed, this principle later became the basic claim of the original Wright patent, and the claim was sustained, as covering the idea of the aileron control, in all countries where the Wright patents were adjudicated.)

Orville made a rough sketch of a wing, showing a stationary section at the center, consisting of approximately one-third of the wing, measured from tip to tip, with two adjustable sections, one at either side. These sections were carried on shafts interconnected by cogs mounted on the center section and extending toward the wing tips. The movement of a lever attached to one of the shafts would cause one wing section to rotate in one direction while the other wing would turn in the opposite direction. Thus a greater lift could be obtained on whichever side it was needed.

The Wrights soon saw, however, that for two reasons this particular design did not provide a good structure for a gliding machine. First, with two-thirds of the entire weight of the machine and operator carried by the two shafts, the structure would be weak; and, second, with the ends of the wings free to turn about the shafts, there would not be enough rigidity for a machine that would have to be toted about.

Then one night, some five or six weeks later, Wilbur came home from the bicycle shop, to tell Orville enthusiastically of an idea he had hit upon. A customer had dropped in to buy an inner tube for a tire. Wilbur had taken the tube from the pasteboard box it came in and was toying with the box while talking to the customer. As he twisted the box he observed that though the vertical sides were rigid endwise, the top and bottom sides could be twisted to have different angles at the opposite ends. Why, he thought, couldn't the wings of a gliding machine be warped from one end to the other in this same way? Thus the wings could be put at a greater angle at one side than at the other, without structural weakness. That plan seemed so satisfactory that the Wrights did not look for or consider any other method.

A few weeks later, in August, 1899, the brothers built a biplane kite, and Wilbur, with a group of small boys as spectators, flew it on a common at the edge of town. This kite had wing surfaces five feet from tip to tip by thirteen inches wide. The warping of these surfaces could be accomplished by the use of four cords reaching from the kite to the ground. Two of the cords were attached to the forward corners of the right wing tips, one to the upper and one to the lower; the other ends of the cords, at the ground, were tied to opposite ends of a short stick to be held in the operator's hand. The cords tied to the left wing were arranged in the same way. With a stick in each hand, the operator could move the wings as he desired. The upper wing could be moved farther forward or farther backward than the lower wing, according to the direction in which the two sticks were simultaneously inclined, by movement of the wrists. By inclining the two sticks in opposite directions it was possible to draw one upper wing tip farther forward than the lower at that end, while at the other end of the kite the lower wing tip would be the one farther forward. This moving of the wing tips in opposite directions caused a twisting or warping of the wings. Then the wing at one end would be presented to the wind at a different angle from that at the other end. If one end of the kite started to sink, sidewise balance could be restored by exposing the wing at that end at a greater angle, thus getting more lift.

Balance from front to rear was to be maintained by inclining the two sticks in the operator's hands in the same direction—to move the upper wing either forward or backward over the lower wing, to change the center of lift.

But in addition to this moving of the wings forward and backward, the Wrights added an "elevator" at the rear. It was held by a pair of wooden rods attached at right angles to the uprights that connected the wings. When the upper wing was pulled forward, to turn the kite upward in front, the elevator met the air at its top side and was pressed downward, which helped to turn the wings upward—as the rear elevator does on planes today.

Though their interest did not lag, the Wrights did nothing more for some time about kite experiments, except to seek information in regard to wind velocity in different parts of the country. They wrote to the Weather Bureau at Washington, in December, 1899, and Willis Moore, chief of that Bureau, sent them a number of government bulletins that included statistics on wind velocities at various places. They looked these over, but at that time made no further investigation of any of the places mentioned.

In May, 1900, Wilbur Wright wrote a letter to Octave Chanute, living in Chicago, who had written *Progress in Flying Machines*. Though Chanute was better known in engineering circles by his work for certain western railroads, as well as for having built the Kansas City bridge and the Chicago stockyards, his book, a reprint of his articles published from 1891 to 1893, had made him probably the best authority on the history of aeronautics. Thinking Chanute would be interested, Wilbur told him in his letter of a plan he had for experimenting with a man-carrying kite by means of which, Wilbur thought, one would be able to get hours of practice in operating a machine in the air. He proposed the use of a high tower from the top of which a cable would lead to the man-carrying kite. He described to Chanute, in his letter, the system of control to be used in the kite —the warping of wings for lateral control, and the shifting of the upper surface backward and forward for longitudinal control—the same system used in the five-foot kite tested the previous August. Then he asked Chanute if he had any information as to locations where winds suitable for carrying on such experiments might be found. (This letter from Wilbur marked the beginning of an acquaintance and correspondence with Chanute that lasted for a number of years.) Chanute suggested San Diego, California, and St. James City (Pine Island), Florida, to be considered because of the steady sea breezes. But, on the other hand, he pointed out that, since those places were deficient in sand hills, perhaps

THE FIRST CAMP AT KITTY HAWK. *Top:* The 1900 camp. *Bottom:* Kitty Hawk Bay as seen from the 1900 camp.

THE 1902 GLIDER. The Wrights are testing the efficiency of the 1902 glider by flying it as a kite—September 19, 1902.

even better locations could be found on the Atlantic coast of South Carolina or Georgia.

When the rush of the spring trade in bicycles began to subside, giving them more time for other interests, the Wrights again took up with enthusiasm the study of equilibrium. Each day they proposed and discussed new devices. Orville thought the shifting of the upper surface backward and forward over the lower one, for longitudinal equilibrium, though successful in their kite, would not be practical for a man-carrying glider, which would start and land on the ground. He suggested that the wing surfaces be fixed one above the other, and that an elevator be placed some distance in front of the wings, instead of at the rear. In this position there would be less danger of the elevator touching the ground in starting; and if from any cause the elevator were disabled it would be discovered before the machine got into the air. Wilbur then proposed that, since curved surfaces were more efficient than flat planes, the front rudder, or elevator, should be made flexible. Then it could be bent to present a concave surface on whichever side a pressure was desired, but would be flat when moving edgewise through the air.

The Wrights did not at first think an elevator in front would provide inherent stability—that is, it would not give the machine the desired tendency to restore its own balance just from the arrangement of its fixed parts. But Wilbur shortly afterward developed a theory that led him to believe the machine would have that quality.

Having read that the center of pressure moves toward the front edge of the wings whenever the wings are turned more nearly horizontal in flight, he thought inherent longitudinal stability could be obtained if the front elevator were set at a negative angle—that is, with its front edge lower than its rear edge. With such an arrangement of wings and elevator, every time the wings became more nearly horizontal in flight and met the air at a smaller angle on their under sides, the elevator would meet the air at a greater angle on its upper side. So, he reasoned, whenever, by becoming more nearly horizontal, the wings caused the center of pressure to move forward, tending to turn the machine upward in front, the front elevator would receive a greater downward pressure on its upper side and so counteract the disturbing pressure on the wings.

Actual tests later proved that the negative angle of the front elevator did not provide the inherent stability expected. The explanation was that the center of pressure on cambered wings traveled in the opposite direction from that which Wilbur's reading had led him to expect. The Wrights later were to discover that Wilbur's reasoning was correct; but because the travel of the center of pressure was rearward instead of forward the elevator had to be set at a positive instead of at a negative angle.

The Wrights' elevator possessed three features not found in the gliders of any of the earlier experimenters. It was in front of the wings, where it was less liable to damage by striking the ground in take-off and landing; it was operable, instead of fixed as in other machines; and it flexed to present a convex surface to the air, instead of a flat surface. At this early stage of their work the Wrights considered this front elevator their most important invention, because, from their reading, they thought it was solving a problem more difficult than that of lateral control.

Though the Wrights' reasons for placing the elevator in front of the wings were at first those just mentioned, they afterward found that this arrangement had much greater importance for two reasons not at first discovered. One of these was that it eliminated all danger of a nose dive when the plane got into what is known as a "stall"—when the speed became too slow. The other reason was that the elevator in front, set at a positive angle with the pressure on its under side, not only produced inherent stability, but also carried part of the load, and so relieved the wings to that extent. (An elevator in the rear, set at a negative angle to provide inherent stability, carries a pressure on its upper side, which adds just that much to the load the wings must carry.)

Around the first of August, 1900, the brothers decided to build a man-carrying glider on which to try out their inventions. To get practice in operating it they would first fly it as a kite. For such kite flying, flat open country would be needed; and for the gliding, sand hills free from trees or shrubs. Once again they examined the reports they had received from the Weather Bureau at Washington. Several of the places where winds might be suitable were in the Far West, but one in the East, much nearer to Dayton, was a place with an odd name, Kitty Hawk, North Carolina. They decided to write at once to Kitty Hawk for further information.

Wilbur Wright addressed a letter to the chief of the Kitty Hawk weather bureau station, asking for various details about the locality, explaining that he might wish to go there shortly to conduct experiments with a man-carrying kite. He inquired, too, if it would be possible for him and his brother to obtain board and lodging in the vicinity until they could get themselves established in a camp.

Joseph J. Dosher, in charge of the Kitty Hawk station, who received the letter, replied briefly, on August 16, giving the direction of the prevailing winds; and he described the nature of the land for many miles.

After writing his reply, Dosher handed Wilbur Wright's letter to a neighbor, William J. Tate, with the request that he also make a reply. "Bill" Tate (later known as Captain Tate) was probably the best-educated man in that locality. He lived about a mile inland from the weather station, in the hamlet or settlement of Kitty Hawk, where he had formerly been the postmaster. For all practical purposes he still was the postmaster, though the office was in his wife's name. Endowed with a gift for expressing himself readily in either speech or writing, Tate did a creditable job when he wrote to Wilbur Wright on August 18. Not only did he tell about the suitability of the Kitty Hawk region, because of the prevailing high winds, for the kind of experiments Wilbur had mentioned, but he went into details about the treeless sand hills and the general terrain. And he said arrangements could undoubtedly be made for the Wrights to obtain board for as long as desired.

The letters from Dosher and Tate—particularly the

one from Tate—convinced the Wrights that Kitty Hawk was the place for their experiments. Almost immediately they decided they would go to Kitty Hawk as soon as they could build their glider.

The work at Dayton, getting parts and material ready for the glider, required only a few weeks. Only the cutting and sewing of the cloth covering for the wings, the bending of the ash ribs into shape, and making the metal connections, took much time. The cost of the whole machine in actual money outlay was trifling, probably not more than $15.

It was arranged that Orville should stay in Dayton, to look after the bicycle shop until Wilbur got settled at Kitty Hawk, and then join him there.

Wilbur set out on a September day, taking with him parts of the glider and all material needed to assemble it except some spruce lumber he expected to obtain nearer his destination.

The journey proved to be more of an undertaking than Wilbur expected.

V

GLIDING AT KITTY HAWK

ONE must look at a map of North Carolina to get an idea of the isolation of the long strip of sandy beach that separates the Atlantic Ocean from Albemarle, Pamlico, and Roanoke Sounds. At the time the Wrights went there, no bridges connected this beach with any part of the North Carolina mainland or even with nearby Roanoke Island, seat of Sir Walter Raleigh's "Lost Colony." At one point on the beach was the Kitty Hawk life-saving station, and alongside of it a government weather bureau. About a mile back from the ocean was the hamlet of Kitty Hawk which, though it had a post office, was little more than a settlement, with only about a score of dwelling houses, most of them as widely scattered as in an ordinary farming community. Four miles south was the Kill Devil life-saving station.

It was not surprising that when Wilbur Wright, on September 9, 1900, reached Elizabeth City, North Carolina, the nearest railroad point to his destination, the first persons he chanced to ask about Kitty Hawk had never heard of the place. Then he learned that a boat made weekly trips to Roanoke Island; but it had gone the day before. Not liking delay, he went to the water front to inquire if another boat might be available. There he met one Israel Perry, formerly a resident of Kitty Hawk, who lived the year round on his little flat-bottomed schooner. As no other boatman showed any interest in making the trip, Wilbur booked passage with "Captain" Perry, despite the boat's dirty, forbidding appearance. After loading parts of the glider and other goods that had been shipped from Dayton, he set out with Perry on the morning of September 10 for the forty-mile voyage to Kitty Hawk. Wilbur noticed that the small boat they used to go from the wharf out to where the schooner was anchored was leaking badly and he asked if it was safe.

"Oh," Perry assured him, "it's safer than the *big* boat." That didn't inspire too much confidence in what was in store, and Wilbur soon learned that any misgivings he felt were amply justified. Toward the middle of the afternoon they met a strong head wind that forced them to seek a smooth water haven in North River where they anchored to await better weather. By that time Wilbur had worked up a good appetite; but he discovered that neither the food nor the kitchen met even minimum standards of cleanliness and he made excuses, as politely as he could, for not eating. All he had with him against hunger was a small jar of jelly his sister Katharine had slipped into his suitcase.

The weather was not favorable for continuing the voyage until the afternoon of the second day, and the boat reached a wharf, where there was a small store, on Kitty Hawk bay, at about nine o'clock that night. Not knowing where else to go, Wilbur stayed aboard until the next morning. A small boy named Baum agreed to guide him to the home of William J. Tate, about a quarter of a mile away. By the time Wilbur arrived there, on that morning of September 12, it was just forty-eight hours since he had tasted food other than his little supply of jelly.

After introducing himself, and in response to "Bill" Tate's inquiries about how he enjoyed his trip, Wilbur spoke of his back being sore from lying on deck and of how his arm ached from holding on when the boat rolled. Then it came out that he had been unable to bring himself to eat the food provided on the Perry schooner.

"You mean to tell me," asked "Bill" Tate, greatly concerned, "that you've eaten no victuals for two days?"

Here was a situation that called for quick action in a hospitable home. It was after the Tates' breakfast hour, but Mrs. Tate soon had a fire in the kitchen stove and prepared a great platter of ham and eggs that the guest seemed to relish.

Then Wilbur inquired if it would be possible for him to obtain board and lodging there for the week or more until his brother "Orv" arrived.

Tate went into an adjoining room to ask his wife. As the door was ajar, Wilbur could hear what was said. Mrs. Tate was a bit alarmed. Here was a man able to devote time and money for weeks at a time to sport. Doubtless he must be a person of great wealth, accustomed to every luxury. Would he be satisfied with the best they could offer?

Wilbur stepped to the door, explaining that he could not help overhearing their conversation, and said it must be understood that if he were accepted as a paying guest he would not expect any extra frills, but would greatly appreciate the courtesy.

"This fellow's a real gentleman," thought Tate, and by way of settling the question, without waiting to hear any more from his wife, he said to Wilbur:

"You must be tired. Why don't you come into our spare bedroom and take a nap?"

By the next day Wilbur was at work. The cloth covering for the glider—white French sateen of extra good quality—had already been shaped and sewed at Dayton, except at the ends, to permit fitting it over the framework. But now he had to make changes in the covering, because the glider was going to be smaller than originally planned. The longest timbers, for the wing spars, that he had been able to find in either Norfolk or Elizabeth City were only sixteen feet long instead of the eighteen-foot length he desired. Thus it was necessary to cut out strips from the middle of the lengths of cloth for both upper and lower wings. For resewing the cloth where necessary, Wilbur borrowed Mrs. Tate's machine. But all the rest of the work of assembling the glider was done at a tent Wilbur set up, about half a mile from the Tate home, at a spot where there were a few trees and a view of the bay. He dragged the crates, containing various parts and tools, to the tent and hoped to have everything in readiness when Orville arrived. But the heat was intense, the job of carrying water to the camp used up much energy, and when Orville got there, on September 28, Wilbur told him regretfully that much work on the glider was still to be done.

Orville's trip had been uneventful. Indeed, though he came on a better boat than Israel Perry's, he had struck such a calm sea that his voyage from Elizabeth City took two days, the same as Wilbur's. For the first five days after Orville's arrival, both brothers stayed at the Tate home. Then they established themselves in camp. One end of their tent, twelve by twenty-two feet, was tied to a tree for anchorage. The tree was headquarters for a mocking bird that sometimes joined in the harmony when Orville twanged at a mandolin he had brought from home.

Not many visitors came to the camp from near-by Kitty Hawk. One reason for this was that the camp was considered dangerous after news got about that the Wrights used a gasoline stove. "Bill" Tate was favorably impressed, though, with an acetylene lamp, intended for a bicycle, that the Wrights used for lighting. He said he had a notion to install such a system of gas lighting in his house.

It was necessary to carry water about one thousand feet over the sand. Orville volunteered to do the cooking—and he continued to do so during all their experiments at Kitty Hawk. But he always felt that he had the better of the bargain, for the dish-washing job was Wilbur's. As it was impossible to obtain fresh bread, Orville learned to make biscuits, and without use of milk. They were good biscuits, too—better, his father afterward insisted, than anyone else could make. To simplify operations, Orville always mixed at one time enough flour and other dry ingredients to last for several days, as biscuits had to be baked three times daily.

Working together, the brothers soon had the glider assembled. When completed it weighed about fifty-two pounds. Though the main spars were only sixteen feet long, the "bows" at the ends of each wing surface brought the total span to nearly seventeen and one-half feet. The total lifting area was 165 square feet instead of 200 as intended. A space eighteen inches wide at the center of the lower surface where the operator would lie, with feet over the rear spar, was left free of covering. The apparatus had no rear vanes or tail of any kind; but it had two important features never used by previous experimenters. One was the front rudder, or "elevator," the rear edge of which was about thirty inches from the nearest edge of the wings; the other was the wing warping. By an ingenious arrangement of the trussing, the wings could be twisted into a helicoidal warp from one end to the other, thus exposing one wing to the air at a greater angle than the other. This was to be used for bringing the machine back to the level after it was tipped up sidewise by a gust of wind.

The Wrights' first surprise at Kitty Hawk was that the winds there were not what they had counted on. United States Weather Bureau reports had led them to think they would have winds of about fifteen miles an hour almost every day. But now it dawned on them that fifteen miles an hour was simply the daily average for a month. Sometimes the wind was sixty miles an hour, and the next day it would be entirely calm. It now began to look as if they might frequently have to wait a few days for suitable conditions, which meant that their experiments would require more time than they had expected.

Almost as soon as they began their trials of the glider, the brothers got another surprise. According to the Lilienthal tables of air pressures, their machine of 165 square feet needed a wind of only from seventeen to twenty-one miles an hour to support it as a kite with a pilot aboard. But they found that much stronger winds were needed to lift it. Since suitable winds would not be plentiful, their plan of practicing by the hour aboard the glider while flying it as a kite would have to be postponed. Instead, they flew it as a kite, loaded with about fifty pounds of chain, but with no man aboard. They held it with two ropes, and operated the balancing system by cords from the ground. Though the results were promising, inspiring confidence in the system of maintaining equilibrium, the brothers knew that only by actual gliding experience could they confirm what the kite experiments had indicated as being true.

One thing that puzzled them was that the machine appeared to be greatly deficient in lifting power as compared with calculated lift of curved surfaces of its size. In wondering what might be the cause of this wide discrepancy between expected and actual lifts, the Wrights considered the possibility that it might be because the curvature of the wings was less than that used by Lilienthal. Or could it be that the cloth covering was too porous and permitted some of the lifting power of the wind to be lost? They wondered, too, if the Lilienthal tables they had followed, relating to air pressure on wing surfaces, could be in error.

They next determined to try gliding on the side of a hill. That meant toting their machine four miles south of their camp to a great sand dune about one hundred feet high, called Kill Devil Hill. On their first day at the hill, the wind was about twenty-five miles an hour. As they lacked previous experience at gliding they decided to wait for less of a blow for their first attempt. The next day the wind had subsided to fourteen miles an hour, and they made about a dozen glides. "Bill" Tate was there and assisted them.

In making these glides, the machine was usually only two or three feet from the soft, sandy ground, and though the brothers repeatedly made landings while moving at a speed of twenty miles an hour, neither operator nor machine was harmed. The slope of the hill toward the northeast was about 9½ degrees, or a drop of approximately one foot in six. After moving at a rate of about twenty-five to thirty miles an hour with reference to the wind, or ten to fifteen miles over the ground, the machine, while keeping its course parallel to the slope, increased its speed, thus indicating that it could glide on a slope less steep.

Their control of the machine was even better than they had dared to expect. They got quick response to the slightest movement of the front elevator, which promised to be satisfactory in maintaining fore and aft balance. At first, they fastened the warping mechanism, to make it inoperable, and had only the elevator to manipulate, for they feared that, inexperienced as they were, if they tried to use both, then they might be unsuccessful with either. But even without the use of the warping mechanism it was possible to make glides of from five to ten seconds before the sidewise tilt of the machine forced a landing. Before making the last three or four flights the Wrights loosened the warping wires to permit the sidewise control to be used.

When these experiments of 1900 ended, instead of the hours of practice in the air the Wrights had hoped to have, they had flown the machine as a kite with a man aboard barely ten minutes, and had had only two minutes of actual gliding.

Now that the experiments for that year were ended and they had no further use for the glider, the brothers weighted the machine with sand and left it on the hill. When "Bill" Tate saw that they were through with the glider he asked if he might have it, and they gladly gave it to him. Mrs. Tate used the sateen that covered the wings to make dresses for her two small daughters. She noted that it appeared to be unusually good fabric, more closely woven and better than she had seen in the stores. Some of her neighbors, when they saw the dresses she made of it, remarked that it seemed too bad to use such excellent material on a kite.

Though the amount of practice was less than they had expected, all the Wrights had learned in that season of 1900 seemed to confirm the correctness of certain opinions held at the beginning. Their method of warping or twisting the wings to maintain lateral balance was better than dependence on either the dihedral angle or shifting the weight of the operator; better than any method yet tried. And their front elevator had been highly satisfactory as a means for directing the machine up and down. Before leaving Kitty Hawk they decided that their next experiments would be with a glider large enough to be flown as a kite, with an operator aboard, in winds ordinarily to be counted on.

When the brothers set to work on their glider for the experiments of 1901, they decided to make it of the same general design as the first one, and with the same system of control. But they carried out their plan to give it considerably more area, to provide greater lifting power. Another change they made was to increase the curvature of the wings to conform to the shape on which Lilienthal had based his tables of air pressures. It had wings of about seven-foot chord (the straight line distance between the front and rear edges) with a total span of twenty-two feet, and weighed ninety-eight pounds. After a section twenty inches wide had been removed from the middle of the lower wing, and the rear corners of the wings rounded off, the total lifting area was 290 square feet, as compared with 165 in the previous glider. The front elevator, with its rear edge about two and one half feet away from the front edge of the wings, had a four-and-one-half foot chord and an area of eighteen square feet.

This was a much larger machine than anyone had ever tried to fly. The Wrights knew it could not be controlled simply by shifting the pilot's weight, as others had done, but they had faith in their own operable front elevator and believed they could manage it. If their calculations were correct, it would be supported in a wind of seventeen miles an hour, with the wing surfaces at an "angle of incidence" of only three degrees. ("Angle of incidence," now more often called "angle of attack," has been defined as the angle at which the plane presents itself to the air in advancing against it.)

As it would be impractical to keep so large a machine with them in the tent, as they had done with the smaller glider, the brothers built near Kill Devil Hill a rough frame shed, twenty-five feet long, sixteen feet wide, and seven feet high at the eaves. Both ends of the building except the gable parts were made into doors, hinged above. When open, the doors provided an awning at each end of the building. For living quarters they still used a tent. By driving a pipe ten or twelve feet into the sand they got a water supply.

Though the great stretch of sandy waste seemed too desolate for anyone to bother about owning, yet it was all under the ownership of one person or another and the Wrights took the precaution to obtain permission to erect their buildings.

This year they were to have company in camp. Octave Chanute, with whom they had been in correspondence for about a year, stopped in Dayton in June, 1901, at their invitation, to get better acquainted. When he learned that the Wrights had carried on their experiments in 1900 without the presence of a doctor in camp, and were intending to do so again, he told them he thought that was too risky, considering the kind of work and the isolation of the experiment ground. He said he knew a young man in Coatesville, Pennsylvania, George A. Spratt, "an amateur" in aeronautics, who had had some medical training. Spratt had never seen any gliding experiments, and Chanute thought he would be eager for the opportunity. If the Wrights would board him at camp, Chanute said, he would be glad to pay Spratt's traveling expenses to Kitty Hawk and would consider himself "compensated by the pleasure given to him." Chanute also proposed that they have in camp with them E. C. Huffaker, of Chuckey City, Tennessee, who was building a glider that Chanute was financing, and the Wrights consented. Thus there were four regularly in camp that season, and for a time Chanute himself was with them as a guest.

The new machine was completed and ready for trial on the afternoon of July 27. Since it was designed to be flown in a wind of seventeen miles, and there was but thirteen miles of wind on that day, the brothers took the machine to the big Kill Devil Hill for its first trial. After five or six short tuning-up flights they made a glide of 315 feet in nineteen seconds. Although several flights on this first day of experiments in 1901 exceeded the best made the year before, yet it was soon evident that in several respects the machine was not as good as the first one. It was found that the wings, with a camber of one to twelve—the camber recommended by Lilienthal, and used by Chanute and others—was not so good as the camber of one to twenty-two, used by the Wrights in 1900. (Camber of one to twenty-two means that the length of the chord, the straight-line distance between the front and rear edges of the wings, is twenty-two times the distance *from* the chord to the deepest part of the wing curve.) This was demonstrated by the fact that the 1901 machine could not glide on a slope as nearly level as had the earlier machine. The

Wrights found, too, that a machine with wings of one to twelve camber was not so easily controlled fore and aft as when the wings were of one to twenty-two camber. They decided therefore to reduce the camber of the wings to make them more like those of the earlier machine. When they resumed their gliding, after the camber had been reduced (one to eighteen), the control of the machine appeared to be as good as it was the year before, and they then made flights in winds of twenty-two to twenty-seven miles an hour, without accident. Though in most of these flights the lateral control was highly effective, in a few others—under conditions seemingly the same—the wing warping appeared to have no effect at all.

The Wrights now made the discovery that in free flight, when the wing on one side of the machine was presented to the wind at a greater angle than that on the other side, the wing with the greater angle, instead of rising as it was expected to do, sometimes descended. The explanation was that the greater angle of the wing at one side gave more resistance to forward motion and thus reduced the speed on that side. This decrease in speed more than counter-balanced the effect of the larger angle of the wing in producing lift. (The Wrights had not discovered this when flying the glider as a kite, because, when held by ropes, the wings always maintained equal air speeds, even when their resistances were unbalanced.)

It was evident to the brothers that their present method of controlling equilibrium was not yet complete. Something was needed to maintain equal speeds at the two wing tips. The idea occurred to them that the addition of a vertical fin attached to the machine at some distance in the rear of the wings might be the solution of the problem. But the test of such a fin had to be left until another season.

The behavior of the glider in these various flights forced the Wrights to give thought to another scientific problem, that regarding the center of air pressure on curved surfaces. Contrary to the teachings of scientific books on the subject, it was becoming more and more evident that the travel of the center of pressure on a cambered surface is not always in the same direction as the travel on a plane surface. When the angle of attack on a plane surface is decreased, the center of pressure moves toward the front edge; but on a cambered surface this is true only when larger angles are being decreased. When the angle of attack on a cambered surface is decreased from, say, thirty degrees to twenty-five degrees, the center of pressure moves forward, as it does on a plane surface; but when a certain angle (between twelve and fifteen degrees) is reached, then the movement of the center of pressure is reversed. From there on, the center of pressure moves toward the rear so long as any further decrease is made in the angle of attack. The Wrights proved this by a series of experiments with a single surface from their plane. Knowledge of the phenomenon of this reversal of center of pressure was of great importance to them in their later work of designing aeroplanes.

Scientific problems were not the only ones to perplex the Wrights. A sore trial were the mosquitoes and sandfleas, particularly numerous and aggressive in that summer of 1901. As Orville Wright recalled in later years, there were times when he thought, while fighting mosquitoes through the night, that if he could just survive until morning he would pack up and return home. Those mosquitoes might have caused a long postponement of the conquest of the air.

By the time they left Kitty Hawk on August 20, the brothers had satisfied themselves that a glider of large surfaces could be controlled almost as easily as a smaller one, provided the control is by manipulation of the surfaces themselves instead of by movements of the operator's body. So far as they knew, judging from figures previously published, they had broken all records for distance in gliding. Chanute, who had witnessed part of the 1901 experiments, insisted that the results were better than had ever been attained before. All that was encouraging. But, on the other hand, if most of the supposedly scientific information available was worthless, then their task was even more formidable than they had expected. With no dependable previous knowledge to guide them, who were they to determine how man should fly? Wilbur seemed much discouraged. Possibly he had entertained hopes of actually flying, though he had always disclaimed having such an idea. He was ready to drop the experiments altogether. On the way home, Wilbur declared his belief: Not within a thousand years would man ever fly!

Chanute urged the brothers not to drop their experiments, arguing that if they did it would be a long time before anyone else would come as near to understanding the problem or how to work toward its solution. Without knowing it, Chanute made a great contribution to aviation history, for the Wrights heeded his repeated admonitions against ceasing their efforts. Without the proddings of Chanute they might not have gone on.

Chanute performed another great service for aeronautics when he, as president of the Western Society of Engineers, invited Wilbur Wright to address that body at a meeting in Chicago, September 18, 1901, on the subject: Some Aeronautical Experiments.

Wilbur shrank from the idea of making such a talk and would hardly have done so except to oblige his friend. He cautioned Chanute, though, not to make the speech a prominent feature of the program, because, he said, he made no pretense of being a public speaker. Chanute did nevertheless plan to use the announcement of the talk as a means to help make the meeting a big success. He wanted to know if it would be all right to make the occasion "Ladies' Night." Wilbur decided that he would already be as badly scared as a man could be and the presence of women would not make the situation much worse. But he insisted on one thing, that he must not be expected to appear in formal evening dress.

In this speech Wilbur boldly declared that the best sets of figures obtainable regarding air pressure against airplane surfaces appeared to contain many serious errors. Orville, at the shop in Dayton, was a little alarmed about that part of the speech. What if something about their own work had been wrong and the figures compiled by various scientists should finally be proved correct? Certainly it was no small responsibility for anyone so little known as Wilbur or he to denounce publicly the work of eminent scientists, dignified by preservation in books long regarded as authoritative. It would be both presumptuous and risky to brand supposedly established facts as untrue unless the person doing so could be unassailably sure of his ground.

In this cautious state of mind Orville rigged up a little wind-tunnel for the purpose of making a series of tests. This tunnel consisted simply of what appeared to be an old starch box, not more than eighteen inches long, that was lying in the shop. In it he placed a hastily constructed apparatus, a main part of which was simply a metal rod pivoted in the manner of a weather vane. Without attempting to give technical details of the method used, it may be said that a curved surface was balanced against a plane surface in an air current passing through the box. As Orville had provided the box with a glass top he could measure the angles to the wind at which the curved surface and the plane surface of equal area produced equal pressures.

The experiments with this crude apparatus lasted only one day. They were conclusive enough so far as they went, indicating errors in published figures relating to air pressure on curved surfaces. But as Orville was later to learn, the published errors were greatest in regard to wing surfaces set at small angles, such as would be used in flying, and he had tested thus far only larger angles. With the tests thus incomplete, Orville and Wilbur decided, on the latter's return from Chicago, that it might be prudent to stay on the safe side and omit from the published record of Wilbur's speech the more severe part of his criticism of available figures. They would wait until further wind-tunnel experiments could give more detailed knowledge. Consequently, when Wilbur's speech appeared in the December, 1901, issue of the *Journal of the Western Society of Engineers*, it was a bit less startling than the one he had actually delivered— though, even after the deletions, there still remained strong hints that accepted tables of figures might be wrong. And the record of the speech was treated as of great importance. It has probably been reprinted and quoted as often as any other article ever written on the subject of flying.

The Wrights were not sure they would ever build another glider. But their curiosity, their passion for getting at truth, had now been too much aroused for them to quit studying the problem of air pressures. They decided to build another wind-tunnel, less crude than the one Orville had hastily used, and continue their experiments. The new tunnel consisted of an open-ended wooden box about sixteen inches square on the inside by six feet long. Into one end would come a current of air and the draft thus created would be "straightened," as well as made uniform, by having to pass through a set of small pigeon-holes. It would have been a great convenience to use an electric fan for sending the air into the tunnel. But the Wrights had no electric current in their shop—still lighted by gas—and the fan was driven by a one-cylinder gas engine they had previously made. They attached the fan to a spindle that had held an emery wheel. A new measuring device, or balance, was built of wire intended for bicycle spokes, and pieces of hacksaw blades. These experiments were now done with much more refinement than at first, and the measurements were for both "lift" and "drift." But as each curved surface measured was balanced against the pressure on a square plane, exposed at ninety degrees to the same air current, it was not necessary to know the precise speed of the air current.

During that autumn and early winter of 1901, the brothers tested in the wind-tunnel more than two hundred types of wing surfaces. They set these at different angles, starting with the angle at which the surface begins to lift, and then at 2½ degree intervals, up to twenty; and at five degree intervals up to forty-five degrees. They measured monoplane, biplane, and triplane models; also models in which one wing followed the other, as used by Langley in his experiments. They measured the lift produced by different "aspect ratios" —that is, the ratio of the span of the wing to its chord. They found that the greater the span in proportion to the chord the more easily the wing may be supported. They measured thick and thin surfaces. One surface had a thickness of nearly one-sixth of its chord.

Among other things, these experiments proved the fallacy of the sharp edge at the front of an airplane wing and the inefficiency of deeply cambered wings as then generally advocated by others. Sometimes they got a result so unexpected that they could hardly believe their own measurements—as, for example, when they discovered that, contrary to all previously published figures by students of the subject, a square plane gave a greater pressure when set at thirty degrees than at forty-five degrees.

These wind-tunnel experiments in the bicycle shop were carried on for only a little more than two months, and were ended before Christmas, 1901. The Wrights discontinued them with great reluctance; but, after all, they were still in the bicycle business, still obliged to give thought to their means for earning a living, and with no idea that this scientific research could ever be financially profitable. In those few weeks, however, they had accomplished something of almost incalculable importance. They had not only made the first wind-tunnel in which miniature wings were accurately tested, but were the first men in all the world to compile tables of figures from which one might design an airplane that could fly. Even today, in wind-tunnels used in various aeronautical laboratories, equipped with the most elaborate and delicate instruments modern science can provide, the refinements obtained over the Wrights' figures for the same shapes of surfaces are surprisingly small. But it is doubtful if the difficulties and full value of the Wrights' scientific researches within their bicycle shop are yet appreciated. The world knows they were the first to build a machine capable of sustained flight and the first actually to fly; but it is not fully aware of all the tedious, grueling scientific laboratory work they had to do before flight was possible. Important as was the system of control with which the Wrights' name has been connected, it would not have given them success without their wind-tunnel work which enabled them to design a machine that would lift itself.

The Wrights had a double reason for making sure of their figures. With little money to spend on a hobby, it was much cheaper to rectify mistakes on paper than after the idea was put into material form. They knew that if they should decide to go on to further gliding attempts, they could not afford to spend much more money on apparatus built according to unreliable data.

After compiling their own tables of figures, the Wrights gave copies of them to their friend Chanute and others interested in the problem of aerodynamics. Chanute well knew that the Wrights now had knowledge of aeronautics far beyond that of anyone else in the world, and he felt that for them to go on with their experiments was almost a duty. He much regretted, in the interest of science, he said, that they had reached a stopping-place, for he was sure further experiments on their part promised "important results."

Chanute might well have felt pride in the effectiveness of his insistence that the Wrights should go on experimenting, as well as in the results of his invitation to Wilbur to make that Chicago speech. Except for that speech and its daring statements that Orville thought needed more confirmation, there probably would have been no wind-tunnel tests; and without the kind of knowledge then obtained, neither the Wrights nor anyone else could have built a practical flying-machine. Those wind-tunnel experiments marked one of the great turning points in the long history of attempts at human flight.

It still remained for the Wrights to put their new knowledge to actual test in gliding, and they set out on

August 25, 1902, for their third stay at Kitty Hawk. But not until September 8 were they able to begin the work of assembling their new glider, for the camp, battered by winter gales, needed much repairing; and they decided to build an addition to it for living quarters. They did not have their machine ready for its first trial until September 19.

This new glider was of not much greater lifting area than that of the previous year, though the wing span had been increased from twenty-two to thirty-two feet. But since the wind-tunnel experiments had demonstrated the importance of the "aspect ratio," the total span was now about six times the chord instead of three. One minor change also may be noted. In the earlier gliders, the wing-warping mechanism had been worked by movement of the operator's feet; but now in this 1902 glider it was done by sidewise movement of one's hips resting on a "cradle." The most noticeable change was the addition of a tail, consisting of fixed twin vertical vanes, with a total area of a trifle less than twelve square feet. Its purpose was to correct certain difficulties encountered in some of the flights with the 1901 machine. When the wing surfaces at the right and left sides were warped to present different angles toward the wind, the wing that had the greater angle, and therefore the more resistance, tended to lag behind, and then the slower speed offset what otherwise would have been the greater lifting power of that wing. The tail was expected to counter-balance that difference in resistance of the wing tips. If the wing on one side tended to swerve forward, on a vertical axis, then the tail, more exposed to the wind on that same side, should, it was thought, stop the machine from further turning.

Entirely apart from any advantages to be gained from the use of the tail, the first trials of the new machine were highly encouraging for another reason. It was soon evident that by disregarding all tables of air pressures used by their predecessors and building according to the figures obtained from their wind-tunnel experiments, the Wrights had made a big advance toward flight. Because of the knowledge they now had, not possessed by any previous experimenter, of how the wings should be shaped, this 1902 machine was of just about twice the "dynamic efficiency" of any other glider ever built; it could have been flown with probably less than half the power required for any other glider.

Altogether the Wrights made more than one thousand gliding flights in September and October, 1902. Several glides were of more than six hundred feet, and a number of them were against a thirty-six-mile-an-hour wind. No previous experimenter had ever dared to try gliding in so stiff a wind. That the Wrights were successful at such feats gave proof of the effectiveness of their devices for control. Some of their flights lasted more than a minute and at times it was possible to soar in one spot without any descent. So impressive were such exhibitions that Bill Tate's brother Dan solemnly offered the opinion: "All she needs is a coat of feathers to make her light and she will stay in the air indefinitely."

About one time in fifty, however, the machine behaved in a manner quite mysterious. It would turn up sidewise and come sliding to the ground in spite of all the warp the operator could give to the wing tips. At one trial the lateral control would work perfectly and then the next time, under conditions that seemed to be about the same, it was impossible to prevent one wing end from striking the sand with a kind of spinning movement that the brothers called "well-digging."

This new problem, that had not occurred in their previous gliders, came from the fact that the machine had a tail. Those "well-digging" accidents were tail-spins—though that term did not come into use until several years afterward. But even after it was evident that the tail had something to do with the machine's peculiar behavior, neither brother was prepared to explain *why*. Then one night Orville drank more than his customary amount of coffee. Instead of going to sleep as usual the moment he got into bed, he lay awake for several hours. Those extra cups of coffee may have been important for the future of practical flight for, as he tossed about, he figured out the explanation of the phenomenon caused by the tail. Here it is, as he eagerly gave it to Wilbur, and to their brother Lorin, who was visiting them, at breakfast the next morning:

When the machine became tilted laterally it began to slide sidewise while advancing, just as a sled slides downhill or a ball rolls down an inclined plane, the speed increasing in an accelerated ratio. If the tilt happened to be a little worse than usual, or if the operator were a little slow in getting the balance corrected, the machine slid sidewise so fast that this movement caused the vertical vanes to strike the wind on the side toward the low wing instead of on the side toward the high wing, as it was expected to do. In this state of affairs the vertical vanes did not counteract the turning of the machine about a vertical axis, caused by the difference of resistance of the warped wings on the right and left sides; on the contrary, the vanes assisted in the turning movement, and the result was worse than if there were no fixed vertical tail.

If his explanation was sound, as Orville felt sure it was, then, he said, it would be necessary to make the vertical tail movable, to permit the operator to bring pressure to bear on the side toward the higher wing. (This is the form of the Wright system of control generally used today—the independent control of aileron and rudder.)

Wilbur promptly saw that the explanation was probably correct and nodded approvingly. And he immediately made a suggestion. A particular relation existed, he said, in the desired pressures on the tail, no matter whether the trouble was due to difference of resistance of the wing tips or on account of sliding. Whatever the reason, it was desirable to get rid of the pressure on the side toward the low wing, to which a greater angle of incidence must be imparted in restoring lateral balance, and bring pressure on the side of the tail toward the high wing where there must be a reduced angle. So why not have the mechanism that controlled the wing warping and that which moved the tail operated in conjunction? Then the pilot, instead of having to control three things at once, would need to attend only to the front elevator and the wing-warping device. The brothers at once attached the wires controlling the tail to those that warped the wings—and they also changed the tail from two vertical fins to a single vertical rudder.

After the changes in the 1902 glider, the Wrights had their machine in about the form pictured and described in the drawings and specifications of their patent, applied for on the 23rd of the next March.

With their accurate data for making calculations, and a system of balance effective in winds as well as in calms, the brothers believed that they now could build a successful power-flyer.

VI

FIRST POWER FLIGHT

IMMEDIATELY on their return to Dayton after the 1902 glider flights, the Wrights set to work to carry out plans, already begun at Kitty Hawk, for a power machine. The satisfactory performance of the glider had demonstrated the accuracy of the laboratory work on which its design was based, and they now felt sure they could calculate in advance the performance of any machine they built with a degree of accuracy not possible with the data available to their predecessors.

Early in their preparations, they took steps to obtain a suitable engine. They knew that a steam engine might do well enough for their purpose, but a gasoline engine would be simpler and better. Some time previously they had built an air-cooled, one-cylinder gas engine for operating the machinery of their small workshop; but they did not feel experienced enough to build the kind they now needed and preferred to buy one.

They wanted a motor to produce at least eight horsepower and to weigh, without accessories, not more than twenty pounds per horsepower. It seemed doubtful if such a motor as they required was then being manufactured; but perhaps one of the automobile companies could build one light enough by reducing the weight of the flywheel and using more aluminum than in the regu-

INSIDE THE 1902 CAMP. The kitchen corner of the 1902 camp at Kitty Hawk.

FROM ORVILLE WRIGHT'S DIARY. Part of the entry for December 17, 1903—the day of the first power flight.

lar output. On December 3, 1902, they sent letters to a number of automobile companies, and to gasoline motor manufacturers, altogether to nearly a dozen, asking if they could furnish a motor that would develop eight brake horsepower and weigh not more than 200 pounds. Orville Wright was not sure in after years whether he and Wilbur revealed in their letters the use they planned for the motor they were seeking; but most of the companies replied that they were too busy with their regular business to undertake such a special order. There is reason to suspect the companies may have got wind of the purpose to which the motor would be put and were afraid to become implicated in the project. If a company provided a motor for a so-called flying-machine, and this fact should leak out, it could hurt their business prestige, because it might look as if they considered human flight a possibility.

One company replied, however, that they had motors, rated at eight horsepower, according to the French system of ratings, which weighed only 135 pounds, and if the Wrights thought this would develop enough power for their purpose, they could buy one. After an examination of the particulars of this motor, from which they learned that it had but a single cylinder, of four-inch bore and five-inch stroke, the Wrights decided that its power was probably much overrated.

Finally the brothers decided that they would have to build their motor themselves. They estimated that they could make one of four cylinders, of four-inch bore and four-inch stroke, weighing not more than two hundred pounds, with accessories included. Their mechanic,

Charlie Taylor, gave them enthusiastic help. In its final form, the bare engine, without magneto, weighed 152 pounds; with accessories, 170 pounds. At 1,200 revolutions per minute, it developed sixteen horsepower—but only for the first fifteen seconds after starting; after a minute or two it did not give more than about twelve horsepower. Since, however, they had not counted on more than eight horsepower, for a machine of a total weight of 600 pounds, now they could add 150 pounds for strengthening wings and other parts. Not yet knowing how much power an engine of that size ought to have developed, the Wrights were much pleased with its performance. Long afterward they found out that the engine should have provided about twice as much power as it did. The trouble, as they later said, was their "lack of experience in building gasoline motors."

The wings of this new power machine had a total span of a few inches more than forty feet, and the upper and lower wing surfaces were six feet apart. To reduce the danger of the engine ever falling on the pilot, it was placed on the lower wing a little to right of center. The pilot would ride lying flat, as on the glider, but to the left of center, to balance the weight. To guard against the machine rolling over in landing, the sled-like runners were extended farther out in front of the main surfaces than on the glider. These two runners were four feet, eight inches apart. The tail of the machine had twin movable vanes instead of a single vane as in the 1902 glider.

The Wrights left the designing of the propellers until the last, because they felt sure that part of the job would be easy enough. Their tables of air pressures, derived from wind-tunnel experiments, would enable them, they thought, to calculate exactly the thrust necessary to sustain the machine in flight. But to design a propeller that would give the needed amount of thrust, with the power at their command, was a problem they had not yet considered. No data on air propellers were available, but the Wrights had always understood that it was not difficult to obtain an efficiency of fifty per cent with marine propellers. All that should be necessary would be to learn the theory of the operation of propellers from books on marine engineering and then substitute air pressures for water pressures. What could be simpler or easier? Accordingly, the brothers got several such books from the Dayton Public Library. But when they began to read those books, they discovered to their surprise that much less was known about propellers than they had supposed.

All the formulae on propellers in the books were found to be based on experiment and observation rather than on theory. The marine engineers, when they saw that a propeller would not move a boat fast enough, had then tried one larger, or of a different pitch, until they got one that would serve their purpose. But they could not design a propeller on paper and foresee exactly what its performance on a certain type of motor-boat would be. Exact knowledge of the action of the screw propeller, though it had been in use for a century, was still lacking.

The Wrights knew that rough estimates, which might be near enough for a motor-boat, would not do for an airplane. On a boat a propeller having only a fraction of one per cent of the desired efficiency could move the boat a little; but on an airplane, unless the propeller had the full amount of thrust needed, it would be worthless, for it couldn't lift the plane into the air at all! In short, the Wrights had to have a propeller that would do exactly what was expected of it. And they had neither the time nor money to carry on a long series of experiments with different kinds of propellers until they could hit on one suitable. They couldn't afford to make mistakes except on paper. They must somehow learn enough about how propellers acted, and why, to enable them to make accurate calculations.

It was apparent to the Wrights that a propeller was simply an airfoil traveling in a spiral course. As they could calculate the effect of an airfoil traveling in a straight course, why should they not be able to calculate the effect in a spiral course? At first thought that did not seem too difficult, but they soon found that they had let themselves into a tough job. Since nothing about a propeller, or the medium in which it acts, would be standing still, it was not easy to find even a point from which to make a start. The more they studied it, the more complex the problem became. "The thrust depends upon the speed and the angle at which the blade strikes the air; the angle at which the blade strikes the air depends upon the speed at which the propeller is turning, the speed the machine is traveling forward, and the speed at which the air is slipping backward; the slip of the air backward depends upon the thrust exerted by the propeller, and the amount of air acted upon." It was not exactly as simple as some of the problems in the school arithmetic—to determine how many sheep a man had or how many leaps a hound must make to overtake a hare.

In trying to work out a theory about the action of screw propellers, Wilbur and Orville got into many arguments. Right here it may be noted that this habit the brothers had of arguing technical points was one of the reasons why they were able to accomplish all they finally did in a relatively short time. Neither was a "yes" man to the other. But in their arguments about propellers a peculiar thing happened. "Often," Orville later reported, "after an hour or so of heated argument, we would discover that we were as far from agreement as when we started, but that *each had changed to the other's original position.*"

Many months passed before the intricacies of the problem began to untangle themselves. The Wrights finally got a better understanding of the action of screw propellers than anyone had ever had before. The time came when they felt sure of their ability to design propellers of exactly the right diameter, pitch, and area for their needs.

A calculation indicated that 305 revolutions of the propeller would be required to produce 100 pounds thrust. Later, actual measurement showed that only 302 instead of 305 propeller turns were required, or just under one per cent of the calculated amount. The propellers delivered in useful work 66 per cent of the power expended. That was about one-third more than either

Hiram Maxim or Professor Langley in their attempts at flying had ever been able to attain.

For two reasons the Wrights decided to use two propellers. First, they could in that way obtain a reaction against a greater quantity of air, and at the same time use a larger pitch angle; and, by having the propellers run in opposite directions, the gyroscopic action of one would neutralize that of the other. The propellers were on tubular shafts about ten feet apart, both driven by chains running over sprockets, somewhat as on a bicycle.

L. M. Wainwright, president of the Diamond Chain Company, of Indianapolis, became interested in the Wrights' transmission problem, and gave them valuable advice.

The Wrights found that the chains would have to be run through guides to prevent slapping and to overcome undue stresses on the machine. They adopted tubular guides and found that they could cross one of the chains in a figure eight and thus have the propellers running in opposite directions.

Not until September 23 was all in readiness for the Wrights to set out for Kitty Hawk. They were able to make good connections with a boat and arrived at camp two days later, on a Friday. Discussing en route what they hoped to accomplish, neither had the slightest doubt about the fulfillment of their dreams. Besides being full of confidence they also felt the exuberance of excellent physical condition. Orville was now thirty-two years old and Wilbur thirty-six. Five foot ten and a quarter inches in height, Wilbur was the taller of the two by a little more than an inch and a half. Orville weighed 145 pounds, about five more than Wilbur. Each of them had grayish-blue eyes and they might have been recognized as brothers, though in their own family Wilbur at that time was considered "more of a Wright" in his facial conformation. Orville looked a little more like his mother. Both were suitably built for bird men.

Plenty of annoyances, difficulties, and delays were still to be faced. When they reached their camp near Kill Devil Hill, the Wrights found that a storm had blown it from its foundation posts. They repaired the shed and also built a new one. With two sheds they had enough space for housing both the 1902 glider and the power machine, and also for a better workshop.

Just as the new building was nearing completion, the Kitty Hawk region had one of the worst storms in years. It came without warning, soon blowing forty miles an hour, and increased during the night until the next day the wind was more than seventy-five miles an hour. Orville risked climbing to the roof to nail down some of the more exposed parts. But by the time he got to the roof edge, the wind had blown his coat about him in a manner to pinion his arms and leave him helpless. Wilbur rushed to his assistance and held down his coat, but the wind was so strong that it was almost impossible to swing a hammer accurately enough to hit a nail.

Three weeks were needed for assembling the new machine. From time to time, also, they took out the 1902 glider, still in fairly good condition in the shed where they had left it, and got practice. After the first few trials each brother was able to make a new world's record by gliding for more than a minute.

It was hoped to have the power machine ready for its first trial early in November. But at the first run of the motor on the completed machine, an unexpected strain from back-firing twisted one of the propeller shafts and tore loose the cross-arm to which the propeller was fastened. Both shafts were then sent back to the bicycle shop at Dayton to be made stronger. Dr. Spratt had arrived on October 23 to witness tests of the new machine, but the weather had become so wintry that he started home on November 5, taking with him as far as Norfolk the shafts for shipment to Dayton.

Octave Chanute came, on invitation, the next day, but he too found it difficult to be comfortable with the weather increasingly wintry and he stayed less than a week. Before leaving camp, Chanute had unintentionally given them something else to worry about. He had remarked that at least twenty per cent usually must be allowed in chain transmission for loss in power. As the Wrights had allowed only five per cent, they felt considerable alarm.

Since Chanute was a capable and famous engineer, it seemed prudent to find out whose estimates were more nearly correct. After Chanute had gone, the brothers suspended one of the drive chains over a sprocket and hung a bag of sand at each end of the chain. By measuring the amount of weight on one side needed to lift that on the other, they calculated the loss in transmission. As nearly as they could tell, this loss was even less than the five per cent they had estimated.

The shafts, made of larger and heavier tubing, arrived from Dayton on November 20. When they were tested again, a new difficulty appeared. The sprockets, which were screwed to the shafts and locked with nuts of opposite thread, kept coming loose. This was a small problem, and yet the brothers did not at once see any way to solve it. They went to bed discouraged. The next day, however, they tried, as they often did, something they had learned in the bicycle business. They had found a great variety of uses for the kind of cement intended for fastening tires to rims. Once they had used it successfully in fastening the hands of a stop-watch that several watchsmiths had said was beyond repair. Why not try tire cement on those sprockets? They heated the propeller shafts and sprockets, poured melted cement into the threads and screwed them together. There were no more loose sprockets.

Just as the machine was ready for test, bad weather set in. There was rain or snow for several days and a wind of twenty-five to thirty miles an hour from the north. But while being delayed by the weather the Wrights were not idle. They busied themselves contriving a mechanism to measure automatically the duration of a flight from the time the machine started to move forward to the time it stopped, the distance traveled through the air in that time, and the number of revolutions made by the motor and propeller. A stop-watch took the time; an anemometer measured the air traveled through; and a counter took the number

of revolutions made by the motor. The watch, anemometer, and revolution counter were all automatically
started and stopped simultaneously.

During this time, the Wrights occupied themselves
also in making tests of the strength of the wings, as well
as many satisfactory tests of the engine. During a test
of the engine, on November 28, they discovered that
one of the recently strengthened tubular shafts had developed a flaw and cracked!

With winter almost upon them, there was no time to
trust to express service in getting the shafts to Dayton.
Orville decided he would go there at once. Instead of
tubular shafts, they would use solid tool steel, necessary,
it seemed, to take up the shock of premature or missed
explosions of the engine.

Not until Friday, December 11, did Orville get back
to camp. (En route, he had read in a newspaper of the
last unsuccessful attempt to fly the Langley machine
over the Potomac at Washington.)

It didn't take long to install the new propeller shafts
and the next afternoon, Saturday, the machine was again
ready for trial. But the wind was so light that a start
could not have been made from the level ground with a
run of only sixty feet permitted by the monorail track
to be used. Nor was there enough time before dark to
take the machine to one of the near-by hills, where, by
placing the track on the steep incline, enough speed
could be promptly attained for starting in calm air.

All day Sunday the Wrights just sat at the camp and
read, hoping for suitable weather the next day. They
were now particularly eager to avoid delay because of

their boyish craving to be at home by Christmas. If there should be a spell of bad wintry weather they might have to stay at Kitty Hawk for another two or three weeks.

Monday, December 14, dawned beautifully clear, but cold, and there was not enough wind to permit a start from level ground near the camp. The Wrights therefore decided to attempt a flight from the side of Kill Devil Hill. With a relatively light wind it should be all the easier to handle the machine. The pilot, whichever one of them it should be, ought to be able not only to fly successfully but to go on down far beyond the Kitty Hawk life-saving station, nearly five miles away, before landing.

Contrary to reports of secretiveness, the Wrights, naturally desiring witnesses, had extended a general invitation to people living within five or six miles to come and see their first attempt at flight. But it was impossible for them to send word or give a signal as to the exact time the attempt would be made. They had arranged, however, to put a signal on one of the sheds that could be seen from the Kill Devil Life-Saving Station only a little more than a mile away. Members of the life-saving crew were on the lookout for the signal. Soon after the signal was hung against the wall of the shed, the Wrights were joined by John T. Daniels, Robert Westcott, Thomas Beacham, W. S. Dough, and "Uncle Benny" O'Neal. All helped to get the machine to the place selected, a quarter of a mile away, on the hillside. It would not have been easy to drag the 750-pound machine that distance and the Wrights used a

characteristic bit of ingenuity. They set the machine on
the monorail track they were going to use for the take-
off, slid it along to the end of the sixty-foot wooden
rail, then took up a rear section of the track and added
it to the front end. By thus re-laying the track over and
over, they were able to have the machine run on wheels
all the way. The sled-like skids that were the landing
gear of the machine rested on a truck—a plank about six
feet long, laid across a much smaller piece of wood to
which were attached two small wheels, one in front of
the other. Each was kept on the track by two vertical
guides. These little wheels had ball-bearings. They were
modified hubs from wheels of a bicycle. The rail itself
was two by four inches, set on edge, with the upper
surface covered by a thin strip of metal.

As soon as they reached the hill, the Wrights prepared for the test. Each was eager for the chance to
make the first trial, and they tossed a coin to determine
which of them it should be. Wilbur won the toss.

After the machine had been fastened to the track by
wire to prevent its moving until released by the operator, one of the Wrights started the motor and let it run
for a few minutes to make sure it was working properly. Then Wilbur took his place on the machine. Two
small boys, with a dog, who had come to see what was
going on, were scared away by the noise of the motor.

Here is Orville Wright's own account [1] of what then
happened:

I took a position at one of the wings, intending to help
balance the machine as it ran down the track. But when

[1] First published in *Flying*.

the restraining wire was slipped, the machine started off so quickly I could stay with it only a few feet. After a 35- to 40-foot run, it lifted from the rail.

But it was allowed to turn up too much. It climbed a few feet, stalled, and then settled to the ground near the foot of the hill, 105 feet below. My stop-watch showed that it had been in the air just 3½ seconds. In landing, the left wing touched first. The machine swung around, dug the skids into the sand and broke one of them. Several other parts were also broken, but the damage to the machine was not serious. While the tests had shown nothing as to whether the power of the motor was sufficient to keep the machine up, since the landing was made many feet below the starting point, the experiment had demonstrated that the method adopted for launching the machine was a safe and practical one. On the whole, we were much pleased.

Two days were consumed in making repairs, and the machine was not ready again till late in the afternoon of the 16th. While we had it out on the track in front of the building, making the final adjustments, a stranger came along. After looking at the machine a few seconds he inquired what it was. When we told him it was a flying-machine he asked whether we intended to fly it. We said we did, as soon as we had a suitable wind. He looked at it several minutes longer and then, wishing to be courteous, remarked that it looked as if it would fly, if it had a "suitable wind." We were much amused, for, no doubt, he had in mind the recent 75-mile gale when he repeated our words, "a suitable wind"!

During the night of December 16th a strong cold wind blew from the north. When we arose on the morning of the 17th, the puddles of water, which had been standing about the camp since the recent rains, were covered with ice. The wind had a velocity of 10 to 12 meters per second (22 to 27 miles an hour). We thought it would die down before long, and so remained indoors the early part of the morning. But when ten o'clock arrived, and the wind was as brisk as ever, we decided that we had better get the machine out and attempt a flight. We hung out the signal for the men of the Life Saving Station. We thought that by facing the flyer into a strong wind, there ought to be no trouble in launching it from the level ground about camp. We realized the difficulties of flying in so high a wind, but estimated that the added dangers in flight would be partly compensated for by the slower speed in landing.

We laid the track on a smooth stretch of ground about one hundred feet west of the new building. The biting cold wind made work difficult, and we had to warm up frequently in our living room, where we had a good fire in an improvised stove made of a large carbide can. By the time all was ready, J. T. Daniels, W. S. Dough and A. D. Etheridge, members of the Kill Devil Life-Saving Station; W. C. Brinkley of Manteo; and Johnny Moore, a boy from Nag's Head, had arrived.

We had a "Richard" hand anemometer with which we measured the velocity of the wind. Measurements made just before starting the first flight showed velocities of 11 to 12 meters per second, or 24 to 27 miles per hour. Measurements made just before the last flight gave between 9 and 10 meters per second. One made just afterward showed a little over 8 meters. The records of the Government Weather Bureau at Kitty Hawk gave the velocity of the wind between the hours of 10:30 and 12 o'clock, the time during which the four flights were made, as averaging 27 miles at the time of the first flight and 24 miles at the time of the last.

With all the knowledge and skill acquired in thousands of flights in the last ten years, I would hardly think today of making my first flight on a strange machine in a twenty-seven-mile wind, even if I knew that the machine had already been flown and was safe. After these years of experience, I look with amazement upon our audacity in attempting flights with a new and untried machine under such circumstances. Yet faith in our calculations and the design of the first machine, based upon our tables of air pressures, obtained by months of careful laboratory work, and confidence in our system of control developed by three years of actual experiences in balancing gliders in the air, had convinced us that the machine was capable of lifting and maintaining itself in the air, and that, with a little practice, it could be safely flown.

Wilbur having used his turn in the unsuccessful attempt on the 14th, the right to the first trial now belonged to me. After running the motor a few minutes to heat it up, I released the wire that held the machine to the track, and the machine started forward into the wind. Wilbur ran at the side of the machine, holding the wing to balance it on the track. Unlike the start on the 14th, made in a calm, the machine, facing a 27-mile wind, started very slowly. Wilbur was able to stay with it till it lifted from the track after a forty-foot run. One of the Life Saving men snapped the camera for us, taking a picture just as the machine had reached the end of the track and had risen to a height of about two feet.[1] The slow forward speed of the machine over the ground is clearly shown in the picture by Wilbur's attitude. He stayed along beside the machine without any effort.

The course of the flight up and down was exceedingly erratic, partly due to the irregularity of the air and partly to lack of experience in handling this machine. The control of the front rudder was difficult on account of its being balanced too near the center. This gave it a tendency to turn itself when started, so that it turned too far on one

---

[1] Orville had arranged the camera on a tripod pointing to where he hoped the machine would be after leaving the track. The negative was developed by Orville after his return to Dayton.

side and then too far on the other. As a result, the machine would rise suddenly to about ten feet, and then as suddenly dart for the ground. A sudden dart when a little over a hundred feet from the end of the track, or a little over 120 feet from the point at which it rose into the air, ended the flight. As the velocity of the wind was over 35 feet per second and the speed of the machine over the ground against this wind ten feet per second, the speed of the machine relative to the air was over 45 feet per second, and the length of the flight was equivalent to a flight of 540 feet made in calm air.

This flight lasted only 12 seconds, but it was nevertheless the first in the history of the world in which a machine carrying a man had raised itself by its own power into the air in full flight, had sailed forward without reduction of speed, and had finally landed at a point as high as that from which it started.

With the assistance of our visitors we carried the machine back to the track and prepared for another flight. The wind, however, had chilled us all through, so that before attempting a second flight, we all went to the building again to warm up. Johnny Moore, seeing under the table a box filled with eggs, asked one of the Station men where we got so many of them. The people of the neighborhood eke out a bare existence by catching fish during the short fishing season, and their supplies of other articles of food are limited. He probably never had seen so many eggs at one time in his whole life.

The one addressed jokingly asked him whether he hadn't noticed the small hen running about the outside of the building. "That chicken lays eight to ten eggs a day!" Moore, having just seen a piece of machinery lift itself from the ground and fly, a thing at that time considered as impossible as perpetual motion, was ready to believe nearly anything. But after going out and having a good look at the wonderful fowl, he returned with the remark, "It's only a common-looking chicken!"

At twenty minutes after eleven Wilbur started on the second flight. The course of this flight was much like that of the first, very much up and down. The speed over the ground was somewhat faster than that of the first flight, due to the lesser wind. The duration of the flight was less than a second longer than the first, but the distance covered was about seventy-five feet greater.

Twenty minutes later, the third flight started. This one was steadier than the first one an hour before. I was proceeding along pretty well when a sudden gust from the right lifted the machine up twelve to fifteen feet and turned it up sidewise in an alarming manner. It began a lively sidling off to the left. I warped the wings to try to recover the lateral balance and at the same time pointed the machine down to reach the ground as quickly as possible. The lateral control was more effective than I had imagined and before I reached the ground the right wing was lower than the left and struck first. The time of this flight was fifteen seconds and the distance over the ground a little over 200 feet.

Wilbur started the fourth and last flight at just 12 o'clock. The first few hundred feet were up and down, as before, but by the time three hundred feet had been covered, the machine was under much better control. The course for the next four or five hundred feet had but little undulation. However, when out about eight hundred feet the machine began pitching again, and, in one of its darts downward, struck the ground. The distance over the ground was measured and found to be 852 feet; the time of the flight 59 seconds. The frame supporting the front rudder was badly broken, but the main part of the machine was not injured at all. We estimated that the machine could be put in condition for flight again in a day or two.

While we were standing about discussing this last flight,

a sudden strong gust of wind struck the machine and began to turn it over. Everybody made a rush for it. Wilbur, who was at one end, seized it in front. Mr. Daniels and I, who were behind, tried to stop it by holding to the rear uprights.

All our efforts were in vain. The machine rolled over and over. Daniels, who had retained his grip, was carried along with it, and was thrown about, head over heels, inside of the machine. Fortunately he was not seriously injured, though badly bruised in falling about against the motor, chain guides, etc. The ribs in the surfaces of the machine were broken, the motor injured and the chain guides badly bent, so that all possibility of further flights with it for that year were at an end.

It is unlikely that any of the five spectators who had seen these flights sensed their scientific importance. But some of them felt interested, from one point of view, because they would have the laugh on a number of natives thereabouts who had insisted that these Wright brothers must be a pair of harmless cranks. A common argument had been: "God didn't intend man to fly. If he did, he would have given him a set of wings."

It was the regret of his life to the Wrights' friend, "Bill" Tate, that he missed witnessing that first flight. He had decided that "no one but a crazy man would attempt to fly in such a wind," and made no effort to be there.

After preparing and eating their lunch, and then washing their dishes, Wilbur and Orville set out, about two o'clock that afternoon, to walk over to the Kitty Hawk weather station, four or five miles away, to send a telegram to their father. It must have been about three o'clock when they reached the station. So few telegrams were sent from this locality that no regular commercial office existed and it was permitted to send them over this government wire as far as Norfolk where they would be relayed by phone from the weather bureau to the office of one of the telegraph companies.

Orville wrote out the following message to their father: "Success four flights Thursday morning all against twenty-one-mile wind started from level with engine power alone average speed through air thirty-one miles longest 59 seconds inform press home Christmas. Orville Wright."

What Orville meant when he wrote "against twenty-one-mile wind" was that the wind was at least twenty-one miles an hour during each of the flights. At the time of the first flight it was, as already noted, between twenty-four and twenty-seven miles an hour—probably about twenty-six miles.

After handing the message to Joseph J. Dosher, the weather bureau operator, Orville joined Wilbur over in a corner of the room to examine the record on an instrument that recorded the wind velocity.

Dosher got an almost instantaneous connection with Norfolk, and while the Wrights were still looking at the wind record, he said:

"The operator in Norfolk wants to know if it is all right to give the news to a reporter friend."

But the Wrights replied: Absolutely no! They preferred to have the first news of the event come from Dayton.

Dosher clicked out the refusal.

The operator at Norfolk, however, did not heed the warning.

When they left the weather bureau after sending their message, the Wrights went over to the Kitty Hawk life-saving station, a few steps away, and chatted with members of the crew there. Captain S. J. Payne, in charge of the station, declared that he had seen one of the flights with the aid of a pair of binoculars.

Then the Wrights walked to the post office at Kitty Hawk; and before returning to camp they stopped for a farewell visit at the home of Captain Hobbs, who had often done hauling and other work for them.

Meanwhile, the telegraph operator at Norfolk, disregarding the Wrights' adverse response to his request, had promptly gone ahead and given a tip about the flights to a young friend, H. P. Moore, of the Norfolk *Virginian-Pilot.* Moore was connected with the circulation department of the paper but was breaking in as a reporter and was in the habit of calling at the weather bureau. He made a desperate effort to reach by telephone over the government line someone at Kitty Hawk or elsewhere along the coast who could furnish details about what the flying-machine looked like, and about this Mr. Wright who was supposed to have operated it. Whatever information he got did not come from eyewitnesses of the flights, or from anyone who had ever seen the machine, and the account published the next morning was about ninety-nine per cent inaccurate. It described a flight of *three miles* by Wilbur and told of Orville then running about yelling "Eureka." The machine had one six-blade propeller beneath it, to elevate it, so the story ran, and another propeller at the rear to shove it forward.

"Very little can be learned here about the Wrights," the story said. "They are supposed by the natives of Kitty Hawk to be people of means and are always well dressed."

(When Moore met Orville, years later, and asked him what he thought of the account, Orville good-naturedly replied: "It was an amazing piece of work. Though ninety-nine per cent wrong, it did contain one fact that was correct. There *had* been a flight." Then Moore wrote that Orville had corroborated his story.)

One must give the *Virginian-Pilot* editors credit for treating the news as important. The headline over the flight story the next morning extended clear across the top of the first page.

Moore sent brief "queries," outlining the story, to twenty-one other newspapers over the country, including several in Ohio, one of them the Dayton *Journal*. But nearly all the telegraph editors resented having a correspondent suggest that a human being could fly by machinery. Of the twenty-one newspapers to whom it was offered, only five ordered the story. They were the New York *American*, the Washington (D.C.) *Post*, the Chicago *Record-Herald*, the Philadelphia *Record*, and the Cincinnati *Enquirer*. But not all five papers that received the story published it the next morning. The Chicago *Record-Herald* and the Washington *Post* delayed using it, and the Philadelphia *Record* did not print it at all. Thus only three newspapers in the United States had a report of the great event at Kitty Hawk the next morning. The Cincinnati *Enquirer* was the only one besides the *Virginian-Pilot* that gave space to the account on the front page.

As the Associated Press is a co-operative news-gathering agency and the *Virginian-Pilot* was a member, the story was available to the AP at Norfolk, but the AP was not yet interested in it.

One might have thought the news would especially interest the Dayton *Journal;* but Frank Tunison, the telegraph editor there (who also handled outgoing news for the Associated Press) was a man who took pride in not being easily fooled, and he paid no attention to the query from Norfolk.

Orville's telegram to his father did not reach Dayton until 5:25 that evening. In transmission, errors had got into the message; fifty-nine seconds had become fifty-seven, and the sender's name was spelled "Orevelle."

Katharine Wright immediately sent a message to Octave Chanute that the "boys" had reported four successful flights. Bishop Wright asked his son Lorin to prepare a brief statement with a copy of the message and give it to the Associated Press. After he had finished his dinner, Lorin went to the office of the *Journal* and inquired if the Associated Press representative was there. He was referred to Frank Tunison. Whether Tunison had already received the query from Moore at Norfolk is not certain. But he seemed annoyed over being expected to accept such a tale.

Without looking up from his work, he yawned and said to Lorin:

"Fifty-seven seconds, hey? If it had been fifty-seven minutes then it might have been a news item."

Nothing about the Wrights' feat appeared in the Dayton *Journal* the next morning. But news considered important enough to be displayed on the first page of that same issue included items about a routine weekly meeting of the local united trades and labor council; a colored man named Charles Brown, who admitted pocketbook thefts; the pardoning of a robber from Joliet prison, in Illinois. On the page opposite the editorial page, the biggest, blackest headline was: "Stores Are Filled with Christmas Shoppers."

Dayton afternoon papers on that December 18 did print accounts of the receipt of the telegram by Bishop Wright, as well as other "facts" about the flight. The Dayton *Herald* article appeared to be a rehash of the dispatch from Norfolk in the Cincinnati *Enquirer*. Over the article in the Dayton *Daily News*, on an inside page, alongside of so-called "country correspondence" from near-by towns, the heading was: "Dayton Boys Emulate Great Santos-Dumont." Santos-Dumont had flown in an airship, and now the Wrights had flown in something or other. Therefore the Wrights must be imitators of Alberto Santos-Dumont! Lacking scientific knowledge, the editors failed to distinguish between a flying-machine, heavier-than-air, and an airship consisting of a gas-bag equipped with a propeller. Indeed, from then on, nearly all who had heard of the reported flights, editors included, were in one or the other of two groups of disbelievers: (1) those who refused to believe the flights had taken place at all; and (2) those who thought that even if they had been made they were not of great importance.

The Associated Press, that had declined to accept news of the flights at either Norfolk or Dayton the day before, now sent out for afternoon papers on December 18, a brief report, less than 350 words, from Norfolk. This appeared to be simply a condensation of the article in the *Virginian-Pilot* that morning and contained most of the same inaccuracies. Not more than two or three sentences in the AP dispatch were correct. "The machine flew for three miles," the report said, ". . . and gracefully descended to the earth *at the spot selected* by the man in the *navigator's car* as a suitable landing place. . . . Preparatory to its flight the machine was placed upon *a platform . . . on a high sandhill* and when all was in readiness the fastenings to the machine were released and it *started down an incline*. The navigator, Wilbur Wright, *then* started a small gasoline engine which worked the propellers. When the end of the *incline* was reached the machine gradually arose until it obtained [sic] an *altitude of 60 feet. . . . In* the center is the navigator's car and suspended *just below the bottom plan* [sic] is a small gasoline engine, which furnishes the motive power for the propelling and elevating wheels.

"There are *two 6-blade propellers*," the dispatch said, "one arranged just below the frame so as to exert an *upward force* when in motion and the other extends horizontally from the rear to the center of the car furnishing forward impetus. Protruding from the center of the car is a *huge fan-shaped rudder of canvas*, stretched upon a frame of wood. This rudder is controlled by the navigator and may be moved to each side, raised or lowered." Not all the Associated Press papers printed the brief dispatch in full; in fact, many did not use it at all.

With the first reports "confirmed" by the Associated Press, two papers, the Washington *Post* and Chicago *Record-Herald*, that had withheld the story bought from Mr. Moore at Norfolk, finally printed the Moore dispatch on the morning of December 19. The Washington *Post* even used it on the front page, but cautiously inserted qualifying phrases, saying "it is reported" that a flight was made. And the Chicago *Record-Herald* on December 20 had an editorial about the flights, or about "the" flight. But as the editorial restated many of the inaccuracies contained in the news report, it only added to the general misinformation.

(A few newspaper editors are still touchy about the inadequate reporting of the Wrights' first flights. As recently as January 29, 1941, the Chicago *Daily News* had an editorial of nearly half a column defending the merit of the hopelessly inaccurate Associated Press dispatch from Norfolk on December 18, 1903. And shortly afterward, on February 12, 1941, in connection with a letter from a reader who sought to give the historic facts, the *Daily News* editor, still unwilling to accept the truth, added a note insisting once again that there was "nothing fantastic" about that AP report from Norfolk!)

At a meeting of the American Association for the Advancement of Science, in St. Louis, December 28 to

January 2, Octave Chanute made an address on the subject of Aerial Navigation in which he referred to the Wrights' flights. But little was said about the Chanute speech in the newspapers.

(Chanute used that address as the basis for an article in the March, 1904, issue of *Popular·Science Monthly* in which he said: "Now that an initial success has been achieved with a flying-machine, we can discern some of the uses of such apparatus and also some of its limitations. Its first application will probably be military." He said, too, that "it may even carry mails in special cases, but the useful loads carried will be very small. The machines will eventually be fast, they will be used in sport, but they are not to be thought of as commercial carriers." He did not think it would ever be practical to carry loads "such as a store of explosives, or big guns to shoot them.")

Almost as surprising as the lack of effort by the usually painstaking Associated Press to get the facts about the Kitty Hawk event, was the failure of the AP, or any other press association, or any newspaper, to rush a staff man to Dayton in an effort to obtain the whole amazing story of what the Wrights had done.

Desiring to correct the misinformation that had been printed, the Wrights prepared a statement about their recent flights, and gave this to the Associated Press with the request that it be published. This appeared, at least in part, in probably a majority of the Associated Press newspapers, on January 6; but the initiative, it should be noted, did not come from the press association, but from the Wrights themselves. A few editorial paragraphers made derisive comments on one sentence of the statement which suggested that "the day of flying had arrived."

Exactly one month after the Kitty Hawk flights, on Sunday, January 17, the New York *Herald*, in its magazine section, had an article headed: The Machine That Flies. Despite the time that had elapsed, affording opportunity to get the facts, this article not only contained a mass of preposterous misstatements but even quoted Wilbur Wright for many of them. The article was accompanied by a drawing, an artist's conception of the machine in flight, and a diagram, showing the two "six-bladed propellers," one behind the machine and the other beneath it, to give it elevation!

VII

AFTER THE EVENT

THE Wrights felt a glow of pride and satisfaction in having both invented and demonstrated the device that had baffled the ablest scientists through the centuries. But still they did not expect to make their fortunes. True, they had applied, on March 23, 1903, or nearly nine months before they flew, for basic patents (not issued until May 22, 1906), but that was by way of establishing an authentic record. Thus far they hadn't even employed a patent lawyer.

Long afterward, Orville Wright was asked what he and Wilbur would have taken for all their secrets of aviation, for all patent rights *for the entire world*, if someone had come along to talk terms just after those first flights. He wasn't sure, but he had an idea that if they had received an offer of ten thousand dollars they might have accepted it.

Since the airplane was not yet developed into a type for practical use, ten thousand dollars might have been considered a fair return for their time, effort, and outlay. They had had all the fun and satisfaction and their expenses had been surprisingly small. Their cash outlay for building and flying their power plane was less than $1,000, and that included their railroad fares to and from Kitty Hawk. Of course, the greater part of their expenses would have been for mechanical labor, much of which they did themselves. But skilled labor was low-priced at that time; one could hire a better than average mechanic for as little as $16 a week. Even if the Wrights had charged themselves with the cost of their own work, their total expenses on the power plane would still have been less than $2,000.

Many fanciful stories have been told about the sacrifices the Wright family made to enable the brothers to fly, and of how they were financed by this person or that. More than one man of wealth in Dayton has encouraged the belief that *he* financed them. One persistent story is that they raised money for their experiments by the sale of an Iowa farm in which they had an interest. The truth is that this farm, which had been deeded by their father to the *four* Wright brothers, was sold early in 1902 before Wilbur and Orville had even begun work on their power plane or spent much on their experiments. The sale was made at the request of their brother Reuchlin, and had no relation whatsoever to aviation. Nor is it true that the Wright home was mortgaged during the time of the brothers' experiments. Another story was that their sister Katharine had furnished the money they needed out of her salary as school teacher. Katharine Wright was always amused over that tale, for she was never a hoarder of money nor a financier, and could hardly have provided funds even if this had been necessary. Any rumor that her brothers could have borrowed money from her, rather than lending money to her, as they sometimes did, was almost as funny to Katharine as another report—that her brothers had relied on her for mathematical assistance in their calculations.

The simple fact is that no one ever financed the Wrights' work except Wilbur and Orville themselves. Their bicycle business had been giving them a decent income and at the end of the year 1903 they still had a few thousand dollars' savings in a local building and loan association. Whatever financial scrimping was necessary came *after* they had flown; after they knew they had made a great discovery.

But the Wrights' belief that they had achieved something of great importance was not bolstered by the attitude of the general public. Not only were there no receptions, brass bands, or parades in their honor, but most people paid less attention to the history-making feat than if the "boys" had simply been on vacation and caught a big fish, or shot a bear.

Before the flights, some of the neighbors had been puzzled by reports that the Wrights were working on a flying-machine. One man in business near the Wright shop had become acquainted with an inventor who thought he was about to perfect a perpetual motion machine; and this businessman promptly sent the inventor to the Wrights, assuming that he would find them kindred spirits. John G. Feight, living next door to the Wright home, had remarked, just before the brothers went to Kitty Hawk: "Flying and perpetual motion will come at the same time."

Now that flights had been made, neighbors didn't doubt the truth of the reports—though one of them had his own explanation. Mr. Webbert, father of the man from whom the Wrights rented their shop, said:

"I have known those boys ever since they were small children, and if they say they flew I know they did; but I think there must be special conditions down in North Carolina that would enable them to fly by the power of a motor. There is only one thing that could lift a machine like that in *this* part of the country—spirit power." Webbert was a spiritualist. He had seen tables and pianos lifted at séances!

But even if the boys *had* flown, what of it? Men were flying in Europe, weren't they? Hadn't Santos-Dumont flown some kind of self-propelled balloon?

The one person who had almost unbounded enthusiasm for what the brothers had accomplished was their father. They found it difficult to keep a complete file of the photographs they had made showing different phases of their experiments, because the moment their father's eye fell on one of these pictures he would pick it up and mail it to some relative along with a letter telling with pride what the boys had done.

Two brothers in Boston sensed, however, that, if the scant reports about the Kitty Hawk event were based on truth, then something of great significance had happened. These men were Samuel and Godfrey Lowell Cabot, wealthy and influential members of a famous family. Both of them, particularly Samuel, had long been interested in whatever progress was being made in aeronautics. On December 19, the day after the first news of the flights was published, Samuel Cabot sent to the Wrights a telegram of congratulations. Two days later, his brother Godfrey wrote them a letter. In that letter Godfrey Cabot wanted to know if they thought their machine could be used for carrying freight. He was financially interested in an industrial operation in West Virginia, he said, where conditions would justify a rate of $10 a ton for transporting goods by air only sixteen miles.

One reason why nearly everyone in the United States was disinclined to swallow the reports about flying with a machine heavier than air was that important scientists had already explained in the public prints why the thing was impossible. When a man of the profound scientific wisdom of Simon Newcomb, for example, had demonstrated with unassailable logic why man couldn't fly, why should the public be fooled by silly stories about two obscure bicycle repair-men who hadn't even been to college? Professor Newcomb was so distinguished an astronomer that he was the only American since Benjamin Franklin to be made an associate of the Institute of France. It was widely assumed that what he didn't know about laws of physics simply wasn't in books; and that when he said flying couldn't be done, there was no need to inquire any further. More than once Professor Newcomb had written that flight without gas-bags would require the discovery of some new metal or a new unsuspected force in Nature. Then, in an article in *The Independent*—October 22, 1903, while the Wrights were at Kitty Hawk assembling their power machine— he not only proved that trying to fly was nonsense, but went further and showed that even if a man did fly, he wouldn't dare to stop. "Once he slackens his speed,

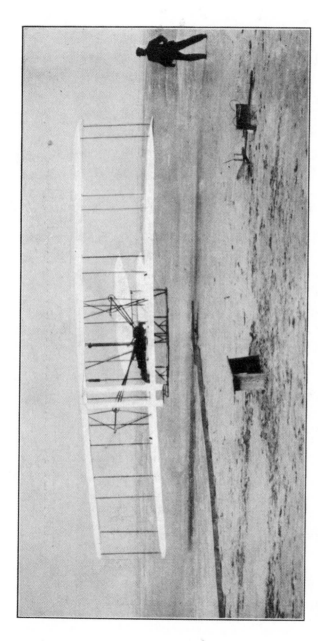

FIRST FLIGHT. The only picture made of man's first flight in a power-driven, heavier-than-air machine, Kitty Hawk, December 17, 1903. The plane, piloted by Orville Wright, has just taken off from the monorail. Wilbur Wright, running at the side, had held the wing to balance the machine until it left the rail.

THE FIRST POWER PLANE. A side view of the 1903 plane at Kitty Hawk.

down he begins to fall.—Once he stops, he falls a dead mass. How shall he reach the ground without destroying his delicate machinery? I do not think that even the most imaginative inventor has yet put on paper a demonstrative, successful way of meeting this difficulty."

In all his statements, Professor Newcomb had the support of other eminent authorities, including Rear Admiral George W. Melville, then chief engineer for the United States Navy, who, a year or two previously, in the *North American Review*, had set forth convincingly the absurdity of attempts to fly.

The most recent Newcomb article was all the more impressive as a forecast from the fact that it appeared only fifteen days after one of Professor Langley's unsuccessful attempts at flight. That is, Langley's attempt seemed to show that flight was beyond human possibility, and then Newcomb's article explained *why* it was impossible. Though these pooh-poohing statements by Newcomb and other scientists were probably read by relatively few people, they were seen by editors, editorial writers, and others who could have much influence on public opinion. Naturally, no editor who "knew" a thing couldn't be done would permit his paper to record the fact that it had been done.

Oddly enough, one of the first public announcements by word of mouth about the Wrights' Kitty Hawk flights was in a Sunday-school. A. I. Root, founder of a still prosperous business for the sale of honey and bee-keepers' supplies at Medina, Ohio, taught a Sunday-school class. One morning shortly before the dismissal bell, observing that the boys in the class were restless, he sought to restore order by catching their interest. Perhaps he wished to show, too, that miracles as wonderful as any in the Bible were still possible.

"Do you know, friends," he said, "that two Ohio boys, or young men rather, have outstripped the world in demonstrating that a flying-machine can be constructed without the aid of a balloon?" He had read a brief item about the Wrights in an Akron paper.

The class became attentive and Root went on: "During the past two months these two boys have made a machine that actually flew through the air for more than half a mile, carrying one of the boys with it. This young man is not only a credit to our state but to the whole country and to the world."

Though this was several weeks after the Wrights had first flown, no one in the class had ever heard about it, and incredulously they fired questions at the teacher.

"Where do the boys live? What are their names? When and where did their machine fly?"

Root described, not too accurately, the Kitty Hawk flights, and added: "When they make their next trial I am going to try to be on hand to see the experiment."

An important part of Root's business was publication of the still widely circulated magazine, *Gleanings in Bee Culture*, and in his issue of March 1, 1904, he told of the episode in the Sunday-school. By printing that story, the Medina bee man may possibly have been the first editor of a scientific publication in the United States to report that man could fly. (The *Popular Science Monthly* in its issue of March, 1904, had an article by Octave Chanute in which the flights were mentioned.)

Root a little later even predicted: "Possibly we may be able to fly over the North Pole."

The Wrights were more amused than disturbed by the lack of general recognition that flying was now possible. They inwardly chuckled when they heard people still using the old expression: "Why, a person could no more do *that* than he could fly!" But they knew they had only begun to learn about handling a flying-machine.

VIII

EXPERIMENTS OF 1904-'05

IN ALL their work on their power plane the Wrights' main incentive had been to gain the distinction of being the first of mankind to fly. They had not designed the machine for practical use. Now, however, even though they did not yet foresee many of the uses for which the airplane was destined, they began to think it could be developed into a machine useful for scouting in warfare, for carrying mail to isolated places, for exploration; and that it would appeal to those who could afford it for sport.

If their machine was capable, as they had demonstrated, of flying by its own power for 852 feet against a 20-mile wind, there was no reason why it shouldn't go many times that far. But if the machine was to be practical, many improvements would be necessary, and they would need more experience in flying. Much practice would be required, and that would mean more expense in proportion to income, for they would have less time for building and repairing bicycles. But they decided to devote to aviation whatever amount of time seemed necessary. A number of bicycles at their shop were in various stages of completion. But no new ones were started after the Wrights' return from Kitty Hawk, though some of those on hand were completed

and sold. The brothers now began to turn over to
Charlie Taylor, their chief mechanic, most of the routine work of the shop.

In January, 1904, the brothers began building a new
plane. It was similar to the one flown at Kitty Hawk,
but there were a number of changes, including more
sturdy construction throughout. The weight exceeded
that of the original plane by about eighty pounds. (In
flight, the weight, including the pilot, and 70 pounds of
iron bars carried on the framework under the front
elevator, was 900 pounds.[1]) The wing camber was
changed from 1-20 to 1-25—that is, the curvature was
decreased; and the ribs were tapered from front to rear
spar instead of being of uniform depth, as in the earlier
model. An entirely new engine went into the 1904
machine. In fact, the Wrights started to build three new
engines. One of these had four cylinders of 4⅛-inch
bore; another, four cylinders of only 4-inch bore, as the
one used at Kitty Hawk; and the third was a V-type, of
eight cylinders. The 4⅛-inch bore was the one installed

[1] The Wrights carried 70 pounds of iron bars in many of the flights
of 1904-'05, and could fly with less power than if that load had not been
carried. Here is the explanation: The center of gravity of their machine
was so far back of the center of pressure on the wings that an air
pressure of 70 pounds was required on the top side of the horizontal
elevator in front, to make the center of lift and center of gravity coin-
cide. Any downward pressure on the elevator, the brothers reasoned,
regardless of whether produced by the air or by a weight, would have
to be supported by the main planes. But if the downward pressure is
obtained by use of the elevator, then two drags are created, one on the
elevator itself, and the other on the wings, in consequence of carrying
that extra pressure on the elevator. On the other hand, an equal downward pressure produced by a weight, carried at the same distance as
the elevator in front of the wings, would add little to the drag on
the elevator, because it would dispose of the necessity for a downward
pressure on that part of the machine, and there would then be only
the drag on the wings.

in the 1904 plane and gave a satisfactory amount of power—but not so much as the Wrights later developed in the other four-cylinder motor of only four-inch bore. That motor they kept in their shop and used for a kind of guinea pig, trying various improvements and refinements until it produced as much power as they had expected from the V-type motor of eight cylinders and twice as much as the original motor used at Kitty Hawk. They then gave up the idea of completing the V-type motor.

Another change in the 1904 machine was using white pine instead of spruce for the front and rear spars in the wings. Spruce was not available in Dayton at that time, and tests the Wrights made at their shop, in the manner usually employed for ascertaining the strength of woods, indicated that the two woods were about equally strong. (But in actual use, when stresses came suddenly, as in landing, the white pine spars snapped "like taffy under a hammer blow," though spruce had always withstood such shocks. The brothers rebuilt the wings, with all spars of spruce.)

To obtain practice, their first need was a suitable field, not too far from home. They found a cow pasture, fairly level, handy to an interurban railway, at Simms Station, eight miles from Dayton, toward Springfield. This field, often called the Huffman prairie, was part of a farm belonging to a Dayton bank president, Torrence Huffman. Compared with a modern flying-field the area of sixty-eight acres they wanted to use was not quite ideal. It contained a number of trees, besides being near power wires and poles. But it was as good as they could find and without delay the Wrights introduced themselves to Mr. Huffman to ask if they might rent his pasture for their experiments. He granted the request and told them they were welcome to use the field free of charge. But he said he hoped they would drive his cows to a safe place and not run over them.

By April 15, 1904, the Wrights had built a rough wooden shed at the Huffman pasture, in preparation for their experiments.

Even if they had tried, the Wrights could hardly have kept secret what they were doing here at the Huffman prairie, with an interurban car line and two highways passing the field they were using. But they took special precautions against being thought secretive, for they knew that the best way to avoid being bothered by newspaper people or others was to make no mystery of what they were doing. Before they had attempted even one trial flight at the Huffman pasture they wrote letters to each of the Dayton papers, as well as to each of the Cincinnati papers, that on May 23 they would attempt to fly and would be glad to have any newspaper representative who felt interested come and watch them. Their only request was that no pictures be taken, and that the reports should not be sensational. This latter stipulation was to avoid attracting crowds, but as it turned out there was no need to be concerned about curiosity-seekers.

About a dozen newspapermen showed up. Also on hand were a number of friends and neighbors of the Wright family. Altogether perhaps thirty-five persons were present—all by invitation.

The Wrights dragged their machine out of the shed to wait for a suitable wind before launching the machine from the short stretch of wooden track. As it happened, the wind was unusually high that day, about twenty-five miles an hour, and the Wrights said they would wait for it to die down a little. When the high wind did cease, it went suddenly to an almost complete calm, and a wind of at least eleven miles an hour was needed to take off from so short a track. The Wrights said they would try a flight if the wind picked up. But the wind failed to do so. The crowd waited and two or three of the reporters—too experienced to be easily fooled— began to make comments to one another. They hadn't wanted to come in the first place. Why had they been asked to waste time on such an assignment? Most of the guests, though, had only sympathy for the brothers. They actually seemed sincere in thinking they *could* fly.

Though sorry to disappoint the spectators, the Wrights showed no signs of embarrassment. They had learned to take events as they came. Finally, after the day had dragged on with no sign of a more favorable wind, one of the brothers announced:

"We can't fly today; but since you've taken the trouble to come and wait so long, we'll let the machine skim along the track and you'll get an idea of what it's supposed to do. With so short a track, we may not get off the ground, but you'll see how it operates."

Then the engine misbehaved. It worked all right in the warming-up period, but began to skip explosions as soon as the machine started down the track. This was caused, the Wrights soon learned, by the flow of air over the mouth of the intake pipe—a trouble never experienced with the engine used at Kitty Hawk.

After running the length of the track, the machine slid off the end without rising into the air at all. That wasn't much of a story for the reporters. Their assumption that they had been sent on a wild goose chase seemed to be confirmed. Would there be a flight the next day? The Wrights couldn't be sure. First of all they must find out what ailed that engine. They might be able to do that overnight, or it might take longer. However, all who wished to return the next day would be welcome. Indeed, the Wrights said, any newspaper representative would be welcome at *any* time.

Two or three of the newspapermen did return the next day. The engine still sulked, but the wind was a bit more favorable and the Wrights decided to show the reporters what they could. This time the machine rose five or six feet from the ground and went through the air for nearly sixty feet before it came down. An electric contact point in one of the engine cylinders had worked loose, and only three cylinders were hitting. The few reporters present, though now convinced that the age of flying had not yet come, wrote friendly articles and made the most of what they had seen. The versions differed widely. One report had the machine rising to a height of seventy-five feet. In the Cincinnati *Enquirer* account was a comment that the machine "is more substantially constructed *than other machines of its kind.*"

None of those newspapermen ever returned. During

all their experiments that year and the next, the Wrights had about all the privacy they needed. They used to smile over a comment by Octave Chanute: "It is a marvel to me that the newspapers haven't spotted you."

Having disposed of the reporters, the inventors resumed their work.

Almost as soon as the new trials began, the brothers encountered a new difficulty. A track 60 feet long had been adequate for launching the machine in the wind at Kitty Hawk; but a track of 160 feet, or even one of 240 feet, was not long enough for use at Huffman field where the winds were usually light.

The Huffman field was covered with hummocks from six inches to a foot high. Only a few spots free from hummocks were suitable for a 240-foot track. And landing wheels, such as were used later, would have been impractical on that uneven ground. Laying 240 feet of track, after finding enough ground space free from hummocks, was a considerable job. But frequently, after the track was laid, the wind would change its direction, and then all the work had to be done over. After a few times, the brothers gave up trying to use so long a track, and ordinarily used one of only 160 feet.

As steady winds of eleven miles an hour, the least that would do for starting from a 160-foot track, were not frequent, the Wrights had to be in readiness to take advantage of occasional gusts of strong wind. With their machine on the track, they waited until they could "see" a flurry of wind coming—that is, until they could see weeds being agitated by the wind in the distance. Then they would start the motor and run the machine down the track to meet the wind gust when it reached the end of the rail. In that way they sometimes succeeded in making a start on a day generally calm. But one such start ended disastrously, and Orville, who was piloting the machine, had one of his narrowest escapes. When the machine first met the flurry of wind, it rose rapidly, but a second later it was on the ground with the wings pointing vertically into the air. It had dived at a steep angle, throwing Orville forward to the ground. The upper wing spar came down across the middle of his back. But luckily, a section about two feet wide, just wide enough to miss hitting him, was broken out. No other damage was done to the spar, and the Wrights could never account for the seemingly miraculous breakage that provided a space for safety over the very place where Orville lay on the ground. After that accident, Charlie Taylor, who had seen other narrow escapes, gloomily told the neighbors across the road that every time he saw one of the brothers start on a flight he felt that he was seeing him alive for the last time.

Early in July the Wrights made alterations in the machine which located the center of gravity farther toward the rear than it had been before. In the first trial after those alterations, the machine, after leaving the track, kept turning up more and more and looked as if it were going to loop the loop. The center of gravity was so far back that the front elevator, even when turned to its limit, could not check the upward turn. While pointing vertically upward, the machine came to a stop and then began to slide backward. By the time it reached the ground it was once more so nearly level that if the skids

had had a slight upward bend at their rear ends, the
landing might have been made without damage. As it
was, the rear ends of the skids dug into the ground; but
the damage was slight.

Before their experiments had progressed far in 1904
the Wrights saw that a better method of launching the
machine was needed. They decided that a derrick with
a falling weight would be the simplest and cheapest
device. A 1,600-pound weight, falling a distance of 16½
feet, was so geared with ropes and pulleys that it produced a 350-pound pull on the machine through a
distance of 49½ feet. By this arrangement the machine
could be put into the air after a run of only 50 feet,
even in a dead calm. Shifting the track was now seldom
necessary.

Up to the time the derrick catapult was ready for its
first trial on September 7, less than forty starts had been
made and many of them failed for lack of speed. But
now the length of the flights increased rapidly. The
shorter flights had been in almost a straight line, but as
the lengths of the flights increased it was necessary to
make turns to stay within the field. Then a new trouble
—or rather an old one that supposedly had been overcome at Kitty Hawk—began to bother the Wrights.
Often in making a short turn they suddenly found themselves in a tail-spin which ended in a crash requiring
days, or even weeks, for repairs. They soon learned
what it was in making the turn that caused the tail-spin;
but they found it difficult to avoid, because they had no
way of knowing at what angle the air was striking the
machine. This led to the "invention" of the first instru-

ment for guidance of a pilot in flying. They simply attached a short piece of string to the crossbar beneath the front elevator. When the machine traveled directly forward the string trailed straight backward; but when the machine slipped to either side the string blew to one side or the other and indicated approximately the amount of the side slip. By close observance of this string it was possible to avoid entirely the danger of tail-spins, but the pilot learning to fly had so many things to attend to, so it seemed to him, that he sometimes neglected to watch the string closely enough.

After it was found that the derrick permitted the plane to be launched at any time, the Wrights often let the machine stand on the track during the day with the weights raised, ready to start at a moment's notice. One day in early November, while idly strolling in front of the track, Orville thought he saw a slight movement of the plane on the track. A more careful look did not confirm his first impression; nevertheless he turned and leisurely walked towards the plane. When within a few steps of it he saw that it actually *was* in motion. The wire that held it against the pull of the 1,600-pound weight was attached to a stake driven into the soft ground several feet. That stake was slowly coming out of the ground! By leaping upon one of the skids, Orville reached the elevator control lever in time to prevent the machine from rising as it rushed down the track. A strained shoulder was the principal damage, though the machine suffered a few slight breakages.

Not until the 51st flight in 1904, when the machine stayed in the air one minute and one second, did the

Wrights beat their best Kitty Hawk record of 59 seconds. The first complete circle was not made until September 20. But toward the end of the 1904 experiments, there were two five-minute flights. In each of these the machine circled the field four or five times without stopping.

The total flying time during 1904 was only 45 minutes. But the knowledge and experience gained from that three quarters of an hour were of almost inestimable importance.

Toward the end of May, 1905, the Wrights began assembling a machine all new with the exception of the motor and the propeller-driving mechanism. Strengthening of the structure at places where the previous machine had been too weak in making landings added about 25 pounds more weight. The principal changes, however, were in wing design, addition of some new features not in the earlier machines, and in making the wing-warping and operation of the tail rudder independent of each other. The camber of the wings was changed from 1-25, used in 1904, back to 1-20 as used in 1903 at Kitty Hawk. This change was to enable the machine to get off at a slower speed.

The most radical change was the addition of two semi-circular vanes, called "blinkers," between the two surfaces of the front elevator. This device was later patented by the Wrights. The purpose of the "blinkers" was to assist the rear rudder in overcoming the unequal resistances of the two wings when they were warped while making a turn. Gliding experiments in 1902 had shown that the pressure on a fixed vane in the rear of the wings tended to speed the higher wing when the machine slipped in the direction of the lower wing, and caused a tail-spin. The vane had to be made movable to relieve this pressure. It now occurred to the Wrights that if a fixed vane were placed in front of the wings, instead of behind them, its effect would be the reverse of that when the vane was in the rear, and that there would be less need of operating the rear rudder to overcome the unbalanced resistance of the two wings. Moreover, when the machine slipped inward while "banking" a turn, the speed of the low wing would be increased and a tail-spin avoided. The operation of the rear rudder could now be made independent of the wing-warp without danger.

It was found that the "blinkers" entirely removed the danger of tail spinning but that they added to the difficulty of steering, both when flying straight and when making turns. Consequently they were not used in all the flights. (In modern planes the effect of the "blinkers" is gained by extending the fuselage far out in front of the wings.)

Though tail-spins could be avoided without use of "blinkers," by carefully observing the little piece of string that indicated side slip, yet they sometimes occurred. In one flight, in September, 1905, when the "blinkers" were not on the machine, Orville suddenly discovered he was in a tail-spin and that he was about to come down in the top of a forty-foot thorn tree. The thorns were several inches long, and the idea of falling through them to the ground was not alluring. Orville quickly turned the machine into an almost vertical dive while turning in a circle 50 to 100 feet in diameter. The inner wing of the machine hit a branch of the tree, imbedding a thorn in an upright, and tore off the branch. In the dive, the higher wing, because of much greater speed, soon passed the lower wing in the downward plunge and itself became the low wing. The machine thus was in a steep bank with the high side toward the tree, just the opposite from what it had been before. When Orville turned the elevator to avoid striking the ground, the machine turned suddenly and unexpectedly away from the tree, because, in this steeply banked condition, the elevator exerted more pressure laterally than it did vertically. (When an aeroplane is banked to 45 degrees the elevator serves just as much for a rudder as for an elevator, and the rudder just as much for an elevator as for a rudder.) Though the machine lightly touched the ground, Orville flew it on back to the hangar, where the branch of the tree was found still clinging to the upright. It had been the practice of the Wrights to dive the machine to recover speed in a stall; but this quick recovery was from an entirely different cause—the great difference in the speeds of the two wings.

An amusing flight by Orville in 1905 was made after some weeks of inactivity in flying and after the machine had undergone a number of changes since his last flight. When the machine left the starting rail it began pitching like a bucking broncho. Orville wanted to stop, but at every plunge the plane came down so steeply he did not dare attempt a landing. As soon as he got control of the machine, after going three or four hundred feet, he did land safely. Wilbur rushed up to inquire why he had stopped just when he had really got going. Orville explained that he would have landed even sooner, but had taken the first opportunity to stop without smashing the machine to pieces.

Though the rudder and wing-warp were entirely independent of each other in all the flights of 1905, the Wrights several years later resumed having the two controls interconnected, to operate together, but with an arrangement needed for modifying their relationship when making turns.

Another change that improved control of the 1905 machine was in giving the wings considerably less angle at the tips than in the central part. By this arrangement, the tips stalled later than other parts of the wings and some lateral control remained even after the central part of the wings were in a stalled condition.

After the Wrights had made the blades of their propellers much wider and thinner than the original ones, they discovered that the performance of the propellers in flight did not agree closely with their calculations, as in the earlier propellers. They could see only one reason for this, and that was that the propeller blades twisted from their normal shape under pressure in flight. To find out quickly if this was the real reason, they fastened to each blade a small surface, like an elevator, out behind the blades, set at an angle to balance the pressures that were distorting the blades. They called the surfaces "little jokers." When they found that the "little jokers" cured the trouble, they dispensed with them and began to give the blades a backward sweep, which served the same purpose.

In the flying season of 1905, the control of the machine was much improved by increasing the area of the front rudder from 50 to 85 square feet, and by moving it to nearly twice the distance from the wings. This added distance made response to the movement of the rudder slower, and control of the machine much easier.

The lateral control also was improved by enlarging the rear rudder from 20 to 34 square feet, and by moving it to a position three feet farther back of the wings.

On account of frequent rains, the soggy condition of the field, and other weather conditions, only nine attempts to fly were made in the first two months of experiments in 1905, and only three of these lasted for as much as ten seconds. But after the first of September progress was rapid.

During all this time, the newspapers had continued to let the Wrights alone. Indeed, the failure of the newspapers in Dayton and elsewhere to say much about the history-making experiments at Huffman field was often used as an argument to prove that there couldn't be any truth in the rumors that men had actually contrived a successful flying-machine. "You couldn't have kept a thing like that *secret*. Some reporter surely would have *heard* about it!"

Dan Kumler, who was city editor of James M. Cox's *Daily News*, in Dayton, during those early years of flying, recalled in 1940, not long before his death, that many people who had been on interurban cars passing the Huffman field and seen the Wrights in the air used to come to the *Daily News* office to inquire why there was nothing in the paper about the flights.

"Such callers," said Kumler, "got to be a nuisance."

"And why wasn't there anything in the paper?" Kumler was asked.

"We just didn't believe it," he said. "Of course you remember that the Wrights at that time were terribly secretive."

"You mean they were secretive about the fact that they were flying over an open field?"

"I guess," said Kumler, grinning, after a moment's reflection, "the truth is that we were just plain dumb."

James M. Cox, owner of the *Daily News*, has likewise confessed that "none of us believed the reports" of flights.

One fact that kept the earlier flights relatively inconspicuous was that much of the time the plane was within 10 or 15 feet of the ground. Only occasionally was it up as high as 50 feet. There were no flights beyond the field itself, because if necessary to make a forced landing elsewhere, dragging the machine back to its shed might not have been easy.

The Wrights had aimed at first to avoid being in the air when an interurban car was passing. But that precaution soon proved to be unnecessary. Few people ever paid any attention to the flights. One day, though, the general manager of the interurban line was on a passing car when the plane was in the air and he ordered the car stopped. He and the chief engineer of the line, who was with him, got off and stayed a while to look at the incredible sight.

Across the Springfield pike from the field lived the Beard family, tenants on the Torrence Huffman farm. Whenever the plane landed abruptly Mrs. Beard was likely to dash across the road with a bottle of arnica, feeling sure it would be needed, as sometimes it was. But there were few other visitors.

Two somewhat mysterious visitors did come, however. The Wrights saw two men wandering about nearby fields during most of one day and thought they must be hunters, though there was not much game thereabouts. Again the next day the two strangers were seen, and finally they came across the field to where the Wrights were adjusting their machine. One of them carried a camera. They asked if visitors were permitted.

"Yes, only we'd rather you didn't take any pictures," one of the brothers courteously replied.

The man with the camera set it down off to one side, twenty feet away, as if to make it plain that he was not trying to sneak any shots. Then he inquired if it was all right to look into the shed. The brothers told him to make himself right at home. Was he a newspaperman? No, he said, he was not a newspaperman, though he sometimes did writing for publication. That was as near as he came to introducing himself. After the callers had gone, Charlie Taylor, the Wrights' mechanic, said: "That fellow's no writer. At least he's no ordinary writer. When he looked at the different parts of the machine he called them all by their right names."

Later the Wrights learned the identity of the visitor.

Orville chanced to see a picture of him in a New York newspaper. His identity was confirmed some time afterward when he and Orville were formally introduced to each other—though neither referred to their previous meeting. The man had been chief engineer for Professor Langley of the Smithsonian Institution.

Toward the end of September, the Wrights were able greatly to increase their distances. On September 26, there was an uninterrupted flight of 11⅛ miles in 18 minutes and 9 seconds; and on September 29, one of 12 miles in 19 minutes 55 seconds. Then, on October 3, there was a new record of 15¼ miles in 25 minutes 5 seconds; another, on October 4, of 20¾ miles in 33 minutes 17 seconds; and finally, on October 5, 24⅕ miles in 38 minutes 3 seconds.

The flights of October 3 and 4 would have been longer except that certain bearings had become overheated. By October 5 the inventors had added more grease cups where needed and also installed a larger gas tank. But the tank was not full when that final test began and the flight ended because the fuel was exhausted. It was the intention of the Wrights to make one more test and put the record at more than an hour; but now for the first time the miracle of flight actually began to attract more spectators and the brothers decided it might be prudent to quit for the season before details of the machine's construction became public knowledge. However, there was one more short flight—just one circle of the field—on October 16.

After the close of the 1905 experiments, a test of the engine showed that it produced more power than when first put into use. This gain was attributed to the increased smoothness of the cylinders and pistons produced by wear.

Looking back over their experiments, the Wrights noted that "in 1903, 62 pounds per horsepower were carried at a speed of 30 miles an hour; in 1904, 53 pounds at 34 miles an hour; and in 1905, 46 pounds at 38 miles an hour." Thus the weight carried per horsepower was in inverse ratio to the speed—the smaller the weight carried per horsepower, the higher the speed. That seems obvious enough now, but at the time the Wrights were making these experiments many scientists still accepted the "Langley Law," that the greater the speed, the less horsepower necessary.

The Wrights now knew that the airplane would have practical use—though they did not foresee how safely trans-Atlantic flights would be made—and not even in their wildest dreams did they think of anyone ever flying at night.

IX

IT STILL WASN'T "NEWS"

THOUGH Dayton newspapermen had not besieged the Huffman pasture for details of the great news story lurking there during 1904-'05, one of their number had occasionally been in contact with the Wrights. That was Luther Beard—no kin to the other Beards mentioned—managing editor of the Dayton *Journal*. Besides being a newspaper editor, Beard also taught school at Fairfield, about two miles from the Huffman farm, and went back and forth by the interurban car line that passed the field where the Wrights were making history. It sometimes happened that on the trip to Dayton he was on the same car with one or both of the Wright brothers, returning from their flights.

"I used to chat with them in a friendly way and was always polite to them," Beard recalled, years afterward, chuckling over the joke on himself, "because I sort of felt sorry for them. They seemed like well-meaning, decent enough young men. Yet there they were, neglecting their business to waste their time day after day on that ridiculous flying-machine. I had an idea that it must worry their father."

In these conversations, neither the Wrights nor Beard was likely to bring up the subject of aviation. The Wrights showed no eagerness to talk about what they were doing, and Beard kept to subjects he considered more sensible. But one day, in the autumn of 1904, several of the school children told him they had seen the Wrights flying all around the field. Maybe, thought Beard, that might make a little local item for the paper. When he next saw Orville Wright on the car, a day or two afterward, Beard asked him if it was true that they had been flying all the way around the field.

Oh, yes, Orville admitted, they often did that. Then Orville began to talk about something else.

Evidently, Beard decided, the fact that an airplane could be flown under perfect control in circles didn't amount to anything after all. Orville Wright himself didn't seem to think it was unusual or important. There was no use putting it in the paper. One more reason perhaps for not printing much in the *Journal* about what the poor, misguided Wrights were doing was that such items were annoying to Frank Tunison, another of the editors—the same Tunison who had turned down the story of the first flight at Kitty Hawk. Having decided that the Wrights were not news, he was naturally irritated to see any reference to them, even on an inside page. "Why do we print such stuff?" he would ask.

However, Beard said to Orville, as they rode along on the car: "If you ever do something *unusual* be sure and let us know." From time to time he went or telephoned to the Wright home to find out if by remote chance the brothers had done anything worth mentioning.

"Done anything of special interest lately?" he asked Orville Wright one evening.

"Oh, nothing much," replied Orville. "Today one of us flew for nearly five minutes."

"Where did you go?" asked Beard.

"Around the field."

"Oh! Just around the field. I see. Well, we'll keep in touch with you."

Doubtless, reflected the newspaperman, the Wrights' circling of Mr. Huffman's pasture for five minutes was pretty good for two local boys. But it was hardly a thing to take up space in the paper. Hadn't Santos-Dumont circled the Eiffel Tower, and flown all around Paris? One more newspaper writer, like hundreds of others, had failed to distinguish between an airship with a gas bag and a flying-machine heavier than air. (At the time of the thirty-eight-minute flight in 1905, however, Luther Beard was among the spectators at the field.)

Another bright young newspaperman in that vicinity didn't grasp quite the full significance of what the Wrights were doing. The Dayton *Journal* had a branch office at Xenia, about eleven miles from where the Wrights did their flying. The reporter in charge of that branch office was an enterprising lad, just out of college, who answered to the name of Fred C. Kelly. His eagle eye spotted an item about the Wrights and their flying-machine in a country weekly, the Osborn *Local*, published in a village a mile or two from the Huffman field. Did he investigate the story? No, he didn't need to investigate it to feel sure it must be nonsense.

The fact of human flight was still unacceptable and ridiculous even to professional humorists. The humorous weekly, *Puck*, in its issue of October 19, 1904—

nearly a month after that first circular flight—published a joke, inspired presumably by absurd reports about two young men at Dayton:

"When," inquired the friend, "will you wing your first flight?"

"Just as soon," replied the flying-machine inventor, "as I can get the laws of gravitation repealed."

The significance of the first complete circular flight, on September 20, 1904, was not overlooked, however, by one man who witnessed it. That was A. I. Root, the Medina bee man. He had traveled by automobile the day before to Xenia, where he had a relative, and then went to the Huffman field, only a few miles away, to become better acquainted with the Wrights. His trip of 175 miles from Medina without serious difficulty with his machine was then almost a feat in itself. He had not needed any repairs until he reached Xenia. (Incidentally, he had remonstrated with the repair man he dealt with there, Mr. Baldner, for his frequent use of profanity; and he was impressed by the fact that no matter how puzzling or discouraging the problem, the Wrights never uttered a profane word.) After going to Huffman field, Root became more than ever interested in the Wrights and as he wished to see all he could of their work for a few days, he arranged for board and lodging at the Beard home across the road. (A little later he even offered to pay the Wrights $100 for material he had obtained from them for articles about their work—but they refused to accept any payment.)

Root knew that the circular flight he had just witnessed was of prime importance, for it demonstrated that the airplane would have practical use. He wrote an eye-witness account of what the Wrights had done for the January 1 (1905) issue of his magazine, *Gleanings in Bee Culture*, and sent a marked copy to the editor of the *Scientific American*, with a letter telling the editor he was free to reprint the article. The editor wrote back that he had not received the marked copy. So Root sent another. But when the editor of the *Scientific American* saw what Root had printed he paid no attention to it.

Root continued to print articles about the Wrights in his magazine. In December, 1905, he published the fact that a great number of long flights had been made during the previous season, "one of 24 miles in 38 minutes," probably the first publication of that event in the United States. At about the same time, in its issue of December 16, 1905, the *Scientific American* said, in an editorial headed "Retrospect for the Year": "The most promising results (with the airplane) to date were those obtained last year by the Wright brothers, one of whom made a flight of over half a mile in a power-propelled machine." Previously in the same editorial, though, was the assertion: ". . . the only successful 'flying' that has been done this year—must be credited to the balloon type." By that time, the Wrights' total flying distance was about 160 miles.

In its issue of January 13, 1906, in an article headed "The Wright Aeroplane and Its Fabled Performances," the *Scientific American* commented skeptically on a letter written by the Wright brothers which had been published in a Paris automobile journal. In that letter the Wrights had given details of the long flights of late

September and early October, 1905. In expressing its disbelief in the "alleged" flights described in the Wright letter, the *Scientific American* said: "If such sensational and tremendously important experiments are being conducted in a not very remote part of the country, on a subject in which almost everybody feels the most profound interest, is it possible to believe that the enterprising American reporter, who, it is well known, comes down the chimney when the door is locked in his face—even if he has to scale a fifteen-story skyscraper to do so—would not have ascertained all about them and published them broadcast long ago?"

A few weeks later, in February, 1906, the editor of the *Scientific American* wrote to the Wrights to inquire if there was any truth in reports that they were negotiating with the French Government. He enclosed in his letter a clipping of "The Wright Aeroplane and Its Fabled Performances."

The Wrights wrote in reply that since the *Scientific American* obtained the data of what it termed "alleged experiments" directly from a published letter signed by the Wright brothers, and since it did not discredit the authenticity of the letter, but only the truthfulness of the statements, they were at a loss to understand why the editor should desire further statements from such a source. They did not answer the inquiry about the negotiations with the French Government.

Most of the long flights in late September and early October, 1905, had been seen by Amos Stauffer, a farmer working in an adjoining field. But he went right ahead husking corn. Another witness, however, was more of a gossip. At one of the October flights, William Fouts, a Dayton druggist, was present, and the Wrights cautioned him not to say anything about what he had seen. But Fouts must have taken a few people into his confidence. In the afternoon of October 5, the Dayton *Daily News* had an article saying the Wrights were making sensational flights every day. The Dayton correspondent for the *Cincinnati Post* reported this to his paper which printed it the next day. A fairly good-sized crowd then went to the Huffman pasture. But when they found nothing going on there most of them decided that the reports must have been much exaggerated. Nothing more was said about the Wrights in Ohio papers for some time. John Tomlinson, a reporter on the Dayton *Journal*, and correspondent for out-of-town papers, offered $50 to Henry Webbert, friend of the Wrights, to let him know the date of their next flight. There was one more short flight on October 16, but no newspapermen or other onlookers were at the field.

On March 12, 1906, the Wrights had sent to the Aero Club of America the following list of names of reputable men who had seen one or more of their flights: E. W. Ellis, assistant city auditor; Torrence Huffman, bank president; C. S. Billman, secretary, and W. H. Shank, treasurer of the West Side Building & Loan Association; William, Henry and Charles Webbert, in the plumbing business; Frank Hamburger, hardware dealer; Howard M. Myers, post-office employee; William Fouts and Reuben Schindler, druggists; William Weber, plumber; Bernard H. Lambers, of Dayton Malleable Iron Works. Besides those living in Dayton, were: O. F. Jamieson, traveling salesman, of East Germantown,

Ohio; David Beard and Amos Stauffer, of Osborn; and Theodore Waddell, of the Census Bureau at Washington. The Wrights had a list of about sixty persons who had witnessed flights.

Those witnesses named in the published list got requests for confirmatory letters from the *Scientific American* whose editor finally had decided that reports of what the Wrights had done might be worth looking into. Then, in the issue of April 7, 1906, the magazine reported the long flights of the previous autumn and quoted in full a letter from one of the witnesses. More than six months later, on November 21, 1906, the Aero Club itself wrote to the various persons named in the list received from the Wrights, asking for letters about the flights they had seen.

As late as October, 1906, the *Scientific American* had devoted more than a column to a letter from J. C. Press, of South Norwalk, Connecticut, who presented arguments to justify his belief that "man may fly within a few years." But, on the other hand, the letter-writer quoted the editor of *Collier's Weekly* as expressing "disbelief in even the ultimate possibility of flight."

At last, however, in the issue of December 15, 1906, or nearly three years after the Wrights' first flights, the *Scientific American* printed an editorial which indicated that the editor was now becoming aware of the facts. The editorial said: "In all the history of invention, there is probably no parallel to the unostentatious manner in which the Wright brothers of Dayton, Ohio, ushered into the world their epoch-making invention of the first successful aeroplane flying-machine."

X

U. S. ARMY NOT INTERESTED

FROM the time that they knew their invention was practical, the Wrights wished to offer to their own government a world monopoly on all their patents and, still more important, all their secrets relating to the airplane. They thought it might be useful to the Army for scouting purposes. But as they had greater interest at first in learning more about flying and improving their machine than in making money out of it, they did not at once attempt negotiations with government officials at Washington. When they did make such an effort they received a rude shock. The United States Army not only didn't believe there was any such device in existence as a practical flying-machine, but was not disposed to investigate.

At least one foreign government showed more awareness and more curiosity. In the autumn of 1904, the Wrights got a letter from Lieutenant Colonel J. E. Capper, of the Royal Aircraft Factory (a government experimental laboratory dealing with aeronautics) at Aldershot. He wrote on shipboard en route to the United States, and enclosed a note of introduction from another Englishman whom the Wrights knew, Patrick Y. Alexander, member of the Aeronautical Society of Great Britain. (Alexander had called upon the Wrights at

Dayton in 1902, with a letter of introduction from Octave Chanute.) Colonel Capper wanted to know if he
might see the Wrights in Dayton when he returned east-
ward from a visit to the St. Louis Exposition. They told
him they would be glad to see him and he came to Dayton, accompanied by his wife, in November.

Soon after his arrival, Colonel Capper frankly said
that he was there at the request of his government. The
Wrights told him of what they had accomplished during that previous season of 1904 at the Huffman field.
Before leaving, Colonel Capper asked them to make his
government some kind of proposal.

The Wrights made no haste about submitting a proposal to the British, but, on January 10, 1905, about two
months after the Capper visit, they wrote to him asking
if he was sure his government was receptive to an offer.
In this letter they suggested that a government in possession of such a machine as they now could furnish,
and the knowledge and instruction they could impart
might have a lead of several years over governments
which waited to buy a perfected machine before making
a start in this line. The letter was signed: Wright Cycle
Company.

Whatever the British Government might desire, the
Wrights did not intend to take any steps that could prevent the United States Government from having opportunity to control all rights in their invention for the
entire world; and before having any further word from
the British it seemed wise to learn from Washington
just what our own government might want. They

THE HUFFMAN PASTURE. This rough field, eight miles from Dayton, where the Wrights made their important experiments of 1904 and 1905, is now a part of Patterson Field.

THE WRIGHT PATENT. Facsimile of the Letters Patent awarded Wilbur and Orville Wright on May 22, 1906, for their invention, the "Flying Machine."

wrote, on January 18, 1905, to their member of Congress from the Dayton district, R. M. Nevin, as follows:

The series of aeronautical experiments upon which we have been engaged for the past five years has ended in the production of a flying-machine of a type fitted for practical use. It not only flies through the air at high speed, but it also lands without being wrecked. During the year 1904 one hundred and five flights were made at our experimenting station, on the Huffman prairie, east of the city; and though our experience in handling the machine has been too short to give any high degree of skill, we nevertheless succeeded, toward the end of the season, in making two flights of five minutes each, in which we sailed round and round the field until a distance of about three miles had been covered, at a speed of thirty-five miles an hour. The first of these record flights was made on November 9th, in celebration of the phenomenal political victory of the preceding day, and the second, on December 1st, in honor of the one hundredth flight of the season.

The numerous flights in straight lines, in circles, and over "S"-shaped courses, in calms and in winds, have made it quite certain that flying has been brought to a point where it can be made of great practical use in various ways, one of which is that of scouting and carrying messages in time of war. If the latter features are of interest to our own government, we shall be pleased to take up the matter either on a basis of providing machines of agreed specification, at a contract price, or of furnishing all the scientific and practical information we have accumulated in these years of experimenting, together with a license to use our patents; thus putting the government in a position to operate on its own account.

If you can find it convenient to ascertain whether this is a subject of interest to our own government, it would oblige us greatly, as early information on this point will aid us in making our plans for the future.

Respectfully yours,

WILBUR AND ORVILLE WRIGHT

Mr. Nevin forwarded the letter to the Secretary of War who turned it over to the Board of Ordnance and Fortification. That Board evidently regarded the letter simply as something for their "crank file." They had received many proposals in the past from inventors of perpetual motion machines and flying-machines and had stock paragraphs to use in reply.

Their response to Nevin, signed by Major General G. L. Gillespie, of the General Staff, the President of the Board of Ordnance and Fortification, said:

I have the honor to inform you that, as many requests have been made for financial assistance in the development of designs for flying-machines, *the Board has found it necessary to decline to make allotments for the experimental development of devices for mechanical flight,* and has determined that, before suggestions with that object in view will be considered, *the device must have been brought to the stage of practical operation* without expense to the United States.

It appears from the letter of Messrs. Wilbur and Orville Wright that their machine has not yet been brought to the stage of practical operation, but as soon as it shall have been perfected, this Board would be pleased to receive further representations from them in regard to it.[1]

It will be noted, of course, that what the letter said bore almost no relation to anything the Wrights had written.

---

[1] All italics used in letters quoted in this chapter are supplied.

Having thus been brushed aside by their own government, the Wrights now might have been conscience
clear to do as they saw fit with a foreign government.
But nevertheless they determined that, no matter how
public officials at Washington behaved, they would take
no steps which could shut off their own government
from use of the airplane if Army people ever got around
to understanding the machine's potential importance.

On February 11, 1905, the Wrights received a letter
from the British War Office, asking them to submit
terms, and March 1, without giving formal terms, they
outlined in a general way what they were willing to do.

"Although we consider it advisable," they wrote to
the British War Office, "that any agreement which may
be made at present be based upon a single machine and
necessary instruction in its use, we would be willing, if
desired, to insert in the contract an option on the purchase of all that we know concerning the subject of
aviation . . .

"We are ready to enter into a contract with the British Government to construct and deliver to it an aerial
scouting machine of the aeroplane type . . ."

Specifications included these: The machine to be capable of carrying two men of average weight, and supplies of fuel for a flight of not less than fifty miles; its
speed, when flying in still air, to be not less than thirty
miles an hour; the machine to be of substantial enough
construction to make landings without being broken,
when operated with a reasonable degree of skill.

Another provision was that the purchase price should
be determined by the maximum distance covered in one

of the trial flights; £500, or about $2,500 for each mile. If none of the trial flights was of at least ten miles, then the British Government would not be obligated to accept the machine.

There were further exchanges of letters between the Wrights and the British (altogether twenty-four letters in the years 1905-6), but the brothers began to suspect that the British were mainly interested in prolonging the negotiations as a means of keeping in touch and knowing what progress was being made in aviation. Probably, thought the Wrights, the British shrewdly foresaw that the flying-machine would not add to the isolation of the British Isles, and did not wish to hasten its development. But they doubtless wished to be well informed about whatever was happening in the conquest of the air.

The British War Office wrote on May 13, 1905, that they were asking Colonel H. Foster, their military attaché, in Washington, to call upon the Wrights at their "works"—meaning, presumably, at their shop—and to see their machine in flight.

The brothers were urged by their friend Octave Chanute on one of his visits to Dayton, to make another offer of their machine to the United States Army. Because of the treatment they had received from the War Department, the Wrights were naturally reluctant to expose themselves to further rebuffs, but Chanute was insistent that such behavior by Army people surely would not occur again. Thus prodded by Chanute, the Wrights, on October 9, 1905, wrote to the Secretary of War:

Some months ago we made an informal offer to furnish to the War Department practical flying-machines suitable for scouting purposes. The matter was referred to the Board of Ordnance and Fortification, which seems to have given it scant consideration. We do not wish to take this invention abroad, unless we find it necessary to do so, and therefore write again, renewing the offer.

We are prepared to furnish a machine on contract, to be accepted only after trial trips in which the conditions of the contract have been fulfilled; the machine to carry an operator and supplies of fuel, etc., sufficient for a flight of one hundred miles; the price of the machine to be regulated according to a sliding scale based on the performance of the machine in the trial trips; the minimum performance to be a flight of at least twenty-five miles at a speed of not less than thirty miles an hour.

We are also willing to take contracts to build machines carrying more than one man.

Respectfully yours,

WILBUR AND ORVILLE WRIGHT.

Once again the Secretary of War referred their letter to the Board of Ordnance and Fortification. Major General J. C. Bates, member of the General Staff, had become president of the Board since the previous correspondence, and he signed the reply. The Wrights blinked at the familiar phrases in the opening paragraph:

"I have the honor to inform you," said the Major General, "that, as many requests have been made for financial assistance in the development of designs for flying-machines, the Board has found it necessary to decline to make allotments for the experimental development of devices for mechanical flight, and has determined that, before suggestions with that object in view will be considered, the device must have been brought to the stage of practical operation without expense to the United States."

The letter went on: "Before the question of making a contract with you for the furnishing of a flying-machine is considered it will be necessary for you to furnish this Board with the approximate cost of the completed machine, the date upon which it would be delivered, and with such drawings and descriptions thereof as are necessary to enable its construction to be understood and a definite conclusion as to its practicability to be arrived at. Upon receipt of this information, the matter will receive the careful consideration of the Board."

In other words, the Board would have to see drawings and descriptions to determine if the machine the Wrights had been flying could fly!

Regardless of whatever irritation they felt, the Wrights wrote to the Ordnance Board on October 19. In that letter they said:

We have no thought of asking financial assistance from the government. We propose to sell the results of experiments finished at our own expense.

In order that we may submit a proposition conforming as nearly as possible to the ideas of your board, it is desirable that we be informed what conditions you would wish to lay down as to the performance of the machine in the official trials, prior to the acceptance of the machine. We cannot well fix a price, nor a time for delivery, till we have your idea of the qualifications necessary to such a machine. We ought also to know whether you would wish to reserve a monopoly on the use of the invention, or whether you would permit us to accept orders for similar machines from other governments, and give public exhibitions, etc.

Proof of our ability to execute an undertaking of the nature proposed will be furnished whenever desired.

Here is what Captain T. C. Dickson, Recorder of the Board, wrote in reply:

The Board of Ordnance and Fortification at its meeting October 24, 1905, took the following action:

The Board then considered a letter, dated October 19, 1905, from Wilbur and Orville Wright requesting the requirements prescribed by the Board that a flying-machine would have to fulfill before it would be accepted.

It is recommended the Messrs. Wright be informed that the Board does not care to formulate any requirements for the performance of a flying-machine or take any further action on the subject *until a machine is produced which by actual operation is shown to be able to produce horizontal flight and to carry an operator.*

Such letters did not encourage the Wrights to press their offer further. As Wilbur expressed it, they had taken pains to see that "opportunity gave a good clear knock on the War Department door." It had always been their business practice, he said, to sell to those who wished to buy instead of trying to force goods upon people who did not want them. And now if the American Government had decided to spend no more money on flying-machines until their practical use should be demonstrated abroad, the Wrights felt that there wasn't much they could do about it.

Chanute, too, was now convinced that the seeming

stupidity of War Department officials was not accidental. His comment was: "Those fellows are a bunch of asses."

On that same day, October 19, when they wrote to the Ordnance Board, the Wrights had sent a letter also to the British War Office amending their earlier proposal. They said that recent events justified them in making the acceptance of their machine dependent upon a trial flight of at least fifty miles, instead of only ten miles as in the original offer.

Shortly afterward, on November 22, 1905, the Wrights received a letter from Colonel Foster, the British military attaché in Washington, asking if it would be possible for him to see the Wright machine in flight. Experiments for that year had been completed; but, the Wrights replied, if Colonel Foster came to Dayton he could meet and talk with many persons who had witnessed flights. That didn't satisfy Colonel Foster. He wrote again on November 29 that the War Office had had many descriptions of airplane flights by persons supposed to have witnessed them. What the War Office wanted, he said, was for him to *see* a flight.

The Wrights made it plain to the Colonel that they saw no point to making a demonstration of their machine unless negotiations had reached a point where a deal could be closed if the machine's performance was as represented. They reminded him that it wasn't necessary for the British War Office to put up any money in advance—only to sign an agreement that a deal would be closed after the Wrights had shown what their machine could do. Communications continued to pass between the Wrights and the British. Colonel Foster was succeeded as British military attaché at Washington by Colonel Gleichen and the latter made a trip to Dayton. But nothing came of the negotiations. In December, 1906, the British finally wrote to the Wrights that they had decided not to buy an airplane.

Meanwhile, in the spring of 1906, the War Department at Washington heard once more about the Wrights in consequence of an exchange of letters between the Wrights and Godfrey Lowell Cabot, of Boston, who, it will be remembered, had written to them just after the Kitty Hawk flights in 1903. Cabot had seen a bulletin published by the Aero Club of America, on March 12, 1906, that told about the progress the Wrights had made during the season of 1905 at Huffman field. He had learned also, from his brother Samuel, a little about the Wrights' offer to the U. S. War Department. Samuel Cabot got the news, presumably, from Chanute, with whom he from time to time exchanged letters. (He had written to Chanute asking if the Wrights needed any financial assistance for carrying on their experiments, and Chanute told him they did not.) Godfrey Cabot wrote to the brothers (in April, 1906) saying that he supposed they had offered their machine to the U. S. Army "with negative results," but that if they ever decided to form a company to exploit the machine's commercial possibilities, he wished they would send him a prospectus.

In their reply to Cabot (May 19), the Wrights confirmed the reports about their correspondence with the Ordnance Board. Cabot was so astounded over the treatment they had received that he promptly sent the facts to his relative, Henry Cabot Lodge, United States Senator from Massachusetts. Lodge forwarded Cabot's letter, along with one of his own, to the Secretary of War—who sent it to the Board of Ordnance and Fortification. Brigadier General William Crozier, president of the Ordnance Board, wrote to Senator Lodge, on May 26, acknowledging his letter to the Secretary of War, and stating that "if those in control of the flying-machine invented by the Wright brothers will place themselves in communication with the Board of Ordnance and Fortification, War Department, Washington, D. C., any proposition they may have to make will be given consideration by the Board."

Shortly afterward, Godfrey Cabot called upon General Crozier in Washington and showed him copies of the Aero Club Bulletin which told about the Wrights flying twenty-four miles in 1905. Since this was convincing evidence that the Wrights' machine was capable of horizontal flight, General Crozier may have been somewhat embarrassed. He said the Ordnance Board would be glad to receive a proposition from the Wrights! He said, too, that he might send a representative to see the Wrights in Dayton.

In reply to a letter from Cabot reporting his talk with Crozier, the Wrights (on June 21) wrote:

If General Crozier should decide to send a representative to Dayton we would be glad to furnish him convincing proof that a machine has been produced which by actual operation has been shown to be able to produce horizontal flight and to carry an operator.

This letter also said:

We are ready to negotiate whenever the Board is ready, but as the former correspondence closed with a strong intimation that the Board did not wish to be bothered with our offers, we naturally have no intention of taking the initiative again.

General Crozier did not send any representative to Dayton.

Several months later, in November, 1906, newspapers got wind of the fact that there had been some kind of correspondence between the Wrights and the War Department. On November 29, many newspapers carried a dispatch from Washington which said: "While General Crozier will not discuss negotiations with the Wrights, he said today: 'You may simply say it is now up to the Wright brothers to say whether the government shall take their invention. They know the government's attitude and have its offer.'"

There had been no Government offer. The last communication the Wrights had received from the War Department was the one, more than a year before, in which the Ordnance Board said it did not wish to take any further action.

The Wrights felt sure that the War Department no longer doubted the existence of a successful flying-machine. It appeared, though, that certain Army officers still were unwilling frankly to admit their blundering behavior and come down from their high horse. There was reason to believe that the Ordnance Board would welcome a face-saving opportunity and hoped the Wrights would once again take the initiative by making a new proposal. But the Wrights were not ready to do so. Their advances had too often been spurned. The next move, they thought, should come from the War Department.

In that frame of mind, early in the spring of 1907, the inventors evolved a plan for bringing their machine to the attention of the War Department in a manner quite dramatic.

An exposition was going to be held on the Virginia coast that year to celebrate the three hundredth anniversary of the founding of the first English colony, at Jamestown. In connection with this Jamestown Exposition there would be a great naval review, April 26, at Hampton Roads. President Theodore Roosevelt and other important government people, including Army and Navy officers, would be present. What would be the matter, the Wrights asked themselves, with appearing there unexpectedly in their flying-machine? They could equip their machine with hydroplanes and pontoons for starting and landing on water, take it to Kitty Hawk, and then fly it, over Currituck Sound and beyond, to the scene of the naval review. After circling a few hundred feet above the battleships, the machine would disappear as suddenly and as mysteriously as it had come. No newspaper people or anyone else would know where it came from or how to get in touch with those who knew about it, and the mystery would grow.

Officers of the Army and Navy would be asked embarrassing questions. Had they arranged for the flying-machine to appear, and had it been adopted for use in time of war? Those who still "knew" there was no practical flying-machine would be set to wondering.

The Wrights had many a quiet chuckle at the thought of the effect of their practical joke if it could be carried out. It was not too dangerous a project. Much of the flight could be made over shallow water in Currituck Sound. It would easily be possible to fly as far as the scene of the naval review and out of sight on the return trip before coming down.

They put an engine, with propellers attached to it, on pontoons, and placed this experimental outfit on the river at Dayton for preliminary trials. After a day or so of these tests it was evident that the plan of mounting their machine on hydroplanes and pontoons and taking off from the water was practical. But the inventors took aboard a passenger who tried to be helpful. In his efforts to throw his weight where he thought it would help the balance, he succeeded only in tilting the machine so steeply that it dived below the surface. The propellers were damaged. Before repairs could be made, something broke the dam in the river. The Wrights had to abandon their plans for a prank that might have been a national sensation.

Only a short time after the Wrights were planning their surprise flight, in that spring of 1907, Herbert Parsons, a member of Congress from New York, sent to President Roosevelt a clipping from the *Scientific American*—whose editor now knew about the Wrights.

Roosevelt sent the clipping, with a note signed by his secretary, to Secretary of War Taft. The note suggested a talk with Representative Parsons to discuss the idea of experimenting with the Wright flying-machine. Taft sent the clipping and White House note to the Ordnance Board, with a note signed by his own secretary and headed "Endorsement."

The personnel of the Ordnance Board had changed, at least partly, since the earlier correspondence with the Wrights. But the same attitude of aloofness regarding flying-machines still existed. The Board could not, however, ignore a letter from the office of the President of the United States, Commander-in-Chief of the Army and Navy, with an endorsement from the Secretary of War. It might have been expected that the Board members would feel bound to investigate the reported flying-machine. But they couldn't bring themselves to go that far. All they did was to send, on May 11, a brief letter to the Wrights, signed by Major Samson M. Fuller, Recorder of the Board. The letter said:

I am directed by the President of the Board to enclose copies of two letters referring to your aeroplane, for your information, and to say that the Board has before it several propositions for the construction and test of aeroplanes, and if you desire to take any action in the matter, will be glad to hear from you on the subject.

Accompanying the letter were copies of the notes from the White House and the office of the Secretary of War. The Wrights believed they knew why those copies were sent. It was to let them know that the Ordnance Board was writing only because of orders from higher up.

Though the letter from the Board was standoffish enough, yet it did not imply, as some of the earlier letters did, that the Wrights were a pair of beggars, or cranks, seeking funds. The Wrights thought the letter had been forced and that it really was a mere gesture, but nevertheless they treated it as if the Ordnance Board might now be seriously interested.

In their reply, May 17, the Wrights said they had some flying machines under construction and would be glad to make a formal proposal to sell one or more of them to the Government if the War Department was interested. They said the machine would carry two men and a supply of fuel for a flight of 200 kilometers; that a trial flight of at least 50 kilometers, at a speed not less than 50 kilometers an hour, would be made before representatives of the Government before any part of the purchase price was paid. They suggested a conference for the purpose of discussing the matter in detail. And they said they were willing to submit a formal proposition, if that was preferred.

In the next letter from the Ordnance Board, dated May 22, 1907, nothing was said about the Wrights' suggestion for a conference; but the Wrights were requested to make a formal proposal incorporating the specifications and conditions contained in their letter to the Board, dated May 17.

The Wrights sent a formal proposal on May 31. In this proposal they repeated all the specifications and conditions mentioned in their letter of the 17th, and in addition agreed to the following: to teach an operator to fly the machine; to return to the starting point in the 50 kilometer test flight; and to land without any damage that would prevent the machine being started immediately upon another flight. The price stated was $100,000 for the first machine; others to be furnished at a reasonable margin above the cost of manufacture. They added that they were willing to make the contract speed 40 miles an hour, provided an additional sum would be allowed for each mile in excess of that speed in the trial flight, with a forfeit of an equal amount for every mile below. Again the Wrights made it plain that nothing was to be paid to them until after a trial flight had met all contract requirements.

The next letter from the Ordnance Board dated June 8 said that $100,000 was more than the Board had available, and that such an amount could not be obtained without a special appropriation by Congress at its next session. Then the letter went on to ask what the price would include; whether the United States would be granted exclusive use, or whether the Wrights contemplated commercial exploitation of their machine, or negotiations with foreign governments.

The Wrights wrote in reply explaining just what was included in the price. They said it did not include any period during which the use of the invention would belong exclusively to the United States, since a recent contract precluded such an offer, and that it was their intention to furnish machines for military use before entering the commercial field. The letter repeated what the Wrights had said before, that when a contract had been signed they would produce a machine at their own expense and make flights as specified in the contract in the presence of representatives of the War Department before any money whatever was paid to them.

That was the last letter to pass between the Ordnance Board and the Wrights for some time. But while the Wrights were in Europe, the Board undoubtedly began to hear from military attachés and others about the brothers' negotiations abroad. At any rate, the Board began to show signs of uneasiness and they wrote a letter, signed by Major Fuller, October 5—received by the Wrights in Europe—to say that the Wright proposal of June 15 had again been given consideration by the Board at its meeting of October 3, 1907, but that nothing definite could be done before a meeting of Congress, as Congressional action would be necessary to accept the proposition, since the funds at the Board's disposal were insufficient.

The Wrights' reply, from London, on October 30, made it clear that if the price was the only thing in the way, that could probably be satisfactorily adjusted.

Wilbur Wright started home from Europe ahead of Orville, but before he left, it was agreed between the brothers that their price for an airplane to the United States Government would be $25,000.

XI

EUROPE DISCOVERS THE WRIGHTS

THOUGH the importance of the Wrights' achievements was unrecognized in the United States until long after their first power flights, reports about their gliding prior to those flights had aroused much interest abroad.

In the spring of 1903, the Wrights' Chicago friend, Octave Chanute, had gone to his native France in the interest of the St. Louis Exposition to be held the next year. One purpose of his visit was to arrange with Alberto Santos-Dumont, the Brazilian aeronaut, who lived in Paris, to make flights at St. Louis with his dirigible balloon. While in Paris, Chanute was invited by the Aéro Club to give a talk regarding aviation in the United States. In this talk, on April 2, he told of his own gliding experiments in 1896 and of those of the Wright Brothers in 1901 and 1902, illustrated by photographs. Then in the August, 1903, issue of *L'Aérophile* Chanute published an article on the same subject, with photographic illustrations, scale drawings, and structural details of the Wright 1902 glider. In the *Revue des Sciences* of November, 1903, he again published photographs and description of that machine. This 1902 glider far surpassed any that had ever been built before, and in it the problem of equilibrium had practically been solved. That glider was the basis of the specifications in the Wright patent. Chanute's revelations therefore were sensational. And they did not fall on deaf ears.

Until this time, about the only man in France who was showing any interest in aviation was Captain Louis Ferdinand Ferber of the French army, who himself had made gliding experiments as a hobby while serving in an Alpine artillery corps. As early as 1901 he had begun an exchange of letters with Chanute, after having read in the *Illustrierte Aeronautische Mitteilungen*, a German magazine devoted mainly to ballooning, a brief article, supplied by Wilbur Wright, about the 1900 experiments at Kitty Hawk. A little later he wrote for information to the Wrights themselves. But now after the Chanute speech, Ferber was no longer alone among Frenchmen in thinking the Wrights' experiments might be significant. Though belief in the possibility of a successful flying machine had been at lowest ebb in France, the information now made available by Chanute caused a greatly revived interest. Heretofore the Aéro Club had devoted its attention almost entirely to balloons and dirigibles, but it considered the French as leaders in every line pertaining to aeronautics. Immediately following the Chanute address telling of the Wrights' gliding experiments in America, several members of the Aéro Club, led by Ernest Archdeacon, decided to organize a special committee on aviation. Archdeacon also made a warm appeal in favor of organizing contests for gliders to show that the French did not intend to allow anyone to surpass them in any branch of aeronautics. He subscribed three thousand francs for the organization of such contests and for prizes. *L'Aéro-phile*, official organ of the Club, which up to this time had published little about aviation, now suddenly began to carry many articles and items of news concerning projected experiments in gliding.

But it was some months before the French actually passed from the "talking" to the "doing" stage in gliding. In the meantime a brief dispatch about the Wrights' power flights on December 17, 1903, had appeared in French and other European daily papers. Though the reports of these power flights were received with considerable skepticism, nevertheless they created such a furore in French aeronautical circles that before the end of January, 1904, no less than six gliders of the Wright 1902 type were being built in France from data furnished by Chanute.

Ernest Archdeacon, of the Aéro Club, placed an order with M. Dargent, a model maker of Chalais-Meudon, to build a copy of the Wright 1902 glider. Early in 1904 (January 28), Captain Ferber delivered a lecture at Lyon on the subject of gliding experiments, and a young man named Gabriel Voisin, just finishing his course in a technical school, came to him to ask advice about how to get into the field of aviation. He said he wished to "consecrate his life" to aviation. Ferber suggested that he should go to see Archdeacon. Voisin did so, and Archdeacon employed him to test the glider built by Dargent. Ferber gave Voisin his instructions in gliding. Then Archdeacon employed Voisin to build still another glider like the Wright machine. That contact with Archdeacon gave Voisin

his start toward becoming a famous airplane manufacturer. And it was from that glider *"du type de Wright,"*
as the French papers called it, tested by Voisin, that
grew the first Voisin machines, soon to be followed by
those of other copyists. Here was the real beginning of
French—indeed of European—aviation.

Articles about the Wright power flights were appearing in the French, English and German aeronautical magazines. A longer article about the Kitty Hawk
event was printed in the March, 1904, issue of *Illustrierte Aeronautische Mitteilungen* from Carl Dienstbach,[1] a musician in New York, who as a side line was
the magazine's correspondent.

One copyist after another began to use devices and
technical knowledge invented or discovered by the
Wrights. When Ferber received a letter from the
American publication, the *Scientific American,* asking
for an account of his own gliding experiments, he wrote
to them that he was simply a "disciple of the Wright
Brothers." But these copyists were not content to follow the Chanute revelations and build gliders just like
that of the Wrights. Instead, they tried to improve
upon the Wrights' work. The "improvements" were
not successful, because the builders did not have the
Wrights' knowledge and wind-tunnel data, except that
used in the 1902 glider, to guide them. So great were
their difficulties that some of the experimenters began
to place blame on Chanute. They thought Chanute
must have misrepresented what the Wrights had done
—maybe purposely. That was the only way they could

[1] Dienstbach was still a resident of New York in 1943.

account for their failure to get the good results obtained by the Wrights.

Robert Esnault-Pelterie, a member of the Aéro Club, pointed out that they had not put to a fair test the information on the Wright glider that Chanute had given them, because, he said, in building their gliders they had not strictly adhered to Chanute's description and specifications. Since they had all the data needed to reproduce the glider that Chanute had reported as having been so successful, Esnault-Pelterie said, the way to determine the value of the information was to build a Wright glider exactly like Chanute had described and then test it to see how it performed. He himself then built such a machine, in 1904, and reported that he got the same performance as had the Wrights.

While the French were carrying on these experiments with copies of the 1902 Wright glider, the Wrights themselves were busy with their power machine with which they made more than 100 starts in 1904. It was not until late October, 1906, or nearly three years after the Wrights' first power flights, that a French power machine was flown. (This machine, piloted by Santos-Dumont, was reported to have made a hop of 200 feet, about ten feet above the ground.)

Before long, Archdeacon and another member of the Aéro Club, Henri Deutsch de la Meurthe, were offering aviation prizes, and doing all they could to encourage someone to try to build a successful power plane. But as Captain Ferber later made clear to Georges Besançon, editor of L'Aérophile, in a letter

Besançon published in his issue of June, 1907, this revival of interest in aviation in France, and whatever was accomplished, was all a direct outgrowth of information about what the Wrights had done in America.

In October, 1905, reports about the long flights accomplished that year by the Wrights with their power machine were received in France. They created an even greater stir in French aeronautical circles than had the earlier reports. Just at the time these reports reached France an organization was formed there to be known as the Fédération Aéronautique Internationale, the purpose of which was to verify and record the truth about reported aeronautical flights. The Aero Club of America, formed at about the same time, was made the official representative of the F.A.I. in America. No flight had as yet been made in France with a motor plane. Long afterward, many uninformed persons, even in the United States, declared that the flights by the Wrights prior to 1908 really should not count, as they had not been officially witnessed by any representative of the F.A.I.—the organization that came into being after the flights had been made!

As the tempo of interest increased, the Wrights were kept fairly busy writing letters to France in reply to requests for information. At the time of the first reports of the 1903 flights at Kitty Hawk, probably the only person in France inclined to believe them was Captain Ferber. Knowing what he did, from correspondence with Chanute, and with the Wrights themselves, he was not too incredulous. If he had said at first that he believed human flight might have occurred, he doubtless would have been laughed at—especially by those who had been most busily experimenting. But as early as May, 1905, Captain Ferber had written to the Wrights, asking if they would sell a power plane and at what price. They were not ready to discuss such a project at that time and, though Ferber wrote a second letter prodding them, they did not reply until October 9, four days after they had completed their most important flying experiments for that year.

In that letter, after telling of their recent long flights, the Wrights said they were prepared to furnish machines on contract, to be accepted only after trial trips of at least forty kilometers, the machine to carry an operator and enough supplies of fuel for a flight of 160 kilometers. They said they would be willing to make contracts in which the minimum distance of the trial trip would be more than forty kilometers, but that the price of the machine would then be greater. They were also ready, the letter added, to build machines carrying more than one man. No figures as to price were given.

Hoping to have the French War Department buy a plane, Ferber went to his chief, Colonel Bertrand, director of the laboratory of research pertaining to military aeronautics. But Colonel Bertrand told him the French Government could not commit itself to pay a sum "probably enormous" for an invention not yet authenticated. All that it was possible to do, said Bertrand, was to appoint and send a commission to see the Wrights.

Again Ferber wrote to the Wrights, on October 21, asking what the price for a machine would be. He said he didn't think his government would any longer be interested in paying so great a sum as it had been when he had first asked for a price.

The Wrights replied, on November 4, saying they would consent to reduce their price to the French Government to one million francs—$200,000—the money to be paid only after the genuine value of their discoveries had been demonstrated by a flight of one of their machines in the presence of French Government representatives. Ferber had not told in his letter what the French Government had been willing to pay and the Wrights did not say what the price of one million francs was reduced *from!* The price was to include a complete machine, and instruction in the Wright discoveries relating to the scientific principles of the art; formulas for the designing of machines of other sizes and speeds; and personal instruction of operators in the use of the machine.

At the time Captain Ferber was thus dickering for the possible purchase of a Wright flying-machine, others in France who were interested in aeronautics still doubted if such a machine existed.

About the middle of October, Frank S. Lahm, a member of the Aéro Club of France, had a chance meeting with his friend Patrick Y. Alexander, of the Aeronautical Society of Great Britain, who had visited the Wrights as recently as the previous April. Alexander expressed to Lahm his strong belief that the Wrights had actually been making power flights in America.

Lahm was an American. After going to France from Mansfield, Ohio, many years before, he had introduced the Remington typewriter to Europe. As a hobby he had taken up ballooning and held a pilot's license. It was of more than casual interest to him that Alexander believed successful flights had been made in America. Lahm then made an effort to learn the facts from a source right in Dayton, Ohio. He wrote to Nelson Bierce, a manufacturer there whom he knew, asking what sort of people the Wrights were and what was known about their reported experiments. Bierce didn't make any investigation, but wrote to Lahm, late in November, that the Wrights were considered men of good character, and that they were said to be carrying on some kind of flying experiments near Dayton; but, he said, no one seemed to know much about the nature of these experiments.

Before there was time for Bierce's letter to reach him, Lahm got other news about the Wrights. A letter they had sent on November 17, to Besançon, editor of *L'Aérophile*, giving a detailed account of their most recent experiments, had been published on November 30 in *L'Auto*, a Paris daily dealing with sports. Besançon had given the letter to *L'Auto* because his own next monthly issue would not go to press for a week or more and he was afraid a rival German publication might print, before he could, similar information from the Wrights.

That letter to Besançon, containing much specific information, created a sensation. There was much animated talk about its contents that night of November 30 at the Aéro Club. Indeed, that date is noteworthy in aeronautical history, for publication of the letter to Besançon led to several important investigations.

News about the Wrights' recent flights that the letter revealed was taken up by one or two of the wire services and cabled back to the United States where it reached various newspapers, including those in Dayton. But Dayton editors couldn't understand why the Wrights should have stirred up so much excitement in France.

One investigation was started by Lahm, now determined to get the facts. He had a brother-in-law in Mansfield, Ohio, Henry M. Weaver (a manufacturer of cash carriers for department stores); and Weaver had a son, Henry, Jr., perhaps not too busy to go to Dayton and find out all about the Wrights. Immediately after leaving his friends at the Aéro Club, Lahm sent this cable to the younger Weaver: "Verify what Wright brothers claim necessary go Dayton today prompt answer cable."

The young man in Mansfield, never having heard of the Wrights, supposed the message must be for his father, then away on a business trip, and he forwarded it to him at the Grand Pacific Hotel in Chicago. It was received by the father on December 1, shortly after he had retired for the night. Weaver, Sr., didn't at once recall ever having heard of the Wrights, but if they had a "claim" against his brother-in-law, he would see what could be done about settling it. As the question must be important he sent a wire to Dayton that very night. Having no street address for them, he addressed it simply to "Wright Brothers." This message was not clear to the Wrights and their reply the next morning was as

puzzling to Weaver as his had been to them. To get
down to dots and make sure he was addressing the
people he sought, Weaver then sent another telegram
asking the Wrights if they knew F. S. Lahm, of Paris.
The Wrights didn't know Lahm but they knew *of* him
and replied: "Yes Lahm French aeronaut." When he
noted that word "aeronaut," Weaver began to remember vaguely having heard some years previously about
two brothers who had experimented with a glider somewhere in the Carolinas. The mystery seemed to be lifting. Doubtless the Wrights had made a glider for
Lahm and now there was some misunderstanding about
the price. He immediately telegraphed again to the
Wrights, saying he would arrive in Dayton the next
morning (Sunday), and asking the Wrights to meet him
at the Algonquin Hotel.

When he reached the hotel in Dayton, Weaver discovered that there was no firm of Wright Brothers in
the telephone book or city directory. The hotel clerk
had never heard of them. Others whom he asked if they
knew of anyone in Dayton having a flying-machine
looked at him blankly and shook their heads. Well,
these Wrights must be somewhere, Weaver reflected,
for they had replied to his two earlier telegrams. He
may have feared that their place of business was closed
for the week end before they could have received his
telegram asking them to meet him. At any rate, he went
to the office of the telegraph company. There he met
the messenger boy who had delivered his message. The
boy explained that the brothers had their office at the
Wright Cycle Company but that, since it was Sunday,

they could not be reached except at their home. Weaver then returned to his hotel. There he found Orville Wright waiting for him.

As soon as they began to talk, Weaver said: "You made a glider, I believe, for Mr. Lahm, in Paris."

Orville, of course, shook his head. No, he said, they had never made a glider for Mr. Lahm.

"Then," asked Weaver, even more puzzled, "what in the world can be the meaning of this cable?" And he handed to Orville the message from Paris.

Orville then understood. Evidently, he said, Lahm, a member of the Aéro Club of France, wished to find out if the report of their flights sent to the Aéro Club by the Wright brothers was true.

As Weaver later reported in a letter to Lahm, he was already impressed by this younger Wright brother. "His very appearance would disarm any suspicion—with a face more of a poet than an inventor or promoter. In contour, head and face resemble Edgar Allan Poe . . . very modest in alluding to the marvels they have accomplished . . ."

Orville, somewhat amused, said if an investigation was desired, they might as well get right at it. It was too late in the season for flying, and the machine had been taken apart, but he could introduce the visitor to many responsible people who had seen them fly.

Orville took him to the home of C. S. Billman, of the West Side Savings and Loan Company. The Billmans were a fairly large family and nearly all had seen the Wrights fly. When the callers were taken into the sitting-room the first member of the family to appear was a four-year-old boy. "Son," asked Weaver jokingly, "have you ever seen a flying-machine?" He wasn't expecting to get evidence just yet; but the boy began to run around the room, trying to imitate with his hands the motion of a propeller and to make a noise like the machine.

Turning to Orville, Weaver laughingly observed: "I'm about convinced already. That boy couldn't be a bribed witness."

They also went, by interurban car, to talk with the Beard family, across from the flying field, and with Amos Stauffer, the nearest farmer up the road.

As Weaver reported: "On October 5, he [Stauffer] was cutting corn in the next field east, which is higher ground. When he noticed the aeroplane had started on its flight he remarked to his helper: 'Well, the boys are at it again,' and kept on cutting corn, at the same time keeping an eye on the great white form rushing about its course. 'I just kept on shocking corn,' he continued, 'until I got down to the fence, and the durned thing was still going round. I thought it would never stop.' I asked him how long he thought the flight continued, and he replied it seemed to him it was in the air for half an hour."

Then Orville and Weaver returned to Dayton and called on William Fouts, West Side druggist, who had witnessed the long flight on October 5.

Later they went to the Wright home. Of that visit Weaver wrote: "The elder brother, Wilbur, I found even quieter and less demonstrative than the younger. He looked the scholar and recluse. Neither is married.

As Mr. Wright expressed it, they had not the means to support 'a wife and a flying-machine too.' "

Weaver was completely convinced before he left Dayton, and on December 3, cabled to Lahm: "Claims completely verified." A few days later, on December 6, back at his home in Mansfield, he rushed a letter to Lahm giving his evidence of what the Wrights had done.

In a little more than a week after Weaver's visit to Dayton, another investigator appeared there, Robert Coquelle, representing *L'Auto*, of Paris. He had been in New York attending the six-day bicycle races and arrived in Dayton on December 12. Since his paper and *Les Sports* had taken opposite sides regarding the possibility that the Wrights had flown, and *L'Auto* had been pro-Wright, Coquelle wished to report on these "*deux marchands de cycles*" in a way to make a sensation. The imaginative tale he wrote about how "mysterious" were the Wrights was almost worthy of his compatriot, Dumas. The Wrights gave him names of people who had witnessed flights but it is believed he didn't bother to consult many of them, evidently feeling sure he could invent a better story than they could tell him. However, Coquelle was convinced that the reports about the Wrights' flights were not exaggerated and he cabled a preliminary dispatch to his paper: Wright brothers refuse to show their machine but I have seen some witnesses it is impossible to doubt.

On December 13, the day after Coquelle's visit to Dayton, the Wrights sent another letter to M. Besançon, editor of *L'Aérophile*, in reply to questions of his, and gave him details of their recent flights, distances, height at which they flew, size of field, and so on. Incidentally the closing paragraph of that letter contained a statement in contradiction of a myth, still widely accepted:

The claim often made in the 19th century that the lack of sufficiently light motors alone prohibited man from the empire of the air was quite unfounded. At the speeds which birds usually employ, a well-designed flyer can in actual practice sustain a gross weight of 30 kilograms for each horsepower of the motor, which gives ample margin for such motors as might easily have been built 50 years ago.

Before Besançon could have received this letter, with its details of recent flights, Robert Coquelle arrived in Paris, having taken a boat from New York only a day or two after his stay in Dayton, and his sensational story was published. Much of this report seemed so incredible that one member of the Aéro Club said it almost made him wonder if the Wright brothers existed at all.

What Weaver had written in his letter seemed convincing enough to Lahm and he prepared a French translation of it to read to the aviation committee of the Aéro Club of France at a meeting on the night of December 29, 1905. That meeting, as Lahm later told about it to friends, and in an article he gave to the Mansfield (Ohio) *News*, published October 24, 1908, was a memorable one. The skeptical members of the committee, greatly in the majority, having heard of Weaver's telegram, assumed the more elaborate report would be favorable to the Wrights, and were prepared to combat it. Characteristic of the French, there was almost cere-

THE U. S. ARMY TEST. Preparing the Wright plane for a test at Fort Myer.

AT FORT MYER. Lieutenant Frank P. Lahm and Orville Wright with the *Wright* plane during the test at Fort Myer. Lieutenant Lahm was the first army officer to fly as a passenger in a plane.

monious politeness at the beginning of the meeting because everyone supposed there might be less politeness as the discussions went on.

By the time Lahm had finished reading the letter, everyone began to talk at once. Archdeacon, who presided, was famous for a high-pitched staccato voice and it could be heard calling for order as he also rapped on the table before him with a flat metal ruler.

One member observed that they had seen nothing about the Wrights' flights in American newspapers, recognized as enterprising. He found himself incapable of believing, he said, that all the journalists in America would permit so important a piece of news to escape them.

Another remarked that they had heard the Wright brothers were of modest enough wealth. Who, he asked, is their financier? It would be interesting to talk with him.

Lahm was hard put to it to explain the lack of news about the flights in the American papers. He himself didn't understand that. But he tried to explain that since the brothers did most of the mechanical work on their machine themselves they did not require financial assistance. His voice, however, was drowned in the hubbub. As the discussion continued, so vehement were the contradictions of the Weaver letter that Lahm, Ferber, Besançon, and Coquelle, the only ones present who seemed to believe it, hardly dared express themselves at all. Someone turned to Coquelle and asked him if he really accepted the stories of the Wrights' flights.

"I do," he said—but in a low voice.

All conceded that Lahm's friend Weaver had doubtless been sincere in what he wrote but they insisted that he had somehow been fooled. They "knew" flight was impossible with a motor of only twelve horsepower. Indeed, many had decided that power flight would always be an impossibility. This belief was all the stronger because a number present had personally done enough in attempts to fly to know the difficulties.

One member after another strolled into an adjoining room where they could argue without being called to order. Finally Archdeacon found himself nearly alone. When, long after midnight, the meeting finally broke up the one thing all were agreed upon was that human flight, if true, was of vast consequence.

When the Wrights learned how great was the incredulity at the Aéro Club in France they were only amused that the stories seemed to the French too wonderful to be true.

On December 31 the Weaver letter to Lahm was published in full in *L'Auto.* The next day it appeared in the Paris edition of the New York *Herald* and also in *Les Sports,* competitor of *L'Auto.*

Though the Aéro Club did not yet know it, Captain Ferber in November had started still another investigation. He had written to the Wrights on November 15, asking permission to send an "official" commission to see them. The Wrights answered on December 5 that they thought it highly advisable that the French Government send a commission to make a thorough investigation of their claims, and that it should be done at once. Eight days later the Wrights received a cable from Ferber saying: "Friend with full powers for stating terms of contract will sail next Saturday." Ferber also sent a letter, a copy of which, he said, would be carried by Arnold Fordyce as his means of identification, but this letter did not reach the Wrights until after the visitor had arrived. As Ferber only a few weeks before had asked permission to send a military commission, the brothers supposed the man en route to Dayton represented the War Ministry.

Arnold Fordyce, the French emissary, arrived in New York on the *Lorraine*, and reached Dayton shortly after Christmas, 1905. He was about thirty-five years old, formerly an actor, of characteristic French politeness, and he spoke English. His first meeting with the Wrights was in their office over the old bicycle shop.

To the Wrights' surprise he told them, in reply to a question, that he had no connection with the French War Ministry. He had come, he said, on behalf of a syndicate of wealthy men who wished to buy a flying-machine and to present it to the French Government for the national defense. He said he was secretary to M. Letellier, member of the syndicate and owner and editor of the Paris newspaper, *Le Journal*. He went on to explain that Letellier and his associates in the syndicate were presenting the plane to the Government with the hope they might receive decorations of the Legion of Honor. His story seemed to the Wrights a bit fishy. They thought it more probable that he was really representing the French War Ministry, but that the War Ministry did not wish to appear directly in negotiations for a flying-machine. The Wrights went ahead, though, to give him the information he sought. First of all, he wished to make sure that they really had a machine that would fly. They arranged for him to meet a number of trustworthy persons who had witnessed flights, among them bankers, other prominent businessmen, and county officials.

Fordyce was soon convinced that the machine would do all that had been claimed for it, and he wanted a contract to take back with him to his principals. Though Ferber's cable had stated that Fordyce was coming with "full powers" he did not have a power-of-attorney to represent his principals. Still believing that Fordyce's true mission was in the interest of the French War Ministry, the Wrights had no objection to entering into a contract with him granting an option for a short period. They made it clear, however, that they reserved the right to deal with their own Government at any time, even though the United States War Department had not seemed appreciative of their former offers of exclusive rights to the aeroplane. They also made it clear that Letellier and his associates in the "syndicate" would have no rights whatever in the machine except the right to pay for it. The machine would be delivered only to the French Government.

The Fordyce option was for the purchase of one flying-machine at a price of 1,000,000 francs, or $200,000, the price the Wrights already had set in a letter to Captain Ferber. The option was to become void if the holder failed by February 5, 1906, to deposit in escrow with J. P. Morgan & Co., New York, 25,000 francs ($5,000) to the joint credit of the Wright brothers and

Arnold Fordyce. It was provided that the contract would become null and void if the holder failed to make a further deposit in escrow with J. P. Morgan & Co. by April 5, 1906, to bring the total to 1,000,000 francs. But if the holder failed to deposit altogether 1,000,000 francs, as stipulated, then the first deposit of 25,000 francs would belong to the Wright brothers. If on the other hand the Wrights failed to carry out any part of their own obligations under the contract they would receive nothing.

On February 5, 1906, the date stated in the option for the first deposit, the Wrights received a telegram from Morgan, Harjes & Co., Paris, stating that 25,000 francs had been deposited with them in escrow to the joint credit of the Wright Brothers and Arnold Fordyce. This seemed to confirm the suspicion held by the Wrights that Fordyce represented the French Ministry of War and not a syndicate. But this suspicion later proved to be false.

Some time after the Wrights had given this option they heard an entirely different story about the nature of Fordyce's mission. According to this story, Captain Ferber, unable to persuade his superior officers in the War Ministry to send an official investigator to Dayton, had hit on the idea of having an investigation made by a Paris newspaper. He then went to see Letellier, owner of *Le Journal*. Letellier saw the possibilities of prestige for his paper by being able to print the facts about the Wrights. If they really had flown, that would be of great interest, and if they were only "bluffers," as many in France thought they were, the truth about them would still be worth publishing. Letellier could well have afforded the gamble of sending an investigator to Dayton. Aside from his ownership of *Le Journal*, he was a man of considerable wealth, having made his money as a contractor. He had built the main fortresses at Liège.

Whatever the truth may have been, if Letellier had intended to publish what Fordyce learned about the Wrights, he did not at once do so. He took the Fordyce option and presented it to the War Ministry and he received in return a letter from the Minister of War stating that if a Wright plane were acquired by the Ministry the purchase would be made through *Le Journal*. Thus *Le Journal* not only would have a big "scoop" on news of the purchase, but would receive credit and acclaim for a big patriotic act. Perhaps the owner of the paper would be decorated!

For some time war clouds had been gathering over Morocco and it looked as if there might be trouble between France and Germany. If war should come, a flying-machine for scouting purposes would be of great value. But in spite of the fact that a Frenchman, Fordyce, had been to see the Wrights and reported favorably about them, the French war chiefs couldn't bring themselves to accept as a certainty the existence of a practical flying-machine. The story seemed too incredible. There must be a "catch" somewhere. Still, the War Ministry was willing to risk making the down payment of 25,000 francs.

But when M. Etienne sent the down payment of 25,000 francs to Morgan, Harjes & Co., the Paris branch of the banking firm of J. P. Morgan & Co., on the last day of the allotted time, he nearly lost the option, for an unexpected reason. Morgan, Harjes & Co. did not wish to accept the money. Though the bank was under American control, French procedure prevailed, and its officers were reluctant to hold money in escrow. They feared there might be a dispute as to whether it finally would belong to the War Ministry that deposited it, or to the Wrights. It required eight hours of perspiring persuasion on the part of a War Ministry representative before the bankers agreed to accept the money and the option became binding.

After the option was in force, but before the date set in the contract for the final payment, the French War Ministry sent a commission to Dayton for the purpose of obtaining some amendments to the contract, pertaining to the test flights.

This commission, which sailed from Cherbourg on the *Saint Paul*, was headed by Commandant Bonel, of the Army Engineer Corps. Another member was Arnold Fordyce. They reached New York on March 18, 1906. The other two members were Captain Fournier, military attaché of the French Embassy at Washington, and Walter V. R. Berry, an American subject, who was legal counselor to that embassy. Though Fordyce was by now zealously pro-Wright, the men at the War Ministry had no fear of his exerting too much influence on the others, because of the presence of Commandant Bonel, who was outspokenly skeptical. He had witnessed tests by the French Government of the unsuccessful machine designed by Clement Ader, a few years previously, and was convinced that no heavier-than-air machine had ever flown or ever could. Bonel would hardly let the commission make a fool of itself. Since he was the only one of the four who spoke no English, he would need to have everything explained to him—all the more reason why he would not be easily imposed upon.

Before the French quartet had been in Dayton long, however, Bonel was the most enthusiastic convert of all. The visitors met dependable witnesses of flights who had previously talked to Fordyce; and photographs of the machine in flight could hardly be fakes. Most of all, they were impressed by the obviously high character of the Wrights themselves. In cables to France they strongly recommended that the deal be closed.

But while the commission was still in Dayton, the European war crisis had subsided. Even before the formal settlement of the dispute, at the close of the conference at Algeciras, Spain, on April 7, it was known that France would still have a favored position in Morocco, and the need for a scouting plane by the French Army became less pressing. The War Ministry now began to demand more and more in airplane performance. They would cable asking if the plane could fly at an altitude of at least 1,000 feet; if the speed could be greater than hitherto mentioned. Then the next day there would be a request for greater weight-carrying capacity. The Wrights, slow as always to make rash promises, said frankly that they had never flown much higher than 100 feet, but that the plane could fly at much more than 1,000 feet, though they would probably need additional practice before making a demonstration. They could increase either the speed or the weight-carrying capacity, too; but it would not be easy to do both in the same machine—no more than one could produce a draft horse and a race horse in the same animal.

The demonstrations of the machine the Wrights agreed to make were already stiff enough, and if they failed on any one of them, within the allotted time, even if only on account of delay caused by accident, their contract would be broken; but they felt sure of what they could do and were willing to take the chance.

When the time limit for the deposit of the rest of the 1,000,000 francs with J. P. Morgan expired, on April 5, the commission was recalled. Before leaving Dayton the visitors expressed their own vexation over the rejection by the Paris officials of their recommendations.

The members of the commission still believed, though, that when Bonel and Fordyce were back in Paris and presented all the facts to the War Ministry, there would be an extension of time and the deal carried out. But it never was. The French Minister of War agreed, however, that the Wrights were entitled to receive the forfeit money of 25,000 francs held in escrow by J. P. Morgan & Co.

Before leaving Dayton, the Frenchmen said they believed they knew what was back of the failure to close the deal. They said frankly that it was probably the present attitude of Captain Ferber, the man who had been instrumental in starting the negotiations. Ferber, they thought, with the Moroccan question no longer pressing, had now decided that with his knowledge of the Wright plane he could build one himself, and so become the French pioneer in aviation—a greater honor than being merely the instrument of introducing the aeroplane into France.

During the time the Frenchmen were at their hotel in Dayton, it might have been expected that their presence would become known to local newspapermen and that the world would have learned of what was going on. To avoid attracting attention they had taken the precaution to avoid the Hotel Algonquin where Fordyce had stayed on his earlier visit, and were at the Beckel House. They were unmolested there until an employee of one of the telegraph offices "tipped off" a reporter friend. The telegrapher had noticed various cables in code going to France and felt sure the Frenchmen must be carrying on an important deal. A reporter nabbed Fordyce and Bonel one evening in the hotel lobby on their return from a theater. As Bonel spoke no English, Fordyce parried the reporter's questions. He thought a plausible explanation of their presence would be that they were studying the water system of a typical American city. But what he said was that they were studying Dayton's "water pipes." That satisfied as well as amused the reporter and nothing about the French commission got into the papers.

The local newspapermen had failed to note that, after Fordyce's previous visit, the New York *Herald* of January 4 had printed a brief item about his having seen the Wrights to discuss a contract. It never occurred to anyone in Dayton that the Wright brothers could have attracted visitors from across the Atlantic, for the Wrights still were not "news." If the Frenchmen had made a statement that they were there dickering with the Wrights for a $200,000 contract, it is possible that the local papers would not have printed it. They might not have believed such a tale.

Only a few days after the French commission had left Dayton, another foreign visitor dropped in on the Wrights—the Englishman, Patrick Y. Alexander.

After some casual talk, he inquired with seeming innocence, as if just to make conversation: "Is the French commission still here?"

The Wrights were startled. So great had been the secrecy about the visit of the Frenchmen that not many even in the French Government were permitted to know about their trip to Dayton. How did this mysterious Britisher know about it? The Wrights assumed that he must have been a volunteer worker in the British secret service. It was now obvious that he had crossed the Atlantic for no other purpose than to call on the Wrights and had hoped to burst in upon them while the Frenchmen were still there. After a stay of only one day in Dayton he hastened back to New York to sail on the next boat. His call made it all the more clear that the British were then more interested in what other European governments were doing about planes than in acquiring an air fleet of their own.

Incredulity about the Wrights' power flights continued at the Aéro Club and in newspaper circles in France. In November, 1906, the Wrights received a visitor in Dayton, Sherman Morse, representing the New York *Herald*. His introduction was a cabled message to his managing editor from the owner of the paper, James

Gordon Bennett, in Paris. The message said: Send one of your best reporters to Dayton to get truth about Wright brothers' reported flights.

The reporter got the truth and wrote intelligent articles that appeared in the New York *Herald*. These included reports of men who had witnessed flights. Parts of the Morse articles appeared in the *Herald's* Paris edition on November 22 and 23. But evidently those in charge of the Paris *Herald* still were not convinced by the reports from Dayton by their own man. On November 28, the Paris *Herald* had an editorial about the Wrights which included the statement that in Europe curiosity about their machine was "clouded with skepticism owing to the fact that information regarding the invention is so small while the results which its inventors claim to have achieved are so colossal." And the next day, the Paris *Herald* gave space to a news item in which Santos-Dumont was reported as saying that he "did not find any evidence of their [the Wrights] having done anything at all."

Late in 1906, Frank S. Lahm, who had cabled his brother-in-law, Weaver, to make an investigation, was in the United States, and he, accompanied by Weaver, went on November 22 to see the Wrights in Dayton. He was convinced, of course, that their statements could be relied upon, but he made further investigation of his own, interviewing witnesses not previously seen by Weaver. After his return to Paris, he prepared a long letter to the Paris *Herald*, in which he expressed his belief in the reported flights. The newspaper devoted a column to the Lahm letter on February 10,

1907. But having distrusted what their own representative had written, it was not to be expected that the editors would give full belief to what Lahm now told them. In the same issue as his letter, was an editorial headed "Flyers or Liars." "The Wrights have flown or they have not flown," the paper profoundly stated. "They possess a machine or they do not possess one. They are in fact either flyers or liars. . . . It is difficult to fly; it is easy to say 'we have flown.' "

XII

THE WRIGHTS IN EUROPE

THE Wrights were at work in 1906 developing a new engine having vertical instead of horizontal cylinders. Though they were doing no flying, brief references to them occasionally appeared in newspapers. These caught the attention of a New York businessman, U. S. Eddy, who thought the Wrights and their patents might be of interest to Charles R. Flint & Company, New York bankers and promoters. Eddy was a former partner of Flint in a shipping line and knew that they were constantly on the lookout for new inventions worthy of their consideration. Partly to do a favor for an old friend and associate, he decided to go to Dayton for a talk with the Wrights.

Eddy arrived in Dayton on Thanksgiving Day and saw the Wrights the next day. They did not discuss business at this meeting. Eddy simply got acquainted with them, and satisfied himself that any statements they made about their invention could be depended upon; but he did tell them he felt sure the Flint firm would be much interested in helping them to develop the machine's financial possibilities.

The Wrights left Dayton on December 5 for New York, to attend an exhibit to be given by the newly formed Aero Club of America. Before leaving New

York they went with Eddy to meet F. R. Cordley, a member of the Flint firm. At this time Flint was in Europe, but the Wrights met him in New York not long afterward. Flint was often over-enthusiastic about new projects, and Cordley was the more cautious member of the firm. His job was to hold Flint in check. But he, as well as Flint and other associates, was favorably impressed by the Wrights, and they began to talk business. On December 26, 1906, George H. Nolte, an employee of the firm, went to Dayton to work out preliminary details. At first the Flints spoke of the possibility of buying all European rights to the airplane; but the deal finally made was that the Flints should be the Wrights' business representatives, on a twenty per cent commission basis, in all countries except the United States. A year or two later it was agreed that the Wrights should manage their own affairs also in Great Britain and its colonies.

The Flints proposed that they would have the Czar of Russia, and certain other crowned heads, request private demonstrations of the flying-machine. But the Wrights were not impressed by such suggestions and in a letter to the Flints said they thought it would be better for them to "look the ground over first before making arrangements with the Czar."

The Flints had an associate in Europe, Hart O. Berg, who, in 1899, had helped to introduce American electric automobiles on the continent. He had acted, too, for Simon Lake, inventor of the submarine, in dealing with Russia and other foreign governments. They thought Berg might be able to start negotiations for forming a European Wright company. But Berg, not knowing the Wrights, and feeling scant confidence in what they were reported to have done, was less than lukewarm over the idea. Flint suggested that it would be well for at least one of the Wrights to go to Europe, with expenses paid, to discuss their invention with Berg and give him more faith in it. The Wrights themselves, said Flint, could do more than anyone else to implant in Berg the wholehearted enthusiasm he would need to convince possible buyers.

On May 15, 1907, a telegram came from the Flint office urging that one of the Wrights should start to Europe at once. Wilbur "grabbed a few things" and prepared to go to New York the next day, to sail on the *Campania*. As he planned to tarry abroad only a short time—only long enough to convince Berg—his baggage consisted of one suit case. He would stop first in England for a brief stay before going to Paris.

Wilbur was to land in Liverpool on a Saturday. Berg, eager to see one of the Wrights face to face and settle in his own mind if these inventors were really dependable, went to London to meet him.

"I knew him the minute he stepped from the train," said Berg long afterward. "To begin with, it is always easy to spot an American among Englishmen, and I saw no other American coming down the platform. But even if there had been other Americans I'm sure I would have known which one was Wilbur Wright. There was a modest self-assurance about him that tallied with his character as I had heard about it."

After the first greetings, Berg said: "Now let's see about picking up the rest of your luggage."

But Wilbur smilingly explained that the one suit case was all he had brought.

On the way to the hotel, Wilbur decided that it might be advisable for him to buy a suit of evening clothes and they went at once to a tailor shop on the Strand.

It didn't take Berg long to convince himself that Wilbur Wright was no slicker, but decidedly on the level, and that if he said his machine would fly, then it must be true.

A day after their first meeting, Berg and Wilbur were joined by F. R. Cordley, of the Flint firm, in Europe on a vacation trip, and the three went to Paris together. They "descended," as the French say, at the Hotel Meurice, on the rue de Rivoli.

It was still broad daylight when they arrived and Berg almost immediately led Wilbur across the street into the Tuileries gardens. They strolled to the Place de la Concorde and looked up the length of the magnificent Avenue des Champs Elysées to the Arc de Triomphe. The horse chestnut trees were still in blossom, and Berg, a resident of Paris during most of his life, was feeling happy over the opportunity to show this stranger his first glimpse of the most beautiful city on earth at its loveliest season.

Before he had been long in Paris, Wilbur attended a balloon meet at St. Cloud, and a few days later made his first trip in a balloon.

A Paris *Herald* reporter, who talked with Wilbur at

St. Cloud, was impressed by his reticence and made this statement: "Mr. Wright talked carefully, as if all was mapped out in advance. It was obvious that he feared to be caught in a trap concerning his remarkable machine and what he wants to do with it. At the end of each question his clean-shaven face relapsed into a broad, sphinx-like smile."

It now seemed wise to try to form a company to buy European rights to the airplane, or to sell the rights to a private financier, rather than to deal with the Government, through politicians; and a wealthy man had become interested: M. Henri Deutsch de la Meurthe, an oil magnate, who had also been a patron of ballooning.

When Wilbur Wright met Deutsch de la Meurthe, the latter, a cautious trader, said that before investing any money he wanted to make sure the French Government would be interested in buying airplanes.

Wilbur then decided that it would be both discourteous and imprudent not to have a talk with Letellier or Fordyce, with whom there had been previous negotiations, and let them know what was going on—particularly since Deutsch de la Meurthe was known to have close relations with *Le Matin*, a rival of Letellier's newspaper, *Le Journal*. He got in touch with Fordyce, and told him a little of the current situation. Shortly afterward, Letellier invited Wilbur to lunch. Letellier seemed indignant that the Wrights had not resumed negotiations with him. Wilbur told him he could doubtless be included if a company should be formed. But that didn't suit Letellier. He didn't care to join a company organized by Deutsch de la Meurthe; if a company was formed he wanted to be the prime mover in it himself. He said nothing, however, about interfering with efforts being made to form a company—possibly because he thought they would not be successful.

Deutsch de la Meurthe now went to call upon the Minister of Marine, with whom he was well acquainted, and was escorted by him to meet the Minister of War, General Picquart, a hero of the Dreyfus case.

General Picquart was not familiar with what had previously been done regarding the possible purchase of a Wright machine, as the negotiations had been carried on during the regime of his predecessor. But he had Commandant Bonel bring the records to him and when he looked them over was impressed by the fact that the Wrights' invention had been considered seriously. No less impressed was Deutsch de la Meurthe. General Picquart said he realized the importance of the Wright invention and was disposed to take favorable action toward buying planes, provided the Wrights would guarantee that their machine could fly at a height of 300 meters.

That was enough encouragement for Deutsch de la Meurthe. In fact, he became highly enthusiastic over the outlook. He had not before appreciated the seriousness of the previous negotiations. Now he began to talk about details of the articles of incorporation of a proposed company.

Commandant Bonel was elated over the news that his government might at last be buying Wright airplanes. His pride and prestige had been hurt by the failure of his recommendations to be accepted. Moreover, for patriotic reasons, he wanted the French Army to be the first to adopt what he regarded as an epoch-making new invention. Now that the outlook was once again more favorable, he was in a communicative mood when he chanced to meet Fordyce, with whom he had traveled to Dayton.

Fordyce showed his surprise at what Bonel told him. He went at once to tell this news to his employer, M. Letellier. Now Letellier expressed great indignation. He had an agreement in writing, he said, that if the War Ministry bought any Wright airplanes the purchase should be made through *Le Journal*, and any departure from that plan he must construe as an unfriendly and illegal act. Immediately he went to the office of the Minister of War where with great politeness he showed to General Picquart a letter obtained from his predecessor.

Since the option the Wrights had given to Fordyce had expired, the agreement between the War Ministry and Letellier was no longer in force. But General Picquart, if he understood that, after a hasty examination of the records, did not argue the point. Possibly he was too practical a politician to enter a controversy with an influential publisher. At any rate, he asked Deutsch de la Meurthe to withdraw from the negotiations.

It was Deutsch de la Meurthe's turn to be indignant. He believed at first that the Wrights had simply used him for a tool. But later, when he understood the facts and saw that the Wrights were not to blame for what had happened, he once more was friendly with them.

The Wrights saw that their most promising opportunity for an immediate contract was through Letellier and *Le Journal.* Consequently, Fordyce, representing that newspaper, came back into the picture. Within a day or two after negotiations were thus resumed, Fordyce came to Berg in an apologetic mood, showing deep embarrassment. He said he had been asked to submit a proposal that it hardly seemed worth while to discuss at all; and yet he had no choice but to convey a message, as had been requested of him, by a man high in government circles. The deal might go through at once, said Fordyce, but there would have to be a little re-wording of the contract. The Wrights must not ask 1,000,000 francs but 1,250,000 francs. Then they would receive their million francs.

Berg knew well enough what would happen when he told this to Wilbur.

There would be no objection to having the contract call for more money than the Wrights were to receive, said Wilbur calmly, *but* the contract must give the name of the man who would receive that additional sum.

Berg went to the office of the man who had communicated, by way of Fordyce, the astounding suggestion. He hoped there had been some misunderstanding. But to Berg's astonishment and disgust, the man said with shocking candor that he would indeed expect 250,-000 francs ($50,000) as his reward for putting through the deal.

Before indignantly walking out of the man's office, Berg told him the Wrights would never be a party to such financial irregularity and that the negotiations with the Minister of War would have to be carried on without the co-operation of anyone in the Government who expected to be paid for his efforts. (After the first World War that same man was tried for treason.)

Meanwhile, Wilbur had cabled to Orville to join him in Paris. And with the prospect that it might be necessary to make a demonstration of what the Wright machine could do, a plane was crated and shipped from Dayton to France.

Orville arrived in Paris around the first of August, and the Wright's chief mechanic, Charlie Taylor, came about a week later.

While crossing the Atlantic, Orville had a talk with another passenger that illustrates his possession of a freakish kind of memory. An Englishman had been introduced to him and, after a few moments of conversation, Orville asked if they had not met before. No, the Englishman said, they had not. He had no recollection of any previous meeting, and he was sure if there had been one he would remember it. The man's face was not familiar, but there was something about his voice and gestures that somehow stirred in Orville old memories. Finally, Orville inquired:

"Were you by any chance at the World's Fair in Chicago back in 1893?"

The Englishman nodded.

"And," asked Orville, "did you ever have occasion to explain to a bystander some kind of device at one of the exhibits?"

Yes, that also might have happened.

"There," said Orville, much relieved that his memory had not played him tricks, "must have been where I saw you. I felt sure I couldn't be mistaken about your voice."

After Orville had joined Wilbur at the Hotel Meurice, the brothers did not find their business affairs too pressing to do a lot of sight-seeing. Neither one spoke French, but Orville had acquired a fair reading knowledge of it. Oddly enough, Wilbur, who had learned Greek and Latin easily, made no effort to learn French. He jokingly said it was a convenience not to know it, as it saved him from a lot of talking.

As they went about their sight-seeing, Wilbur, always a reader of history, was especially fascinated by all places of historic interest. Orville found himself spending much time each day in the Louvre. Those days gave him an appreciation of good paintings that he never lost.

Negotiations with the French Government dragged on. For weeks the Wrights were kept in uncertainty. They never saw any of the people they were dealing with. Their only contact with anyone at the War Ministry was through Fordyce, and they had no way of knowing, except from what he told them, whether any progress was being made.

Nothing came of the long negotiations. The Wrights were not alone in being disappointed. Commandant Bonel, not long afterward, perhaps as a consequence of the failure of his recommendations to be accepted, resigned from the Army.

Late in the summer of 1907, the Wrights left Paris. Orville went first to London, at the suggestion of Flint & Co. to have a talk with the receiver of the Barnum & Bailey circus and the Buffalo Bill Wild West Show, then in bankruptcy. The receiver wondered if the

Wright plane could be flown within an enclosure where an admission fee could be charged.

Wilbur Wright had set out with Berg for St. Petersburg. They changed their minds about going to Russia, however, and, instead, stopped at Berlin where Orville shortly afterward joined them.

As the train on which Wilbur and Berg traveled was passing through Belgium, Wilbur noticed a sign indicating that they were in the little town of Jemappes. Then he recalled that a great battle took place there back in 1792. He began to discuss the battle with an exact knowledge of details that astounded Berg. Wilbur had read about it in his youth. Over and over again, Berg and others who dealt with Wilbur Wright, were similarly impressed not only by the range of his reading but by the fact that no knowledge he had once acquired ever seemed to grow dim.

In Berlin, the brothers were able to gain direct contact with top flight men—with the minister of the Kaiser's war department,[1] and also with the minister of the department of transportation. These German officials were highly intelligent and not slow about recognizing the tremendous importance of the Wright machine if it would perform as the brothers said it could. The

[1] When the airplane was first considered for military purposes, the Wrights thought the plane could be such a destructive instrument in warfare that no nation, no government, would risk subjecting people to the terrors it could create. Another reason why the brothers thought the machine might prevent war was the possibility that it could be used against those persons chiefly responsible for bringing on a war. That is, if one nation started an attack against another, with or without a declaration of war, the nation attacked could drop bombs on, say, assembled members of the legislature, or the buildings housing the highest officials of the aggressor country. That possibility, it was hoped, would deter any nation from taking warlike steps.

Wrights had proposed a contract in which they would agree to furnish a machine capable of carrying, at a speed of forty miles an hour, two men and a supply of fuel for a flight of 125 miles, and to make a demonstration flight of one hour fulfilling every requirement of the contract before one pfennig should be paid to them. The German officials could not deny the fairness of this offer, and could see no reason why the Wrights should have made it unless they could carry it out. Besides, they were not altogether unacquainted with the earlier work of the Wright brothers, accounts of whose glider and power flights had been appearing for five or six years in German technical publications. But in spite of all this the officials were in a quandary. They could not bring themselves to believe that what the Wrights now offered could be possible. They were afraid to sign their names to a contract that generally would be considered as foolish as a contract for a perpetual motion machine. They might become the laughingstock of the world.

On the other hand, these officials did not want to let an invention of such potentialities, if it really existed, slip through their fingers. They therefore gave, instead of a signed contract, their solemn verbal promise that if the Wrights would make a flight before them, such as had been offered in the proposed written contract, they would buy planes on the terms the Wrights had offered.[1]

---

[1] Though there was no agreement in regard to the altitude at which the machine would fly, the Wrights were willing to guarantee 1,000 feet, and said that so far as the machine itself was concerned it could be flown at an altitude of a mile. One of the Germans remarked that half a mile from the ground should be enough, as no gun in existence would be likely to hit so swiftly moving a target at that height.

The Wrights felt that these officials, being at the head of important departments, could be relied upon, and they were willing to take their verbal guarantee to buy planes upon the successful demonstration of the machine. When they left Germany, they fully expected to return the next March to make such a demonstration. (They could not foresee that they would have too many other engagements in definite contracts elsewhere before another four months had passed.)

Wilbur Wright returned from Europe in November of 1907. But Orville remained a little longer to attend to having a number of engines built in Paris by the firm of Barriquand & Marre. The Wrights wanted to have in reserve duplicates of their American engine, at that time in customs, at Le Havre, for use the next year. Barriquand & Marre were manufacturers of precision instruments and had built light motors. They doubted if the Wright motor gave as much power as was claimed for it, but they felt sure that if it did, the copies they made of it—on account of more careful workmanship—would give considerably more power than the original. But as later events showed, they gave less. At that time it was not known that when one motor is made as an exact copy, to the thousandth of an inch, of another motor, of supposedly the same steels and other metals, but from different foundries and mills, months of experiment are required before the new motor can be made to work properly.

XIII

A DEAL WITH THE U. S.

WHILE in Paris, in 1907, the Wrights naturally had visits with Frank S. Lahm, who had arranged with his brother-in-law, Henry Weaver, of Mansfield, to investigate the reports from America of human flight. Lahm invited the inventors to his home and there they met his son, Lieutenant Frank P. Lahm,[1] who was recuperating from an attack of typhoid fever. The younger Lahm, a former instructor at West Point, had recently spent a year at the French Cavalry School at Saumur. He, as well as his father, was much interested in aeronautics. The previous October he had won the James Gordon Bennett balloon race by starting at Paris and landing in England. Probably the only American Army officer who recognized that the airplane should now be taken seriously, he was delighted to meet the Wright brothers, with whom he now began a lasting friendship. After he had learned a little about their negotiations in France, he began to urge the United States War Department to take more interest in the airplane.

It so happened that, in September, 1907, only a few weeks after this meeting, Lieutenant Lahm was transferred by the War Department from the Cavalry to the Signal Corps, to be stationed at Washington. His first

[1] Afterward a major general.

assignment was to make a tour of Europe, before returning to Washington, and report on the situation regarding dirigible aircraft in several countries. Soon afterward
he returned to Washington. The presence of a man in
the War Department there who felt enthusiasm for the
airplane's possibilities, and who had strong faith in the
Wrights, may have had its effect on his associates. At
any rate, there was now in the War Department a man
who believed in the Wrights.

When Wilbur stopped in Washington shortly before
Thanksgiving, 1907, en route to Dayton, on his return
from France, he had a talk with General Crozier and
Major Fuller of the Ordnance Department, and with
General Allen, head of the Signal Corps—the organization that would conduct tests of the airplane and use it
if the Ordnance Board sanctioned and provided funds
for its purchase. At this meeting Wilbur stated the price
the Wrights would accept ($25,000) and the perform-
ance of the machine that they were willing to guarantee.
These terms, agreed upon between the brothers before
Wilbur left France, were stiff enough, it was thought,
to bar any competition. The Ordnance Board was to
have a meeting on December 5, and Wilbur was invited
to appear before it. He did so; but the meeting did not
inspire him with confidence that an early contract could
be obtained at the price of $25,000. The Wrights were
not willing to accept less, because they thought they
had better prospects abroad. However, the Signal Corps
soon began drawing up specifications, and, on December 23, advertised for bids.

Inasmuch as the Wright machine was the only one in

existence that could meet these requirements, and the price was understood in advance, advertising for bids may have been superfluous; but it was considered necessary to meet demands of red tape. Among specifications set forth in the advertisement for bids were these: the plane must be tested in the presence of Army officers; it must be able to carry for one hour a passenger besides the pilot, the two weighing not less than 350 lbs.; it must show an average speed of forty miles an hour, in a ten-mile test, and carry enough fuel for 125 miles. Also, the machine must have "demountability"; that is, it should be built in such a way that it could be taken apart, and later reassembled, without too much difficulty, when necessary to transport it on an army truck from one place to another.

Almost from the day the advertisements for bids appeared, the War Department was subject to editorial attacks—not because it had been so slow about interesting itself in the airplane, but because it had done so at all!

The New York *Globe* said:

One might be inclined to assume from the following announcement, "the United States Army is asking bids for a military airship," that the era of practical human flight had arrived, or at least that the government had seriously taken up the problem of developing this means of travel. A very brief examination of the conditions imposed and the reward offered for successful bidders suffices, however, to prove this assumption a delusion.

A machine such as is described in the Signal Corps' specifications would record the solution of all the difficulties in the way of the heavier-than-air airship, and, in fact, finally give mankind almost as complete control of the air as it now has of the land and the water. It would be worth to the world almost any number of millions of dollars, would certainly revolutionize warfare and possibly the transportation of passengers; would open to easy access regions hitherto inaccessible except to the most daring pioneers and would, in short, be probably the most epoch-making invention in the history of civilization.

Nothing in any way approaching such a machine has ever been constructed (the Wright brothers' claims still await public confirmation), and the man who has achieved such a success would have, or at least should have, no need of competing in a contest where the successful bidder might be given his trial because his offer was a few hundred or thousand dollars lower than that of someone else. If there is any possibility that such an airship is within measurable distance of perfection any government could well afford to provide its inventor with unlimited resources and promise him a prize, in case of success, running into the millions.

The *American Magazine of Aeronautics* (later called *Aeronautics*) devoted its opening article in the issue of January, 1908, to pointing out the absurdity of what the War Department was trying to do.

There is not a known flying-machine in the world which could fulfill these specifications at the present moment, [declared the editorial]. . . . Had an inventor such a machine as required would he not be in a position to ask almost any reasonable sum from the government for its use? Would not the government, instead of the inventor, be a bidder? . . . Perhaps the Signal Corps has been too much influenced by the "hot air" of theorizers, in which aeronautics unfortunately abounds, who have fathomed the entire problem without ever accomplishing anything; talk is their stock in trade and models or machines are beneath them because beyond their impractical nature. . . . Why is not the experience with Professor Langley a good guide? . . . We doubt very much if the government receives any bids at all possible to be accepted.

To the surprise of nearly everyone, forty-one proposals were received. Most of the bidders were the same kind of cranks the Ordnance Board had at first supposed the Wrights to be; and their bids were rejected when they failed to put up a required ten per cent of the proposed price of the plane, as a sign of good faith. Two other bidders besides the Wrights did make a ten per cent deposit. One of these, J. F. Scott, of Chicago, had made a bid of $1,000, and promised delivery of a plane in 185 days. Another was A. M. Herring. His price was $20,000; delivery to be in 180 days. The Wrights' bid was $25,000, with delivery promised in 200 days.

Receipt of these unexpected bids created a problem. Everyone assumed that none of the bidders except the Wrights had anything practical to offer; and yet the government would be expected to accept the lowest bid and let the winner show what he could do. No matter how dismally he failed to meet requirements, dealing with him would take up time and cause delays.

General Allen, of the Signal Corps, went to Secretary of War Taft to inquire how the War Department might get around the difficulty. Taft said they could accept all legal bids and as only the Wrights could meet the requirements, the others would be eliminated. The only difficulty was that even if no money would ever be paid to the other bidders, yet it would be illegal to accept the bids unless enough money to pay for whatever was ordered was known to be available. However, Taft suggested a way around that. He knew that the President had at his disposal an emergency fund to do with as he saw fit. If the President wished to he could guarantee that all bidders would be paid if they met the tests.

General Allen, accompanied by Captain Charles De Forest Chandler and Lieutenant F. P. Lahm, Signal Corps officers, called upon President Roosevelt who promptly agreed with Taft's suggestion. He told them to accept all bids and that he would place funds at their disposal to meet legal technicalities. The Signal Corps then agreed to buy planes from all three bidders if they met the necessary requirements.

One of those bidders soon eliminated himself by asking the Government to return his ten per cent deposit. Though the government was not obliged to return the deposit, it nevertheless did so. Herring, the only remaining legal bidder besides the Wrights, hung on a while longer.

What A. M. Herring had in mind was simply to obtain the contract in consequence of his lower price and then try to sublet it to the Wrights. He even had the effrontery to go to Dayton to see the Wrights and make such a proposal. Naturally, they were not interested.

The Wrights' bid was accepted on February 8, 1908.

As it happened, this was not the only important contract the Wrights entered into at about that time. On March 3, three weeks after the Signal Corps had ac-

THE WRIGHT PLANE IN FRANCE. The plane is being hauled from one field to another, near Le Mans, France, in August, 1908.

THE WRIGHTS AND WILBUR'S FRENCH PUPILS. Left to right, Captain Lucas-Girardville, Comte Charles de Lambert, Orville Wright, Wilbur Wright, and Paul Tissandier, at Pau, France, early in 1909.

cepted their bid, they closed a contract with Lazare Weiller, a wealthy Frenchman, to form a syndicate to buy
the rights to manufacture, sell, or license the use of the
Wright plane in France. Upon completion of certain
tests of the machine, the Wrights were to receive a substantial amount in cash, a block of stock, and provision
for royalties. The French company would be known as
La Compagnie Générale de Navigation Aérienne. A
member of the syndicate was M. Deutsch de la Meurthe
who had taken steps toward forming a French company
some time previously.

One provision of the U. S. War Department contract
was that the Government could deduct ten per cent of
the purchase price for each mile per hour that the machine fell short of the forty-mile goal. That is, if it went
only thirty-nine miles an hour, the Wrights would be
docked ten per cent; if only thirty-eight miles, another
ten per cent, and so on. If the machine did not do at least
thirty-six miles an hour, then the Government didn't
have to accept it at all. On the other hand, the Wrights
would receive a ten per cent bonus for each mile per
hour they attained above forty.

It was the intention of the Signal Corps, and the
Wrights so understood it, that these reduced or additional payments would be for either a mile or a fraction of a mile. But a Government legal department
made a surprising interpretation of that part of the contract. If at the time of the tests the plane went $40\frac{99}{100}$
miles, the Wrights would not be paid for more than 40;
but if the plane fell short of 40 miles an hour by only

⅟₁₀₀ of a mile, or even less, then they would be docked for a full mile.

(Orville did not learn of that astounding example of the legal mind at work until after he arrived at Washington to prepare for the tests and it was then too late to build a faster plane. But in the final tests the next year, he had a plane that he knew would give the buyer no opportunity to take advantage of what he regarded as a one-sided interpretation of the contract.)

Though the Wrights had done no flying since October, 1905, they had done much work on improving both plane and engine. Their newest engine, capable of producing about thirty-five horsepower continuously, was also so much better as to reliability that now long flights could be made without danger of failure of the motive power.

During all their experiments at the Huffman pasture they had continued to ride "belly-buster," as a boy usually does when coasting on a sled. Lying flat in that way and controlling the mechanism partly by swinging the hips from one side to the other was good enough for the experimental stages of aviation; but the Wrights knew that if a plane was to have practical use the pilot must be able to take an ordinary sitting position and do the controlling and guiding with his hands and feet as in an automobile. It was not all fun lying flat for an hour at a time with head raised to be on the lookout for possible obstacles. "I used to think," said Orville in later years, "the back of my neck would break if I endured one more turn around the field."

The brothers therefore had adopted a different arrangement of the control levers, for use in a sitting position, and a seat for a passenger. Moreover, the machine could be steered from either seat and thus was suitable for training other pilots if occasion should arise. The plane sent to France for possible trials in 1907 was thus equipped. They revamped the machine they had used at the Huffman pasture in 1905, and installed their later improvements. It now had an engine with vertical instead of horizontal cylinders. With this machine they would go to Kitty Hawk and gain needed practice in handling their new arrangement of the control levers.

The United States Government tests would be made at Fort Myer, Virginia, near Washington. Delivery of the machine had to be made by August 28, and the tests themselves were to begin shortly afterward, in September. But at about that same time, one of the brothers would make a demonstration in France. They had not yet decided which of them would fly at Fort Myer and which should go to France. But both had to be well prepared and there was no time to lose. They must be established at Kitty Hawk as soon as possible.

Wilbur Wright set out for Kitty Hawk ahead of Orville and arrived there April 9, 1908. He was joined within a week by a mechanic from Dayton, Charles W. Furnas. First of all, it was necessary to do much rebuilding of the camp. The buildings had not only suffered from storms, but had been stripped of much timber by persons who supposed the Wrights had permanently abandoned them. The plane was shipped in crates from Dayton April 11, but had to be left for some time in a freight depot at Elizabeth City until the new shed was completed at Kitty Hawk. Both Orville and the plane reached there on April 25.

It might have been expected that with at least two governments now showing interest in the Wright plane, each of the brothers would have been besieged en route by reporters and others. But the general public, including reporters, still seemed disinclined to believe in human flight. At about the same time that the Wrights were preparing to go to Kitty Hawk, a publisher brought out a new novel by H. G. Wells, *Tono-Bungay*, in which the leading character built a gliding machine "along the lines of the Wright brothers' airplane," and finally a flying-machine. That stirred one or two American book reviewers to chide the author for putting such fantastic material into a tale otherwise plausible.

Because of the persistence of that kind of incredulity, the Wrights did not expect many sightseers, least of all newspapermen, at Kitty Hawk during their preparations for government tests. Therefore they did not think it necessary to keep their plans secret. Though they weren't seeking reporters, neither were they trying to avoid them. They simply went ahead without giving any thought to newspapermen one way or another. But the Wrights were about to be discovered.

Not until May 6 did either of the brothers make a flight. But the newspapers, instead of ignoring what the Wrights had done, now began to report what they had *not* done. On May 1, the *Virginian-Pilot*, of Norfolk (the same paper that had reported, not too accurately, the first flight of an airplane), carried a wild tale that one of the Wright brothers had flown, the day before, ten miles out over the ocean! Practically the same story was widely published the next day. Katharine Wright on May 2 telegraphed her brothers that "the newspapers" had reported a flight. As the Wrights later learned, the *B. Z. Mittag*, in Berlin, carried a dispatch from Paris: "From America comes the news that the Wright brothers for the first time have made in public a controlled flight. The flight was made on April 30, at Norfolk, Va., before a U. S. Government Commission."

That same story must have reached London, for the Wrights received a cablegram from Patrick Alexander: "Very hearty congratulations."

Joseph Dosher, who had been the Weather Bureau man at Kitty Hawk in 1903, but was now stationed 30 miles north of Kitty Hawk, telephoned to the Kill Devil life-saving crew, on May 2, seeking information about the Wrights, presumably at the request of some newspaper. That same day, the Greensboro (N. C.) *News* published a telegram from Elizabeth City, dated May 1, saying that the Wright brothers "of airship fame" were at Nag's Head with their "famous flying-machine."

On May 1, the New York *Herald* had wired to the Weather Bureau operator at Manteo, on Roanoke Island, for information. And on May 2, the *Herald* published an item with a Norfolk date line, that the Wrights were reported to have flown "over the ocean." This dispatch appeared also in the *Herald's* Paris edition. Just below the report in the Paris edition was an editorial comment that if the Wrights had actually flown two miles, then they had broken the records of Delagrange and Farman in France. The *Herald* editor evidently was still unaware that long before Delagrange, Farman, or other Wright copyists abroad had even left the ground in flight, the Wright brothers had flown twenty-four miles.

Inasmuch as the Wrights had not yet begun their flights of 1908, it was not easy for the New York *Herald* to obtain confirmation or more details about the imaginary flight out over the ocean. No regularly employed newspaperman at Norfolk wanted to go to Kitty Hawk on what might be a wild goose chase. But D. Bruce Salley, a free lance reporter at Norfolk, was willing to make the trip.

Salley reached Manteo on May 4, and the Wright brothers' records show that he came to their camp the next day. He told the brothers he had been asked by a New York paper to investigate the story of their flight over the ocean. The day after Salley's visit, the Wrights did make their first flight of the season, and though Salley did not see it, he learned about it by phone from one of the men at the Kill Devil life-saving station. His informant told him that one of the Wrights had flown at least 1,000 feet, at about sixty feet above the ground.

Salley immediately sent a query from Manteo, giving briefly the gist of the story, to a list of papers he hoped would be interested. Most of the papers ignored the message; but the telegraph editor of the Cleveland (Ohio) *Leader* not only wasn't interested but was indignant that his intelligence should be insulted by the offer of so improbable a tale. He declined to pay the telegraph toll for the short message, even though at the night press rate of only one-third of a cent a word the cost could hardly have been more than a dime. His only reply to Salley was an admonition to "cut out the wild-cat stuff." Salley, now equally indignant, wired back offering to give names of well-known persons who could testify to his reliability; but the Cleveland editor paid no further attention.

When Salley's query reached the office of the New York *Herald*, it put the editors in a quandary. Though they had printed the brief report about a flight that hadn't occurred, now they were beginning to wonder if all the reports about the Wrights weren't fakes. Yet they knew that the owner of the paper, James Gordon Bennett, living in Paris, would almost certainly discharge any editor responsible for omitting the story if it *were* true. They decided, with misgivings, to print the story and it appeared the next morning on the first page of the *Herald*, though not in the most prominent position.

Then the editors determined to send a staff man to Kitty Hawk for the facts. They picked for this job their star reporter, brilliant, lovable Byron R. Newton—later to become Assistant Secretary of the Treasury, and afterward Collector of Customs in New York—one of the ablest newspapermen of his time. If the Wrights proved to be fakers no one could do a better job than "By" Newton at exposing them.

Other editors, too, decided that the time had come to get the "lowdown" on the Wright brothers. By the time Newton reached the little boarding place, the Tranquil House, in Manteo, he had been joined by two other correspondents: William Hoster, of the New York *American*, and P. H. McGowan, of the London *Daily Mail.* The next day two others arrived: Arthur Ruhl, writer, and James H. Hare, photographer, for *Collier's Weekly.*

The newly arrived correspondents, noting the desolate isolation of Kitty Hawk, thought it probable enough that the Wrights must prefer to be let alone. Perhaps, they thought, if intruders came, the Wrights wouldn't fly at all. They decided that if the Wrights were secretive, they themselves would be no less so. They would hide in the pine woods, as near as possible to the Wright camp, and observe with field glasses what happened. That meant a short walk to a wharf on Roanoke Island, five miles by sailing boat to Haman's Bay, across the sound, and then a walk of a mile or so over the sand to the place where they should secrete themselves. They made a dicker with a boatman to take them all back and forth each day and act as their guide. Provided with food and water, field glasses, and cameras, they set out about 4 o'clock each morning from May 11 to May 14 to keep their vigil. Hour after hour they fought mosquitoes and woodticks and sometimes were drenched by rain. But to their astonishment they several times witnessed human flight.

The first flight any of them witnessed was early in the morning of May 11. "For some minutes," wrote Newton, "the propeller blades continued to flash in the sun, and then the machine rose obliquely into the air. At first it came directly toward us, so that we could not tell how fast it was going except that it appeared to increase rapidly in size as it approached. In the excitement of this first flight, men trained to observe details under all sorts of distractions forgot their cameras, forgot their watches, forgot everything but this aerial monster chattering over our heads."

However, "Jimmy" Hare got a good photograph of that flight.

On May 14, the correspondents saw what no person on earth had ever seen before—a flying-machine under complete control carrying *two* men. First Wilbur made a short flight with Charles W. Furnas as passenger, and then Orville flew with Furnas for nearly three minutes.

Newton predicted in his diary just after that: "Some day Congress will erect a monument here to these Wrights." [1]

The last flight on May 14, made by Wilbur Wright, ended in an accident. Wilbur had pulled a wrong lever. Repairs would have taken a week, and as the time the brothers could spare had elapsed, the experiments stopped. But after removing the engine and other machinery for shipment to Dayton, the Wrights left the plane in the shed at Kitty Hawk, thinking they might return. The ending of these trials brought no grief to

[1] The Wright monument on top of Kill Devil Hill, ordered by act of Congress and dedicated in November, 1932, is probably the most impressive memorial ever built anywhere in the world to do honor to anyone still living. Reaching sixty-one feet above Kill Devil Hill, with a powerful beacon light at its top, it may be seen for miles. About the four sides of the base reads a legend: In Commemoration of the Conquest of the Air by The Brothers Wilbur and Orville Wright, Conceived by Genius, Achieved by Dauntless Resolution and Unconquerable Faith.

"Anchoring" the once shifting sands of Kill Devil Hill by ingenious planting of suitable grasses and shrubbery provides a memorial in itself, as is the national park of three hundred acres that includes the hill.

the correspondents who had been getting up before day-light each morning, and returning to Manteo late each afternoon, footsore and tired, with their dispatches still to be written.

One night's dispatches had brought unexpected trouble for "By" Newton. Though his report had been filed ahead of McGowan's, in plenty of time to be relayed from his paper's New York office to Paris and appear in the next morning's issue of the Paris edition, a need-less delay occurred in New York. In consequence, Newton, through no fault of his own, was "scooped" by McGowan the next day in the continental edition of the London *Daily Mail*. When James Gordon Bennett, pro-prietor of the New York *Herald*, observed that his Paris *Herald* failed to have any account of the sensational flights at Kitty Hawk the day before, as reported in the rival *Daily Mail*, he was furious. During the two seasons when the Wrights had flown a total of 160 miles at Huffman prairie, Bennett, with scores of reporters at his disposal, had failed to learn the truth of what the Wrights had done. But now when he thought a reporter had missed a story about them, he did not wait to make inquiries but promptly sent a cable to New York order-ing Newton suspended from the staff. Under Bennett's way of conducting his papers, suspension usually was a preliminary to permanent discharge.

Though he was reinstated after he had sent to Bennett a review of the facts, along with some affidavits, New-ton, all the rest of his life, felt a grievance against Ben-nett and the *Herald*.

Incidentally, McGowan's "scoop" in the continental

edition of the *Daily Mail* which had so disturbed Bennett, was not accepted as truth by everyone who read it. Charles A. Bertrand, in one of the Paris papers, May 15, published this comment: "He [McGowan] depicts the flight in a manner that does honor to his imagination. If the Wrights hadn't been seen in Europe, one would be justified in believing their very existence as uncertain as their apparatus."

During the several days the correspondents were at Kitty Hawk, the Wrights knew they were being observed. From time to time they caught glimpses of men's heads over the hilltop in the distance. Moreover, they heard each day, from members of a life-saving crew, just how many visitors had come. But they simply thought it was a good joke on the mysterious observers, whoever they were.

Arthur Ruhl, of *Collier's*, had met the Wrights in Dayton about a year before. On May 14, before the final flight, he came over to the camp. But he said nothing about being a member of the group that had been observing the flights.

The Wrights invited Ruhl to stay for lunch. But he declined. He seemed to the Wrights ill at ease and anxious to get away. At a meeting with him some time afterward they learned why. He had come against the wishes of the other correspondents and was afraid he might give away the fact that they were in the near-by woods.

On May 15, the day after the crash, when it was evident that there would be no more flights, McGowan, of the *Daily Mail*, went to the camp, accompanied by still another correspondent who had just arrived, Gilson Gardner, of the Washington office of the Newspaper Enterprise Association. McGowan remarked that he had once visited Octave Chanute's camp at Dune Park, near Chicago, in 1897 for the Chicago *Tribune*. Another visitor at the camp, a day or two before that, was a young man named J. C. Burkhardt, dressed in a brand-new outfit of hunting togs. He was a college boy who had come all the way from Ithaca just to satisfy his curiosity.

"What would you have done," Orville Wright was asked, afterward, "if all those correspondents had come right to your camp each day and sat there to watch you?"

"We'd have had to go ahead just as if they weren't there," he replied. "We couldn't have delayed our work. There was too much to do and our time was short."

That the Wrights would have treated the correspondents politely enough was indicated in a letter from Orville Wright to Byron Newton, dated June 7, 1908. Immediately after his return to New York, Newton had written graciously to the Wrights, enclosing clippings of his dispatches to the *Herald*, and expressing his admiration for them and their achievements.

"We were aware of the presence of newspapermen in the woods," wrote Orville in reply; "at least we had often been told that they were there. Their presence, however, did not bother us in the least, and I am only sorry that you did not come over to see us at our camp. The display of a white flag would have disposed of the rifles and shotguns with which the machine is reported to have been guarded."

After publication of many dispatches from these eye-witnesses at Kitty Hawk and front page headlines, it might have been expected that the fact of human flight would now be generally accepted. As Newton had written to his paper, there was "no longer any ground for questioning the performance of these men and their wonderful machine." Ruhl in *Collier's* had told how the correspondents had informed the world that "it was all right, the rumors true—that man could fly." Yet even such reports by leading journalists still did not convince the general public. People began to concede that perhaps there *might* be something in it, but many newspapers still did not publish the news. When Newton sent an article, some weeks later, on what he had seen at Kitty Hawk, to a leading magazine, it came back to him with the editor's comment: "While your manuscript has been read with much interest, it does not seem to qualify either as fact or fiction."

XIV

END OF DISBELIEF

THE Wrights decided that Wilbur should go to France to make the demonstrations there. Orville would stay in America to build the machine for the United States Government and test it at Fort Myer, near Washington. Wilbur did not return to Dayton from Kitty Hawk but went to New York where he sailed for Europe on May 21.

Orville arrived at Fort Myer in August. Two mechanics, Taylor and Furnas, who were to assist him, had reached there a few days earlier. Army officers designated a shed on the Fort Myer grounds for use in assembling and housing the plane.

Orville's first flight was on September 3, 1908. He went from the Cosmos Club, where he was staying, to Fort Myer by street car. It is doubtful if any of the others on that car suspected that this fellow passenger was on his way to perform a miracle. When he reached Fort Myer, Orville got the impression that not all the Army officers present thought he would succeed in meeting the tests required by the contract. The area from which the flights would be made was only about 700 by 1,000 feet. Neither of the Wrights had ever before made flights within so small a space.

Considering that this was an opportunity to see the

outstanding wonder of the century, the crowd that strung about the parade ground was small. Theodore Roosevelt, Jr., estimated it for his father, then President, at less than one thousand. Indeed, it was probably much less than that.

Orville circled the field one and one-half times on that first test and was in the air only one minute, eleven seconds; but the crowd "went crazy." "When the plane first rose," said Roosevelt, Jr., in describing the event, years afterward, "the crowd's gasp of astonishment was not alone at the wonder of it, but because it was so unexpected. I'll never forget the impression the sound from the crowd made on me. It was a sound of complete surprise."

When he landed after this flight it was Orville's turn to be astonished. Three or four supposedly "hardboiled" newspapermen who rushed up to interview him had been so stirred by witnessing the "impossible" that each of them had tears streaming down his cheeks.

(Those who witnessed this flight might have been prepared for what they saw and less surprised, since Wilbur Wright for more than a month had been making flights in France—told about in a later chapter—and some of these were reported in the newspapers. But the brief newspaper accounts of Wilbur's flights seldom if ever had first page display and were not treated as important news. On August 9, the day after Wilbur's first flight, the New York *Times* had no mention of the event, though it gave first page space to a dispatch from Canton, Ohio, about a balloon trip, and to a dispatch from

Berlin about the German Kaiser contributing to a fund for building another Zeppelin airship.)

Nor did newspapers show too much excitement about this great public demonstration of practical aviation. It was not considered front page news even by Washington papers. The New York *World* account was on page five and most of the report was not about the wonder of the flying-machine, but about the behavior of the crowd, described as in fear of being hit by what the *World* called "the vessel."

Many thousands were present on the second day of the tests when Orville flew about three miles in four minutes, fifteen seconds. After one of these flights, a reporter, it was said, got in touch with Professor Simon Newcomb who, a few years before, had so irrefutably explained why flying was impossible. The reporter wanted to know if Professor Newcomb thought passenger planes would be the next step.

"No," Newcomb was reported to have replied, "because no plane could ever carry the weight of anyone besides the pilot." It might have been expected that by this time Professor Newcomb would have become more cautious!

Orville made a short flight on September 7, and two flights the next day; one of eleven minutes, ten seconds; the other of seven minutes, thirty-four seconds. On the morning of September 9, he circled the field fifty-seven times in fifty-seven minutes, twenty-five seconds. Later in the day, he circled the field fifty-five times in one hour, two and one-quarter minutes. Then he surprised and delighted his friend, Lieutenant Frank P. Lahm, by inviting him to go with him for a flight. They were in the air six minutes, twenty-four seconds, and circled the field six and one-half times. All three of these flights on the ninth established new world endurance records; two of them for flights with pilot alone, and the third for pilot with passenger. Orville made a flight of one hour, five minutes, fifty-two seconds on September 10, rising to a height of 200 feet and exceeding the world endurance record made by himself the day before. On the next day he again broke the one-man endurance record by flying for one hour, ten minutes, and twenty-four seconds, while circling the field fifty-seven times and describing two figure eights. On the twelfth, he increased the two-man endurance record by taking with him Major George O. Squier, Acting Chief Signal Officer, for a flight of nine minutes, six seconds. Immediately after that, Orville made a flight alone. He circled the field seventy-one times in one hour and fifteen minutes—again breaking the endurance record for one-man flight. It was estimated that he reached a height of 300 feet.

The next and final flight, September 17, ended in tragedy. Lieutenant Thomas Selfridge, a twenty-six-year-old West Point graduate, from San Francisco, had been assigned at his own request to go along as passenger. Before they had been in the air more than three or four minutes, and while in the fourth round at a height of about 125 feet over the field, Orville heard, or felt, a light tapping in the rear part of the machine. He thought it was in the chain drive. A hurried glance revealed nothing wrong there; but he decided to shut off the power and descend. Hardly had he reached this decision when two big thumps, which shook the machine violently, followed by the machine swerving to the right, showed that something had gone wrong. He immediately shut off the motor. Directly ahead was a gulley filled with small trees, a dangerous landing spot. He decided on a half-circle to the left, to land on the parade grounds, and it was then that he discovered that the tail was inoperative. By twisting the wings to give the greatest possible resistance to the left one, he did succeed in turning the machine until it faced directly into the field. In this maneuver the machine had descended about one-third of the way toward the ground without any indication of serious trouble. Orville moved the lever to straighten the wing tips, to proceed straight ahead. Then the machine suddenly turned down in front. For fifty feet it was headed almost directly toward the ground, although the front elevator was turned to its limit. When about twenty-five feet from the ground the machine began to right itself, and if there had been another twenty feet to go, or possibly even ten feet, it might have landed safely.

But the recovery of control came too late. The machine hit the ground with such impact that Lieutenant Selfridge was fatally injured and died a few hours later. His skull had been fractured by a blow against one of the wooden uprights of the framework. Orville, though at first believed to be perhaps fatally hurt, had miraculously escaped with what then appeared to be only a fractured left leg and four broken ribs. He never lost consciousness and his first concern was about Selfridge.

(Not until twelve years later, after suffering severe pains, did Orville learn, from a careful X-ray examination in a famous medical clinic, that the Fort Myer accident had also caused three fractures in the hip bones, besides a dislocation of one of them.)

Now that an airplane passenger had been killed, the Fort Myer demonstrations at last reached the front pages of newspapers.

The day after the accident, the mechanics, Taylor and Furnas, brought the broken propeller and some of the other broken parts to Orville's bedside. From these parts he was able to determine the cause of the accident. A new pair of propellers, several inches longer than any previously used, had been installed just before the flight. The trouble started when a longitudinal crack developed in one blade of the right propeller. This crack permitted the blade to flatten and lose much of its thrust, with the result that the pressures on the two blades became unequal, causing a severe vibration of the propeller shaft housing. The vibration loosened one of the stay wires that held in position the tube in which the propeller-shaft turned. Then the propeller began to swing sidewise and forward until a blade hit and tore loose the stay wire to the vertical tail, permitting the tail to take a nearly horizontal position. A pressure on the tail's underside lifted the rear of the machine, thus causing it to dart for the ground.

While Orville was recovering from his injuries, an acquaintance, C. H. Claudy, visited him and asked:

"Has it got your nerve?"

"Nerve?" repeated Orville, not quite understanding.

"Oh, you mean will I be *afraid* to fly again? The only thing I'm afraid of is that I can't get well soon enough to finish those tests next year."

The cost had been high, but one result of those incomplete tests was that widespread incredulity in the United States about the Wrights' achievements now finally ceased. At last, everyone, including even the most skeptical scientists, was convinced that a practical flying-machine was a reality.

XV

WHEN WILBUR WRIGHT WON FRANCE

WILBUR WRIGHT reached France in May, 1908, to fly the Wright machine that for a year had been in its crate at the customs warehouse in Le Havre. If he accomplished what he expected, final details of the Wrights' business arrangement with the recently formed French syndicate would be carried out.

As during the previous stay, when both the Wright brothers were in Europe, Wilbur kept in close touch with Hart O. Berg, European associate of Charles R. Flint & Co., the Wrights' business representatives in all except the English-speaking countries. One of the first questions to be settled was where the actual demonstration of the Wright plane should take place. Naturally, there were not yet any areas in Europe designated as flying fields.

The locality for the flights was determined in consequence of the courtesies of Léon Bollée, an automobile manufacturer, who had a factory at Le Mans, about 125 miles from Paris.[1] When Bollée learned that Wilbur Wright was in France and looking for a suitable field, he sent a message to Wilbur suggesting that a satisfactory place could doubtless be found near Le Mans where

---

[1] A Wright monument at Le Mans, by the sculptor, Paul Landowski, was dedicated in 1920.

there was a great stretch of level country. He added that
Wilbur would be welcome to use a wing of the Bollée
factory for assembling his plane. Wilbur Wright and
Hart O. Berg took a train to Le Mans where they spent
several hours "looking for a good pasture." The most
nearly ideal field for their purpose was a large open area
at Auvours, about five miles from Le Mans, used by the
French war department for testing artillery; but it was
not then available. Another place they noticed was the
Hunaudières race track. The oval field within the track
appeared to be large enough for their needs. There were
a few trees, but Wilbur said he could easily steer clear
of them. The next day, in Paris, M. Nicolai, president
of the Jockey Club and principal owner of the Hunaudières race track, agreed to the use of the field, at a
monthly rental, for as long as needed.

Now the crated Wright plane was shipped from Le
Havre to the Bollée factory and, late in June, Wilbur set
to work there. He assembled the working parts and put
the motor and cooling system to a series of rigid tests.
On July 4 Wilbur met with a painful accident. A rubber
connection in the cooling system burst and he was badly
scalded on his left arm by hot water. This was one of
several unavoidable delays that made many skeptics
think it would be a long time before Wilbur would attempt a public demonstration. One Paris newspaper said:
"*Le bluff continue.*" Wilbur had been quoted as saying
that the tests would be "child's play," and "*jeu d'enfant*"
was often repeated, with sarcasm, by the incredulous.

Painful as his burns were, Wilbur saw a funny side
to the accident and sent home a hilarious letter about the

French doctor who came "with a keg of oil" to apply to the blisters.

Shortly afterward, Wilbur wanted a coiled wire spring to insert in a hose used in the cooling system, to prevent the hose from collapsing from suction. A French mechanic who had been assisting him went with him to a near-by factory to have the coil made. Not knowing any French, Wilbur could not follow the long conversation he overheard, but they came away without the coil. It seemed strange to Wilbur that the kind of wire needed should not have been easily obtainable and he spoke of this to the man who had been his interpreter.

But, said the Frenchman, the wire *was* available.

"Then," asked Wilbur, in surprise, "why didn't we get it?"

Oh, explained the Frenchman, because when he and the man at the factory talked it over it didn't seem to them that using a coiled wire spring in the way Wilbur had in mind was a sound idea!

While working on his machine at the Bollée factory, Wilbur did something, probably just because it seemed the natural thing to do, with no thought of the impression it would make, that delighted the hearts of the factory employees. He kept the same hours that the others did and his whole behavior was as if he were simply one more workman. When the whistle blew for the noon hour, he knocked off along with the others, and went, in overalls, to lunch. This lack of any sign of aloofness caused much favorable comment.

Wilbur's greatest admirer, however, was Léon Bollée himself. Though they had no common language, they

managed to exchange ideas and formed a warm friendship. Bollée, a jolly rotund man with a saucy little beard,
was ever ready to be of any service. Incidentally, though
Bollée had no thought of personal gain when he generously offered the use of space in his factory, the fact
that Wilbur worked on his plane there did not hurt the
sale of Bollée cars.

But the work was soon transferred from the Bollée
factory to the field at Hunaudières where a hastily constructed hangar had been built. Another item of preparation was the setting up of a launching derrick, similar
to the one the Wrights had first used in their experiments at the Huffman pasture. Huge weights were attached at one end of a rope which ran over pulleys and
had a metal ring at the other end to be caught on a hook
at the front of the plane. When the plane shot forward,
the rope automatically dropped away. As at previous
trials, the plane when ready to take off rested on a small
truck having two flanged wheels that ran on a single-rail,
iron-shod, wooden track, about sixty feet long.

Not until August 8, did Wilbur attempt his first
flight. A good-sized crowd was present, the majority
from Le Mans and the near-by countryside, but it included many members of the Aéro Club of France and
various newspaper representatives from Paris.

In describing the scene, years afterward, Hart O. Berg
said: "Wilbur Wright's quiet self-confidence was re-
assuring. One thing that, to me at least, made his appearance all the more dramatic, was that he was not dressed
as if about to do something daring or unusual. He, of
course, had no special pilot's helmet or jacket, since no

such garb yet existed, but appeared in the ordinary gray suit he usually wore, and a cap. And he had on, as he nearly always did when not in overalls, a high, starched collar."

At least one man among the spectators felt certain the flight would not be a success. That was M. Archdeacon, prominent in the Aéro Club. So sure was M. Archdeacon that Wilbur Wright would be deflated that, as the time set for the flight approached, he was explaining to those near him in the grandstand just what was "wrong" about the design of the Wright machine, and why it could not be expected to fly well.

Wilbur's immediate preparations had been made with great care. First of all, the starting rail had been set precisely in the direction of and against the wind. The engine was started by two men, each pulling down a blade of the two propellers and the plane was held back by a wire attached to a hook and releasing trigger near the pilot's seat. After the engine was warmed up, Fleury, Berg's chauffeur, took hold of the right wing. Wilbur released the trigger and the plane was pulled forward by the falling weights. Fleury kept it in balance until the accelerating speed left him behind. By the time it had reached the end of the rail, the plane left the track with enough speed to sustain itself and climb.

At some distance, directly in front of Wilbur as he started to rise, were tall trees, but they gave him no concern. He bore off easily to the left and went ahead in a curve that brought him back almost over the starting point. Then he swung to the right and made another great turn. Most of the time he was thirty or thirty-five

feet above the ground. He was in the air only one minute and forty-five seconds, but he had made history.

The crowd knew well they had "seen something" and
behaved accordingly. In the excited babel of voices one
or two phrases could be heard again and again. "*Cet
homme a conquis l'air!*" "*Il n'est pas bluffeur!*" Yes,
truly Wilbur had conquered the air, and he was no
bluffer. That American word "bluffer" had been much
used during the time that reports from the United States
about the Wrights had been stirring controversy in
France. Now "*bluffeur*" became, more than ever, a part
of the French language. "To think that one would call
the Wrights '*bluffeurs*'!" lamented the French press
over and over again.

For the next few minutes after Wilbur landed, Berg
was kept busy laughingly warding off agitated Frenchmen who sought to bestow a formal accolade by kissing
Wilbur in the French manner on both cheeks. He suspected that Wilbur might consider that carrying enthusiasm too far.

One of the skeptical members of the Aéro Club,
Edouard Surcouf, a balloonist, had arrived at the field
late, barely in time to see Wilbur in the air. Now he
was about the most enthusiastic of all. He rushed up
to Berg, exclaiming: "*C'est le plus grand erreur du
siècle!*" Disbelieving the claims of the Wrights may not
have been the biggest error of the century, but obviously it *had* at least been a mistake.

The only person who offered criticism or minimized
the brilliance of his feat was Wilbur Wright. When
asked by a reporter for the Paris edition of the New

York *Herald* if he was satisfied with the exhibition, he replied, according to that paper: "Not altogether. When in the air I made no less than ten mistakes owing to the fact that I have been laying off from flying so long; but I corrected them rapidly, so I don't suppose anyone watching really knew I had made any mistake at all. I was very pleased at the way my first flight in France was received."

A crowd of Aéro Club members and other admirers were insistent that Wilbur should go back to Paris with them to celebrate the achievement at the best dinner to be obtained in that center of inspired cooking. But Wilbur just thanked them and said he wished to give his machine a little going over. Early that evening, so the newspapers reported, "he was asleep at the side of his creation."

The French press the next day not only treated the flight as the biggest news, but was unsparing in its praise, as were various rivals in the field of aviation who were quoted. All admitted that there was a world of difference between the best French plane yet produced and the one Wilbur Wright had just demonstrated. The *Figaro* said: "It was not merely a success but a triumph; a conclusive trial and a decisive victory for aviation, the news of which will revolutionize scientific circles throughout the world." *Le Journal* observed that: "It was the first trial of the Wright airplane, whose qualities have long been regarded with doubt, and it was perfect."

Louis Bleriot, member of the Aéro Club, wealthy manufacturer of automobile headlights, and himself a flyer, was quoted in *Le Matin* as saying: "The Wright machine is indeed superior to our airplanes."

As early as May, 1908, when the Wrights were still at Kitty Hawk, the Frenchman, Henri Farman, had issued a challenge to them to participate in a flying contest, for $5,000—later raised to $10,000. But the challenge, made only in public prints, was never sent directly to the Wrights. It may have been simply what today would be called a "publicity stunt." (Farman's best straightaway flight of about a mile and a quarter had been made at Issy, France, on March 21, 1908.) Nothing more was heard of the Farman challenge now. A French paper commented that the Farman plane and also that of Léon Delagrange were approximate copies of the Wright plane but that the Wright machine "seems more solid, more controllable, and more scientific."

Two days after that first demonstration, on August 10, Wilbur made two more short flights, the first one a figure eight, and the other, three complete circles. He flew on August 11 for 3 minutes 43 seconds; the next day, 6 minutes 56 seconds; and on August 13, 8 minutes 13.2 seconds. This time he did seven wide *"orbes,"* as the French described them. In landing that day Wilbur broke the left wing of his plane and repairs kept him from flying until August 21. He took time out on August 24 to attend an agricultural fair where reporters observed that he seemed much interested in pigs and cattle and, as one paper expressed it, "talked much more freely about them than about aviation."

After those first few flights, the army officer in charge

of the artillery testing grounds at Auvours let it be known that the military people at Paris would be proud to have Wilbur Wright's further demonstrations carried on there. As the military field was larger than that at Hunaudières, Wilbur was glad to make the change. The Hunaudières hangar—which Wilbur persisted in calling the "shed"—was torn down and rebuilt within twenty-four hours at Auvours. As the two fields were only about ten miles apart, Wilbur could have flown the plane to the new location; but with so much at stake he was taking no chances. The plane was placed longitudinally on two wheels fastened behind Léon Bollée's automobile and towed to the Auvours field without removing the wings. Within a month after setting up operations at Auvours, Wilbur was flying many times the distance between the two fields.

All parts of France were now flooded with souvenir post cards bearing pictures of Wilbur or of his plane in flight. And the French people gave him all the hero-worship of which they were capable. There was talk of a public subscription for a testimonial to him. When the French ambassador to the United States reached New York a short time later he declared that Wilbur Wright was accepted as the biggest man in France. It wasn't alone his achievements in the air that won the people, but also his modesty, decency, and intelligence. The French papers made enthusiastic comment on the fact that in conversation he seemed to be exceptionally well informed not only about scientific work, but also on art, literature, medicine, and affairs of the world.

Newspapermen liked Wilbur because he always made

it plain that they were welcome. They probably liked him all the more because, as a joke, he usually put them at manual work, to fetch tools, or help drag the plane in and out of the hangar.

Those who had access to the hangar were impressed by the orderliness of the place. Wilbur's canvas cot was hauled up by ropes toward the roof during the day, and the space where he slept was divided from another section of the building by a low partition made of wood from packing cases. Wilbur explained that one room was his bedroom, the other his dining-room. Another trait that appealed to the French was Wilbur's punctuality at all appointments. No one ever had to wait even a minute on him.

Nothing Wilbur was overheard to say by French journalists seemed too trivial to be recorded. One day he said "fine" to an assistant, by way of commendation, and the next day a Paris paper explained that Wilbur meant "*C'est beau.*" "Boys, let's fix these ropes" was promptly translated as "*Allons, jeunes gens, allez disposer les cordes.*"

Wilbur was flooded with letters of all kinds. Some were from scientists seeking information, and hundreds came from women who desired to make his acquaintance. He tried his best to answer all sensible questions from scientists; the others went into the stove. He was equally considerate of scientific-minded people—including those who might be considered rivals in aviation—who came in person. To all who had real interest he patiently explained any detail of his machine. But he was capable of quiet sarcasm toward the ill-informed who started to enlighten him about aerodynamics.

It now became the fashionable thing for Parisians to take a train down to Le Mans and drive from there to the Champ d'Auvours to see Wilbur fly. Amusing episodes grew out of that. Since the flights were not often announced in advance, those who made the sightseeing trip had to take their chances. But some of the callers felt almost a personal affront if Wilbur made no flight on the day they happened to be there. One American society woman living in Paris was bitterly resentful when she was told that Monsieur Wright was taking a nap and therefore would not fly that afternoon. "The idea," said she, petulantly, "of his being asleep when I came all the way down here to see him in the air!"

Cabmen at Le Mans found the sudden influx of visitors so profitable that they tried to make the most of it and encouraged people who had been disappointed to come again the next day. They would always say: "He is sure to fly tomorrow. We have it on good authority."

So grateful to Wilbur were members of the "Le Mans-Auvours Aeroplane Bus Service" for the profitable trade he had created, that they wanted to give a banquet in his honor.

News of Wilbur's flights at Le Mans naturally caused talk in England. Members of the Aeronautical Society of Great Britain, one after another, went to Le Mans in doubt about the flights being as wonderful as reported, but returned convinced that the age of practical flying-machines had come.

One of the first to go from England to investigate

was Griffith Brewer, who had been making balloon ascensions since 1891. Half apologetically, lest he be thought over-credulous, he confided to an old associate of his in ballooning, Charles S. Rolls, founder of the Rolls-Royce motor car firm, that he was going to France to see Wilbur Wright fly. Rolls laughed and said he had just returned from seeing him fly.

On his arrival at Le Mans, Brewer walked to the shed at the edge of the field. Opposite the shed, in the middle of the field, was Wilbur Wright tuning up his machine. As a crowd was about Wilbur, Brewer hesitated to add to it, but sat down by the shed to smoke his pipe. When a mechanic came from the machine over to the shed for a tool, Brewer handed him a calling card with the request that he give it to Wilbur Wright. Wilbur glanced at the card, nodded to Brewer, and went on with his work. There was no flight, but it was some time before Wilbur returned to the shed; and as he stayed inside for what seemed a long time, Brewer began to think there might be an indefinite wait. Then Wilbur came out, putting on his coat, and said: "Now, Mr. Brewer, we'll go and have some dinner."

They went to Madame Pollet's inn near by for a simple meal and Brewer, eager though he was to discuss aviation, wondered if the inventor might not appreciate a rest from the subject of flying. He therefore talked to him of affairs in America. Wilbur liked that, and they formed a friendship.

On September 12, Wilbur was guest of honor at a dinner in Paris given by the Aéro Club of the Sarthe (the governmental department in which Le Mans was

THE OLD AND THE NEW IN TRANSPORTATION.
Two views of the Wright plane in flight at Pau, France, in
1909.

DEMONSTRATION AT PAU. Wilbur Wright explaining
the plane's mechanism to Alfonso XIII of Spain.

located). It was understood that he would not be expected to make a speech, but Baron d'Estournelles, member of the Senate from Le Mans, who presided, did nevertheless call upon him. Wilbur then, in justification of his unwillingness to say much, made a remark that became famous.

"I know of only one bird, the parrot, that talks," he was quoted as saying, "and it can't fly very high."

For the first time in France, Wilbur, on September 16, took up a passenger, a young French balloonist, Ernest Zens.

Two days later, in the early morning of September 18, as he was about to make a flight, Wilbur got word about the tragic accident at Fort Myer the day before, when Lieutenant Selfridge was killed and Orville Wright injured, it was not yet known how seriously.

Within a few hours cables brought word that Orville would recover, and Wilbur was able to fly again the next day. Two days later, on September 21, he flew about forty miles, in 1 hour 31 minutes 25.4 seconds. News of that proved to be better medicine for Orville, in Washington, than anything the attending physician could do.

Many passengers now made short flights with Wilbur. They included, on October 3, Mr. Dickin, of the Paris edition of the New York *Herald,* and Franz Reichel, of the Paris *Figaro.* Reichel was so enthusiastic over his flight of nearly an hour, that on landing he threw his arms about Wilbur.

Léon Bollée had his first flight on October 5, and the next day Arnold Fordyce flew with Wilbur for 1 hour

4 minutes and 26 seconds, the longest flight yet made in an airplane with a passenger.

Now that Wilbur was carrying much weight and on longer flights, the Paris edition of the New York *Herald* became impressed with future possibilities for carrying mail by plane. It predicted that the time might come when there would be special stamps for "aeroplane delivery."

A witness to several of these flights in early October was Major B. F. S. Baden-Powell, President of the Aeronautical Society of Great Britain (and a brother of the founder of the Boy Scouts). He was so impressed by what he saw that he sounded a warning to his fellow countrymen. Major Baden-Powell was quoted as follows in the Paris edition of the New York *Herald* on October 6, 1908:

If only some of our people in England could see or imagine what Mr. Wright is now doing I am certain it would give them a terrible shock. A conquest of the air by any nation means more than the average man is willing to admit or even think about. That Wilbur Wright is in possession of a power which controls the fate of nations is beyond dispute.

Hart O. Berg, on October 7, went for a flight, his first, lasting three minutes and twenty-four seconds. Immediately afterward Wilbur took Mrs. Berg for a flight, of two minutes, three seconds, the first ever made anywhere in the world by a woman. (One or two women were reported to have been in planes that made short hops, but Mrs. Berg was certainly the first woman to participate in a real flight.)

Berg tied a rope about the lower part of his wife's skirt to keep it from blowing. A Paris dressmaker who was among the spectators noted that Mrs. Berg could hardly walk, after landing, with that rope above her ankles. There, thought the *couturière*, was a suggestion for something fashionable. A costume with skirt thus drawn between the ankles and the knees to make natural locomotion difficult should appeal to any customers who happened to be both stupid and rich. Thus was born the "hobble skirt" which, for a short time, was considered "smart."

The next day, October 8, her royal highness, Margherita, the dowager queen of Italy, who was touring France, came to see a flight.

"You have let me witness the most astonishing spectacle I have ever seen," was her comment to Wilbur Wright.

On that same October 8, Griffith Brewer, making his second visit to Le Mans, won the distinction of being the first Englishman ever to fly. He was followed almost immediately by three other British Aeronautical Society members, C. S. Rolls, F. H. Butler, and Major Baden-Powell.

One of the Englishmen remarked: "How decent it is of Wilbur Wright never to accept a fee for any of these flights, when there are scores of persons who would gladly pay hundreds of pounds for the privilege."

Wilbur continued until the end of the year to take up passengers at Auvours. Among them, on October 10, was M. Painlevé, of the French Institute. As they were taking off, M. Painlevé gaily waved his hand at the

crowd and in so doing accidentally pulled a rope over-
head that Wilbur used for stopping the engine. After
another start, the flight lasted one hour, nine minutes,
forty-five seconds, and covered forty-six miles, a world
record for both duration and distance for an airplane
carrying two persons. Two other women besides Mrs.
Berg had short flights—Mesdames Léon Bollée and
Lazare Weiller. A passenger on October 24 was Dr.
Pirelli, leading tire manufacturer in Italy. Later, in
November, F. S. Lahm, one of the first in Europe to
believe the Wrights had flown, had his first ride in a
plane. Among the distinguished people who made passenger flights were two destined to die by assassins'
bullets: Paul Doumer, member of the French parlia-
ment, afterward President of France; and Louis Barthou, Minister of Public Works and Aerial Communications, afterward Premier.

Under the terms of the contract between the Wrights
and the newly formed French company, one of the
Wright brothers was to train three pilots. Wilbur began
this training at Auvours. The students were Count
Charles de Lambert, Paul Tissandier, and Captain Lucas
de Girardville. Both Tissandier and de Lambert had
made flights as passengers on September 28, but did not
begin their training until later. Captain Lucas de Girardville went up as a passenger for the first time on October 12. The first to receive a lesson at piloting was
Count de Lambert on October 28.

The Aéro Club of France had offered a prize of 2,500
francs for an altitude of twenty-five meters. But there
was a "catch" to that offer. A little clique in the Aéro

Club, a bit over-chauvinistic, wanted a native experimenter to win, and that was why the altitude to be attained was fairly low. It was stipulated that anyone competing for the prize must start without use of derrick or catapult. The French experimenters had wheels on their machines and could get as long a start as necessary before leaving the ground. But the Wright machine, designed for the rough, sandy ground at Kitty Hawk, and the somewhat bumpy Huffman field, still had skids instead of wheels. Thus the rules for the contest seemed to be aimed to prevent Wilbur Wright from winning the prize. Members of the Aéro Club of the Sarthe thought their compatriots in the Aéro Club of France were being unsportsmanlike, and they offered a prize of 1,000 francs for an altitude record of thirty meters. Wilbur won it on November 13. In doing so he went three times as high as required, reaching an altitude of ninety meters. Then Wilbur decided that he might as well win the prize of the Aéro Club of France, and do so on their own terms. He arranged for a longer starting track than usual, and, five days after taking the prize for thirty meters, he started without the use of derrick or catapult and won the prize for twenty-five meters. To the delight of his friends in the Aéro Club of the Sarthe, he purposely did not throw in much altitude for good measure and went only high enough to clear safely the captive balloon that showed the height required.

On December 16, Wilbur astounded the spectators by shutting off the motor at an altitude of about 200 feet and volplaning slowly down. And on December 18, he flew for 1 hour 54 minutes 53.4 seconds. Later that same day he won another prize offered by the Aéro Club of the Sarthe for an altitude of a hundred meters. Wilbur went ten meters higher than required. This was a new world's record for altitude. Then on December 31, the last day he ever flew at Auvours, he made what was then an almost incredible record of staying continuously in the air 2 hours 20 minutes 23.2 seconds. For this feat he won the Michelin award of $4,000, or 20,000 francs.

As the weather at Le Mans was no longer ideal for flying, it was necessary to seek a warmer climate, and at the suggestion of Paul Tissandier, Wilbur decided to go to Pau, a beautiful winter resort city of 35,000, at the edge of the Pyrenees. The city of Pau provided a field and a hangar.[1]

At about the same time, Orville Wright, now rapidly recuperating from his injuries at Fort Myer, arrived in Paris with their sister, Katharine, for a reunion with Wilbur. Then Wilbur went on down to Pau, and his brother and sister joined him there a week or two later. En route to Pau, their train met with an accident near the town of Dax, in which two persons were killed. The Wrights escaped injury, but Orville was a bit startled for another reason. When the crash came, his mattress tipped up on one side at the same time that his watch, pocketbook and other articles slid off a stand or shelf beside the bed. His valuables thus got themselves hid beneath the mattress and, until he chanced to find them, it looked as if he had been robbed.

[1] A Wright monument at Pau was dedicated in 1931.

As at Le Mans, Wilbur lived at the hangar, where he had a French cook the hospitable Mayor de Lassence, of Pau, had selected. His brother and sister lived at the Hotel Gassion, not far from the famous old château where Henry IV was born, and within a short stroll from the Place near the center of the city that affords what Lamartine has called the finest land view in all the world. The Wrights were not long in discovering that life here should be ideal. Wilbur's French cook proved to be competent enough at preparing regional and other choice dishes—though Katharine Wright did not think he had quite the best technique with a broom for keeping the quarters clean. A London newspaper photographer gave Orville a photograph of his sister demonstrating to that Frenchman how to handle a broom.

By coming to Pau the Wrights had unintentionally played a joke on James Gordon Bennett, owner of the New York *Herald* and Paris *Herald*. A few years previously, when Bennett was spending the winter there, he had a tally-ho party and someone in the party had attracted the attention of the police. The episode was reported in local newspapers. Bennett was so indignant that he laid down a rule for both his papers to say as little as possible about Pau. But now, with Wilbur Wright flying there, the town could hardly be ignored. Pau date lines were again frequent in the Bennett papers.

Wilbur did not attempt any new records at Pau, but devoted most of his time to teaching the young pilots for the French Wright company.

Count Charles de Lambert continued his training, and his wife, almost equally enthusiastic over aviation, made

a passenger flight. Another woman to make a flight at
Pau was Katharine Wright herself. It was her first trip
in a plane, though, as she laughingly remarked, she had
heard plenty about aviation.

An American multi-millionaire from Philadelphia,
spending some time at Pau, announced, with the self-
confidence money sometimes gives, that he intended to
make a flight with Wilbur. When told that Wilbur was
not taking up any passengers, he replied: "Oh, I daresay
that can be arranged."

"I'd like to be around when you do the arranging,
just to see how it's done," observed Lord Northcliffe,
owner of the London *Daily Mail*, who had recently arrived and become acquainted with the Wrights. The
American went away without having had his ride.

In February, King Alfonso of Spain came to Pau
with his entourage, and the Wrights were formally presented to him at the field. "An honor and a pleasure to
meet you," said the king.

Alfonso showed more boyish enthusiasm about the
plane than almost anyone. He was eager to fly, but both
his queen and his cabinet had exacted a promise that he
would not. However, he climbed aboard the plane and
sat there for a long time fascinated while Wilbur painstakingly explained every detail.

A little later, on March 17, still another king arrived.
Edward VII of England came by automobile with his
suite from near-by Biarritz. The presentation of the
brothers and their sister was made at the field and Edward showed his customary graciousness. He did not
seek any technical details about the machine, but was

much interested in seeing the flights themselves and in meeting the Wrights.

It was during the stay of King Edward that Miss Katharine Wright made her second trip in an airplane.

Other famous personages continued to come to Pau, among them Lord Arthur Balfour, former Prime Minister of England. Sometimes when Wilbur was preparing for a flight, visitors would pull on the rope that raised the weights on the launching derrick. Balfour insisted that he must not be denied this privilege of "taking part in a miracle" and did his share of yanking at the rope. Another man who shared in handling the rope that day was a young English duke.

"I'm so glad that young man is helping with the rope," said Lord Northcliffe to Orville Wright, with a motion of his head toward the duke, "for I'm sure it is the only useful thing he has ever done in his life."

Northcliffe, after his meeting with the Wrights at Pau, became one of their most enthusiastic supporters in England.

Long afterward, he publicly made this comment:

"I never knew more simple, unaffected people than Wilbur, Orville, and Katharine. After the Wrights had been in Europe a few weeks they became world heroes, and when they went to Pau their demonstrations were visited by thousands of people from all parts of Europe —by kings and lesser men, but I don't think the excitement and interest produced by their extraordinary feat had any effect on them at all."

XVI

FURTHER ADVENTURES IN 1909

SHORTLY after they were established at Pau, the Wrights received a call from a German, Captain Alfred Hildebrandt. This was not the first time he had tried to see them. He had stopped in Dayton, on his way homeward after attending the international balloon races at St. Louis, in 1907; but on reaching Dayton he learned that the Wrights were in Europe. Captain Hildebrandt came to Pau on behalf of a newspaper publisher. His principal was Herr Scherl, owner of the *Lokal Anzeiger*, a leading paper in Berlin. Scherl thought it would be a great stroke of advertising for his paper if he could arrange for a big public demonstration of a Wright machine, with the general public invited to be the paper's guests. It was arranged that one of the Wrights should make a series of flights at Berlin, later that year, for a substantial fee. The brothers later decided that the Berlin flights should be made by Orville.

A move had been started in Italy to have demonstrations of the Wright plane in Rome. Dr. Pirelli, Italian tire manufacturer, who had flown with Wilbur Wright at Le Mans, was believed to have made the first suggestion that led to organizing an aviation club at Rome to buy a Wright plane. This "club" was supposed to be backed at least partly by the Italian Government, and the arrangement with the Wrights provided for the training of two lieutenants, one from the Navy, the other from the Army.

Parts and material for six new planes had already been shipped to Europe from Dayton, and the parts for one of these were sent to Pau, where they were built into a complete machine. The machine was then taken down in sections and shipped to Rome. (The one used in the French flights became the personal property of Lazare Weiller, organizer of the French Wright company, and later it went to a museum in Paris.)

In April the Wrights returned from Pau to Paris, and after a brief stay there Wilbur went to Rome. He was joined there later by Orville and Katharine, who went to a hotel opposite the Barberini Palace. Count and Countess di Celleri, of the Italian nobility, had a cottage adjoining their villa near the flying field at Centocelle,, and they offered it to Wilbur. Countess di Celleri later felt more than repaid when she had a passenger flight in the Wright plane.

When the machine shipped from Pau in sections arrived in Rome it was reassembled in an automobile factory, just outside the city limits, on the Flaminian Way. It was then moved across the city on a truck drawn by a magnificent team of gray horses to a military field in Centocelle. As the strange-looking machine was carried through Roman streets past ancient ruins, it is doubtful if amazed beholders had ever seen a greater contrast between old and new.

Almost immediately after his arrival, Wilbur began the training of the Italian flyers, naval Lieutenant Calderara and Lieutenant Savoia, of the army engineering corps. (Calderara was afterward the air attaché at the Italian Embassy in Washington; and Lieutenant Savoia became the head of the well-known Italian aviation company of that name.)

King Victor Emmanuel came to witness flights. As he strolled about the field with a folding camera suspended from his shoulder, he might have been mistaken for just one more tourist. Other sightseers who came to the field were the elder J. P. Morgan and the famous railroader, James J. Hill. Among those who made flights with Wilbur were Lloyd Griscom, the American Ambassador, and Sonnino, former Premier of Italy. Soon after that, for the first time, an operator took a motion picture from an airplane in flight.

While at Rome the Wrights established friendship with another German, Captain von Kehler, whom they had already met in Berlin, and he played an important part in steps toward forming a Wright company in Germany.

Captain von Kehler was managing director of the Studien Gesellschaft, an organization for the study of aeronautics, that had been formed after a meeting between certain outstanding German industrialists and the Kaiser, back in 1906. The Kaiser had called the representatives of the Krupps and other powerful industrialists to Potsdam to give them a big banquet at the close of which he said he thought Germany should be looking into the possibilities of the development of the airship (lighter-than-air). Just what should be done he did not pretend to know. That problem, he said, he would turn over to them. They knew what he meant. They, as a patriotic duty, must provide money for research and experimentation in the lighter-than-air field or else lose standing with their Kaiser. Thus did the Studien Gesellschaft come into being. The organization began experiments by building a dirigible known as the Parseval, named for its designer, Major Parseval. The Parseval turned out to be an expensive experiment. At the end of two years the subscribed funds were nearly exhausted and the project far from completion. The subscribers began to fear another invitation to dinner. Just at this time they began to hear reports about the aeroplane flights of the Wrights in France, and they became much interested. It occurred to them that experiments with the new flying-machine would perhaps be less expensive than experiments with a dirigible, and that prospects for the aeroplane might be greater than for the dirigible.

Captain von Kehler went to Rome to talk with the Wrights. He told them that some of the wealthy men in the Studien Gesellschaft would like to form a German Wright company. Before he left Rome, a preliminary contract was signed. Its terms provided that the brothers should receive cash, a block of stock in the company, and ten per cent royalty on all planes sold. The final contract was closed in August, 1909.

After leaving Rome the Wrights made a brief stay in Paris and went to Le Mans to receive a bronze art piece presented by the Aéro Club of the Sarthe. The work in bronze, by Louis Carvin, showed the Wright brothers at the edge of a chasm gazing upon an eagle in flight.

Above them was a winged figure—the spirit of aviation.

From France the Wrights went to London. There they received gold medals from the Aeronautical Society of Great Britain and from the Aero Club of the United Kingdom at formal banquets. Before going to these dinners Griffith Brewer was describing to Wilbur some of the people he would meet. Of one man he said: "You'll readily recognize him, as he is the ugliest man in the Aeronautical Society." To which Wilbur replied: "He'll lose that distinction on this occasion, because now there will be a pair of us."

On their arrival in New York the Wrights attended a luncheon in their honor given by the Aero Club of America. The Aero Club had awarded medals to the Wrights and these were formally presented a month later by President Taft at the White House.

After an absence of many months, the Wrights arrived in Dayton early in May. Five weeks later the city had a great celebration in their honor. The home town had now recognized the Wrights' importance. This "home coming" for the Wrights lasted two days, June 17 and 18.

At 9 o'clock on that morning of June 17, they heard a deafening sound. It did not at once occur to them what it was. Every factory whistle in Dayton was blowing and every bell ringing—all in their honor. This continued for ten minutes. Bands were playing and cannons booming. At 10 o'clock the brothers rode in a carriage, escorted by bands, to the opening events. Ed Sines, boyhood chum of Orville, and Ed Ellis, long a friend of Wilbur, were in the carriage with them. Sines and Ellis, as a practical joke, gleefully shook hands, as if *they* were the heroes, with all who tried to greet the Wrights along the route, and few knew the difference.

After reviewing a parade in their honor that afternoon, the Wrights returned to their shop. That night they had opportunity to see a display of fireworks that included their own profiles, eight feet high, entwined with an American flag.

During these two days, practically all business in Dayton was suspended—except the sale of souvenir postal cards showing the Huffman pasture, the Hawthorne Street home, the flying field at Le Mans, France, and the parade ground at Fort Myer.

On the second day, the inventors' father, Bishop Wright, gave the invocation preceding the presentation of medals to his sons. One medal that had been ordered by act of Congress was presented by General James Allen, chief signal officer of the Army; another, by the Ohio legislature, was presented by Governor Harmon; and a third from the city of Dayton was presented by the Mayor. The Wrights were alongside of 2,500 school children, dressed in red, white and blue, to represent an immense American flag. Patriotic fervor ran high.

The home folk knew now that the Wrights could fly; they knew, too, that international fame had not changed them. They were the same unassuming pair they had always been.

Before the celebration was quite over, Wilbur and Orville took a train to Washington. The time for completing those Government trials at Fort Myer was approaching and there was much to be done.

Orville made his first flight on June 28, and finished on July 30. One of the most memorable of the flights in this series was on that final day when Orville, with an Army officer, Lieutenant Benjamin D. Foulois, for passenger, made the first cross-country trip yet made in an airplane, a total distance of about ten miles to Alexandria and return—without any suitable landing spots if trouble had occurred. This was the speed test. The machine now used was capable of about four miles an hour greater speed than the one in the tests the previous year. The turning point in Alexandria was at Shuter's Hill, where a Masonic temple now stands. A captive balloon floated above the hill, and a telegraph line had been run to the top of the hill where an operator was stationed to give a signal when Orville had passed that point. But a strong wind that day blew down the telegraph line and also kept the balloon so close to the ground that Orville could not see the turning point in advance and covered more than the required distance. As the plane passed out of sight for a time on the return trip, the crowd feared the worst; but when it reappeared, headed back toward the parade ground, the honking of automobile horns and excited cheering indicated that everyone knew they had all seen an extraordinary event. The time for the ten miles was fourteen minutes, or just under forty-three miles an hour. Thus the Wrights got a bonus of $5,000 more than the basic price agreed upon—ten per cent for each complete mile per hour more than forty—and they received $30,000 for the machine.

Almost immediately after the Fort Myer trials and

formal acceptance of the machine, on August 2, by the United States Government, Orville Wright, accompanied by his sister Katharine, set out for Berlin. Orville would start training a flyer for the German Wright company immediately after giving the exhibition arranged for by Captain Hildebrandt on behalf of the *Lokal Anzeiger*.

These first flights in Germany were to be made at Tempelhof field, then a military parade ground, at the outskirts of Berlin. On the day set for the initial flight, there was a terrible wind and Captain Hildebrandt, who accompanied Orville to the field, was torn between his desire not to disappoint the crowd and his fear of seeing Orville take too great a risk. Orville said he would follow Hildebrandt's wishes.

"No," said Hildebrandt, "don't go up."

The next day even more people were present. Orville made a flight of fifteen minutes. When he landed it was difficult to keep the crowd from almost smothering him with adulation. People clamored for a chance not only to look at him up close, but to *touch* him. Men, women, and children struggled to lay gentle hands on him, even to touch his sleeve or the hem of his coat. Evidently it was some kind of belief in the desirability of physical contact with a miracle man.

After a later flight, when Orville stayed in the air fifty-five minutes, the crowd about him and Katharine, who were accompanied by Mr. and Mrs. Charles R. Flint, was so dense that Orville felt duty bound to move as fast as he could away from his party, to relieve the pressure on them. Thereafter a hollow square of German soldiers kept the crowd at a safe distance.

The German Crown Prince, Frederick Wilhelm, sought to get in touch with Orville to ask the privilege of seeing a flight. He telephoned to the Wrights' suite at the Hotel Esplanade, and the call was answered by a young German woman whom Katharine Wright had employed as interpreter when shopping.

When the girl discovered that the voice over the phone was that of a member of the royal family, she dropped the telephone receiver and almost fainted. Members of the hotel staff were not much less agitated when they learned that royalty might be calling on two of their guests.

Orville Wright and his sister were invited by Kaiser Wilhelm himself to be present—the only civilian guests —on August 29, when Count von Zeppelin would make the first trip in his latest model airship from Friedrichs-hafen, and land at Tegel field, Berlin.

When he met Count von Zeppelin, Orville offered to take him for an airplane ride the next day. The Count, after expressing his appreciation, pleaded lack of time. But he invited Orville to accompany him in the airship on a trip, September 5, from Frankfort to Mannheim, and Orville accepted. In the course of that trip, Orville, by using a stop-watch in his pocket and counting tele-phone poles, was able to tell if the reported speed of the ship was correct. (When the Wrights were in Europe in 1907, they had seen flights by government-owned dirigibles in more than one country, and had noted that the German ship, *Der Gross*, was the only one that made the speed claimed for it. All they needed to learn was the length of the airship. Then by sighting on the corner of a building, while using a stop-watch, they could tell to the fraction of a second how long it took for the ship to travel its own length.)

On the airship's arrival at Mannheim, the crowd was so great that Orville soon became separated from Captain Hildebrandt, who had come along as his interpreter. Here he was, not knowing much German, supposed to be guest of honor at a luncheon, and he didn't even recall the name of the hotel where the affair was to be held. A member of the committee in charge of the luncheon decided that Orville would doubtless make his way to the center of the city, in search of the right hotel, and that there was just one way to locate him—to drive about the principal streets until he caught sight of him. This man had never met Orville but he felt sure he would recognize him from pictures he had seen. The plan, to Orville's immense relief, succeeded.

On September 16, Orville raised the world's altitude record from 100 to 172 meters. Two days later, he made a new world's record for a flight with a passenger. Accompanied by Captain Paul Englehardt, he flew for one hour, thirty-five minutes, forty-seven seconds.

Toward the end of his stay in Germany, Orville's flights were at Bornstedt field, near Potsdam. It was there that he trained two pilots for the German Wright company—Captain Englehardt and Herr Keidel.

Since his first meeting with Orville, the German Crown Prince had made no secret of his eager desire to fly as a passenger. As early as September 9, Orville had made a special flight of fifteen minutes for the Crown Prince to witness. Though he was willing enough to oblige the Crown Prince by taking him for a passenger flight, he hesitated to do so, lest it might be disapproved by the Kaiser, and he made one excuse after another for delay. He had been warned that if he took the Crown Prince as passenger against the Kaiser's wishes, then he might immediately become *persona non grata*. The prudent thing to do, it seemed to Orville, was to give members of the royal family plenty of notification. Different members of the family came to Bornstedt field from time to time, and when he met any of them Orville was sure to remark that he and the Crown Prince were going to have a flight together before long. As no one made any objection, the German Crown Prince finally became, on October 2, the first member of a royal family ever to ride in an airplane. On landing, the Crown Prince handed to Orville, as a token of appreciation, a jeweled stick-pin—a crown set in rubies, with a "W" in diamonds. (The "W" was not for Wright, but for Wilhelm, the Crown Prince's name.)

On that same day, Orville ascended 1,600 feet for a new—though unofficial—world's altitude record.

Orville's farewell ascent in Germany was a twenty-five-minute flight, October 15, for Kaiser Wilhelm to see. The Kaiser was enthusiastic and frankly so. He was outspoken in expressing his belief that the airplane might revolutionize warfare, and talked about the different military uses to which the machine could be put. One thing that impressed him was the maneuverability of the plane. Orville had made complete turns within a space not much more than 100 feet wide.

Now, during the time that Orville was making these sensational demonstrations in Germany, Wilbur Wright, in America, had been doing his share to glorify the brotherly partnership. On September 29, in connection with the Hudson-Fulton Celebration, Wilbur made spectacular flights witnessed by millions of people. Two of these were over Governors Island; and another was from Governors Island around the Statue of Liberty and back again. On October 4, Wilbur flew twenty-one miles from Governors Island up the Hudson River beyond Grant's Tomb and back to the starting point. It was one of the most daring flights yet made in an airplane, and Wilbur had taken the precaution to buy a red canoe which he roped to the lower part of the plane. The part of the canoe ordinarily open was covered with canvas to make it water-tight. Wilbur's idea was that if anything went wrong the canoe might possibly serve as a buoy, or pontoon, to keep the machine afloat. In going up the river he flew over ferryboats, and hot gases from the smokestacks did cause the plane to make what looked like dangerous plunges.

A second flight was planned for that afternoon, and everyone who could exert influence had applied for a pass to the military reservation on Governors Island. But they were disappointed, for the engine blew a cylinder and that brought the series of flights to a close.

Almost immediately after his flights for the Hudson-Fulton Celebration, Wilbur began preparations to train two Army Signal Corps officers, as provided for in the contract for the sale of a plane to the United States Government. This was done at College Park, Maryland, near Washington. The men trained were Lieutenants Frank P. Lahm and Frederic E. Humphreys. Their instruction began on October 8 and was completed October 26. Lieutenant Lahm, who had been the first army officer ever to fly as a passenger in a plane, received the first lesson in pilotage. But Humphreys made the first solo flight, a few minutes before Lahm's.

Wilbur also gave some lessons to Lieutenant Benjamin D. Foulois between October 23 and 27.

Orville and Katharine Wright sailed from Europe on the *Adriatic*, due in New York November 4. After leaving Germany, Orville had investigated the outlook of the recently formed French company. Already it appeared that this company would be a disappointment. Count de Lambert had given the company the best kind of advertising by flying a Wright plane over Paris, around and above the Eiffel Tower. But the French Wright company evidently was depending more on political influence and on entertaining important people than on sound salesmanship. The War Ministry hesitated to buy planes for fear of public criticism. General Picquart, the Army officer who had stood for justice in the Dreyfus case, had become Minister of War. He once inquired of the Wrights if it would be possible to buy their planes directly from them in the United States.

That would have been against provisions of the contract with the company in France, but there was another reason why it could not be done. The Wrights were not yet organized to produce planes in great numbers. Though there were now two commercial companies for the manufacture of Wright planes in Europe, no such company yet existed in America.

XVII

IN AVIATION BUSINESS

AFTER companies to manufacture the Wright brothers' invention had been organized in France and Germany, and a plane had been sold in Italy, it might have been expected that important business people in the United States would see commercial possibilities in the Wright patents. The inventors had, indeed, received offers. One proposal had come from two brothers, in Detroit, influential stockholders in the Packard Automobile Company, Russell A. and Frederick M. Alger—who some time before had been the first in the United States to order a Wright machine for private use. But the first American company to manufacture the plane was promoted by a mere youngster.

That was Clinton R. Peterkin. He was barely twenty-four and looked even younger. Only a year or two previously he had been with J. P. Morgan & Company as "office boy"—a job he had taken at the age of fifteen. But he had intelligently made the most of his opportunities by spending all the time he could in the firm's inner rooms, and had learned something of how new business enterprises were started.

Now, recently returned from a stay in the West because of ill health, Peterkin wished to be a promoter, and he wondered if the Wright brothers would agree to the formation of a flying-machine company. By chance he learned that Wilbur Wright was spending a few days at the Park Avenue Hotel in New York, and in October, 1909, he went to see him.

Wilbur was approachable enough and received Peterkin in a friendly way, though he didn't seem to set too much store by the young man's proposals. In reply to questions, Wilbur said that he and his brother would not care to have a company formed unless those in it were men of consequence. They would want names that carried weight. Then Peterkin spoke of knowing J. P. Morgan, whom he might be able to interest.

Without making any kind of agreement or promise, Wilbur told him he could go ahead and see what he could do—doubtless assuming that he would soon become discouraged. But Peterkin saw J. P. Morgan who told him he would take stock and that he would subscribe also for his friend Judge Elbert H. Gary, head of the United States Steel Corporation.

After seeing Morgan, Peterkin was enthusiastically telling of his project to a distant relative of his, a member of a law firm with offices in the financial district. The senior partner in that law firm, DeLancey Nicoll, chanced to overhear what Peterkin was saying and grew interested. He suggested that perhaps he might be of help. That was a good piece of luck for Peterkin. He could hardly have found a better ally, for DeLancey Nicoll had an exceptionally wide and intimate acquaintance among men in the world of finance. All he needed to do to interest some of his friends was to call them on the telephone.

In a surprisingly short time, an impressive list of moneyed men were enrolled as subscribers in the proposed flying-machine company. A number of them were prominent in the field of transportation. The list included Cornelius Vanderbilt, August Belmont, Howard Gould, Theodore P. Shonts, Allan A. Ryan, Mortimer F. Plant, Andrew Freedman, and E. J. Berwind. Shonts was president of the New York Interborough subway. Ryan, a son of Thomas F. Ryan, was a director of the Bethlehem Steel Corporation. Plant was chairman of the Board of Directors of the Southern Express Company, and Vice President of the Chicago, Indianapolis & Louisville Railroad. Berwind, as President of the Berwind-White Coal Mining Company, had accumulated a great fortune from coal contracts with big steamship lines. Freedman had made his money originally as a sports promoter and then in various financial operations. (He later provided funds for founding the Andrew Freedman Home in New York.)

The Wrights wanted to have in the company their friends Robert J. Collier, publisher of *Collier's Weekly*, and the two Alger brothers of Detroit. Those names were promptly added.

But the names of J. P. Morgan and E. H. Gary were not in the final list of stockholders. The truth was that some of the others in the proposed company did not want Morgan with them because they believed—probably correctly—that he would dominate the company; that where he sat would be the head of the table. One of them phoned to Morgan that the stock was oversubscribed. When he thus got strong hints that his participation was not too eagerly desired, Morgan promptly withdrew his offer to take stock for himself and Gary.

On November 22, 1909, only about a month after Peterkin's first talk with Wilbur, The Wright Co. was incorporated. The capital stock represented a paid-in value of $200,000. In payment for all rights to their patents in the United States, the Wright brothers received stock and cash, besides a provision for ten per cent royalty on all planes sold; and The Wright Co. would thenceforth bear the expense of prosecuting all suits against patent infringers.

From the Wright brothers' point of view, the one fly in the ointment was that they now found themselves more involved than ever before in business affairs. It had been their dream to be entirely out of business and able to give their whole time to scientific research.

The company opened impressive offices in the Night and Day Bank Building, 527 Fifth Avenue, New York, but the factory would be in Dayton. In January, 1910, Frank Russell, a cousin of the Algers, who had been appointed factory manager, arrived in Dayton and went to see the Wrights at their office over the old bicycle shop. As the brothers had no desk space to offer him, they suggested a room at the rear of a plumbing shop down the street where he might make temporary headquarters. According to Russell, Wilbur Wright came there a day or two later carrying a basket filled with letters, directed to The Wright Co., that had been accumulating.

"I don't know what you'll want to do about these," Russell has reported Wilbur as jokingly saying; "maybe

they should be opened. But of course if you open a letter, there's always the danger that you may decide to
answer it, and then you're apt to find yourself involved
in a long correspondence."

At first The Wright Co. rented floor space in a factory building, but almost immediately the company
started to build a modern factory of its own, and it was
ready for use by November, 1910. Within a short time
after the company started operations in its rented space
it had a force of employees at mechanical work and was
able to produce about two airplanes a month.

The Wrights well knew that the time was not yet for
the company to operate profitably by selling planes for
private use. Their main opportunity to show a good return on the capital invested would be from public exhibitions. Relatively few people in the United States had
yet seen an airplane in flight and crowds would flock to
behold this new miracle—still, in 1910, almost incredible.

As soon as they decided to give public exhibitions,
the Wrights got in touch with another pioneer of the
air, Roy Knabenshue, a young man from Toledo, who
had been making balloon flights since his early teens,
and was the first in the United States to have piloted a
steerable balloon. They had previously become acquainted with Knabenshue. Because of his curiosity over
anything pertaining to aerial navigation, he had once
subscribed to a press-clipping bureau which sent him
anything found in the papers about aeronautics; and
in this way he had been able to read an occasional
news item about the two Dayton men said to have
flown. With a fairly irresistible impish grin, Knaben-

shue never had much trouble making new acquaint-
ances, and he decided to call upon the Wrights.

That was before the Wright flights at Fort Myer and
in France, and the brothers were not then interested
when Knabenshue suggested that they sell him planes
for exhibitions.

"Well," he said, "I have been making airship flights
at the big state fairs, besides promoting public exhibitions, and I know how to make the proper contacts. You
may have heard about my flights in a small dirigible at
the St. Louis World's Fair. If you ever decide to give
exhibitions, just let me know."

Though exhibitions had been farthest from the
Wrights' thoughts at the time of that first meeting with
Knabenshue, now the situation was different. Roy Knabenshue would probably be the very man they needed.
They sent a telegram to him and he received it at Los
Angeles. He wired back that he would see them as soon
as he returned to Ohio. This he did soon afterward. The
result of their conversation was that Roy took charge of
the work of arranging for public flights. He had need
of a competent secretary and an intelligent young
woman, Miss Mabel Beck, came to take the job. This
was her first employment and she seemed a bit ill at ease,
lest her work might not be satisfactory; but almost immediately she became an extraordinarily good assistant
—so good, in fact, that Wilbur Wright afterward selected her to work with him in connection with suits
against patent infringers, and after his death she became
secretary to Orville Wright, in which position, at this
writing, she still is.

By the time Knabenshue had started planning for public exhibitions, Orville Wright had begun the training of pilots to handle the exhibition planes being built. The weather was still too wintry for flying at Huffman field, now leased by The Wright Co., and it was necessary to find a suitable place in a warmer climate. The field selected was at Montgomery, Alabama. (Today known as Maxwell Field, it is used by the United States Government.)

Shortly after his arrival at Montgomery, early in 1910, Orville Wright had a new experience in the air. While at an altitude of about 1,500 feet he found himself unable to descend, even though the machine was pointed downward as much as seemed safe. Brought up to have faith in the force of gravity, he didn't know at first what to make of this. For nearly five minutes he stayed there, in a puzzled state of mind bordering on alarm. Later it occurred to him that the machine must have been in a whirlwind of rising air current of unusual diameter, and that doubtless he could have returned quickly to earth if he had first steered horizontally to get away from the rising current.

The first pilot Orville trained was Walter Brookins of Dayton. "Brookie" was a logical candidate for that distinction, for since the age of four he had been a kind of "pet" of Orville's. After Orville had left Montgomery and returned to Dayton on May 8, Brookins himself became an instructor. He began, at Montgomery, the training of Arch Hoxsey, noted for his personal charm and his gay, immaculate clothes; and also that of Spencer C. Crane.

On his return to Dayton, Orville opened a flying school at the same Huffman field [1] the Wright brothers had used for their experiments in 1904-5. Here he trained A. L. Welsh and Duval LaChapelle. When Brookins arrived there from Montgomery, near the end of May, he took on the training of Ralph Johnstone and Frank T. Coffyn, besides completing the training of Hoxsey. Two others trained at the same field later in the year were Phil O. Parmalee and C. O. Turpin.

Orville Wright continued to make frequent flights until 1915, personally testing every new device used on a Wright plane. (He did not make his final flight as a pilot until 1918.) More than one person who witnessed flights at the Huffman field (or at Simms station, as the place was better known) has made comment that it was never difficult to pick Orville Wright from the other flyers, whether he was on the ground or in a plane. Students, and instructors too, would be dressed to the teeth for flying, with special suits, goggles, helmets, gauntlets, and so on; but Orville always wore an ordinary business suit. He might put on a pair of automobile goggles and shift his cap backward, and on cold days he would turn

[1] From Wright Hill, near Dayton, on which there is a memorial monument, one has a view of the great government aviation center of Wright and Patterson fields, the latter of which includes the Huffman tract. The monument bears the legend: "In Commemoration of the Courage, Perseverance and Achievements of Wilbur and Orville Wright. Through Original Research the Wright Brothers Acquired Scientific Knowledge and Developed Theories of Aerodynamics which with their Invention of Aileron Control Enabled Them in 1903 to Build and Fly at Kitty Hawk the First Power-Driven, Man-Carrying Aeroplane Capable of Flight. Their Further Development of the Aeroplane Gave it a Capacity for Service which Established Aviation as one of the Great Forward Steps in Human Progress. As Scientists Wilbur and Orville Wright Discovered the Secret of Flight. As Inventors, Builders and Flyers, they Brought Aviation to the World."

up his coat collar; but otherwise he was dressed as for the street. When he was in the air anyone could recognize who it was—from the smoothness of his flying. And when he wished to test the control and stability of a plane, he would sometimes come down and make figure eights at steep angles with the wing tip maybe not more than a few feet from the grass.

The public was no longer unaware of the significance of the flights at Huffman field. Sightseers began to use every possible pretext to come as close to the planes as possible. One evening as Orville Wright was standing near the hangar, a bystander edged up to him.

"I flew with Orville Wright down at Montgomery," he declared, "and he told me to make myself at home here."

Never before having seen Orville, he had mistaken him for an employee.

Three flights at Huffman field in May, 1910, were especially noteworthy. A short one by Wilbur—one minute twenty-nine seconds—on May 21, was the first he had made alone since his sensational feats starting from Governors Island. And it was the last flight as a pilot Wilbur ever made. But on May 25 he and Orville flew for a short time together—with Orville piloting—the only occasion when the Wright brothers were both in the air at the same time. Later that same day, Orville took his father, Bishop Milton Wright, then eighty-two years old,[1] for his first trip in a flying-machine. They flew for six minutes fifty-five seconds, most of the time

---

[1] Bishop Wright lived to be nearly 89.

TWO ACES AND KING. Orville Wright, Wilbur Wright, and Edward VII of England at Pau, France, March 17, 1909.

THE WRIGHT HOME AND SHOP. The original Wright homestead and Wright bicycle shop, brought from Dayton and restored at Greenfield Village, Dearborn, Michigan.

at about 350 feet. The only thing that Bishop Wright said while in the air was a request to go "higher, higher."

The average charge by The Wright Co. for a series of exhibition flights at a county fair or elsewhere' was about $5,000 for each plane used. At Indianapolis, the scene of the first exhibition, five planes were used. The weather was not ideal for the Indianapolis event, but the crowd was much impressed. Another early exhibition was at Atlantic City, where, for the first time, wheels were publicly used on a Wright machine for starting and landing.

Roy Knabenshue knew from his experience in making public airship exhibitions, that it was not enough to go where a fair or carnival was to be held and suggest airplane flights as a feature. To get all the business possible for his company he must promote exhibition flights in places where no such big outdoor events were yet contemplated. He particularly desired to have flights made in large cities where newspaper reports of the event would attract attention over a large area and aid him in making further bookings. With this in mind he went to Chicago and started inquiries to learn whether public-spirited citizens there would be willing to underwrite a big public demonstration of aviation along the lake front. Several people told him the man he should see was Harold McCormick, one of the controlling stockholders in the wealthy International Harvester Company. He went at once to McCormick's offices in the Harvester Building. But when he reached the outer office, he discovered that it was not easy to get any farther.

"What was it you wished to see Mr. McCormick about?" asked a secretary.

"I don't wish to sell him anything," Roy explained, smiling in a manner that should have won confidence, but didn't. "Please just say to him that there's a man here who has an important suggestion for him."

"But if you'll tell me what the suggestion is," the secretary proposed, "then he can let you know if he is interested."

"No, I'll tell you what you do," countered Roy. "Please hand my card to him and let him decide if he wishes to see me."

The secretary reluctantly took Roy's card which indicated that he represented The Wright Co. of Dayton, Ohio. A moment later the secretary returned to say that Mr. McCormick was too busy to see anyone.

Roy walked out of the building into Michigan Avenue, discouraged.

"No matter how good an idea you've got," he reflected, "and no matter how much some of these big executives might be interested, you don't get a chance to tell them about it."

As he strolled along, his eye chanced to fall on a big sign that read: "Think Of It. The *Record-Herald* Now One Cent." Then he remembered that the Chicago *Record-Herald*, rival of the *Tribune* in the morning field, had recently reduced its price and was making a big bid for increased circulation. He also recalled that H. H. Kohlsaat, owner of the *Record-Herald*, had known his father. Using his father's name for an introduction, he had little difficulty, a half hour later, in gaining access to Kohlsaat's private office to tell him what was on his mind. The publisher grew interested. Yes, it might be a good idea to have some airplane flights along the lake front and invite the public to see them as guests of the *Record-Herald*. Before he left the office, Roy had the preliminary arrangements all made.

On the opening day of the big event, when Walter Brookins, as pilot, was about to take off on the first flight, Knabenshue remarked to him: "That corner window on the fourth floor of the Harvester Building is in the office of a man I hope will see what's going on."

The next day Knabenshue appeared once again at Harold McCormick's office in the Harvester Building and presented his business card to the same secretary he had met on his previous visit.

After looking at the card, the secretary, without waiting to consult anyone, said: "Oh, yes, you're with The Wright Company. I'm sure Mr. McCormick will wish to see you. Just step this way."

Roy had made this call partly as a kind of practical joke—for the satisfaction of entering an office where he had once been denied. But as a result of the talk he then had with McCormick, it was arranged that a committee of Chicago citizens should sponsor, the next year, another aviation meeting there, to be the biggest thing of the kind ever held.

Meanwhile, on the final day of the 1910 exhibitions at Chicago, Brookins made the first long cross-country flight, 185 miles, to Springfield, Illinois. It was not, however, a non-stop flight. He made one landing in a cornfield, and it was necessary to obtain permission from the farm owner to cut a wide strip across the field to provide space for the plane to take off.

In that same year, 1910, Dayton people saw the first flight over the city itself. Thousands had now seen flights at the Huffman field, Simms station, but no flight had ever been made nearer than eight miles to the home town where successful flying was conceived. The Greater Dayton Association was holding, in September, an industrial exhibit, but it was operating at a loss. Those in charge of the exhibit saw that something would have to be done to arouse interest. Orville Wright was asked if he would start at Simms station, fly to Dayton and circle over the city. He agreed and the newspapers announced the flight for the next day. It was stirring news —even to Katharine Wright. She had started to Oberlin to attend a college meeting, but, when on her arrival there she happened to see a newspaper item about Orville's flight scheduled for the next day, she hastened home at once.

Another premier event in 1910 was when an airplane for the first time in the world was used for commercial express service. The Morehouse-Martin Co., a department store in Columbus, Ohio, arranged to have a bolt of silk brought from Huffman field to a driving park beyond Columbus. The distance of more than sixty miles was covered at better than a mile a minute, then considered fast airplane speed; and the "express fee" was $5,000, or about $71.42 a pound. But within a day or two the store had a good profit on the transaction, for it sold small pieces of the silk for souvenirs, and the gross returns were more than $6,000.

Then, at Belmont Park, New York, in late October, 1910, Wright planes participated in a great International Aviation Tournament. All other planes taking part were licensed by The Wright Co.

Orville Wright now devoted his time mainly to supervision of engineering at the factory of The Wright Co. Wilbur was kept busy looking after the prosecution of suits against patent infringers and in March, 1911, he went to Europe in connection with suits brought by the Wright company of France. From France he went to Germany and while there called at the home of the widow of Otto Lilienthal to offer his homage to the memory of that pioneer in aviation whose work had been an inspiration to the Wrights.

After Wilbur's return to America, Orville spent several weeks in October, 1911, at Kitty Hawk, where he went to do some experimenting with an automatic control device and to make soaring flights with a glider. In camp with him were Alec Ogilvie of England, who flew a Wright plane, Orville's brother Lorin, and Lorin's ten-year-old boy, "Buster." On account of the presence of a group of newspapermen who appeared and were at the camp each day during his entire stay at Kitty Hawk, Orville never tested the new automatic device; but before his soaring experiments were over he had made, on October 24, a new record, soaring for nine minutes forty-five seconds. (This was to remain the world's record until ten years later when it was exceeded in Germany.)

That same year, 1911, The Wright Co. benefited from another aviation record. Cal P. Rodgers, who had received some of his flying training at the Wright School, made—between September 11 and November 5 —the first transcontinental airplane trip, from New York to California.

New as their line of business was, The Wright Co. was profitable from the start—especially so during the first year or two when the sight of a flying-machine was still a novelty and contracts for exhibition flights were numerous. (It might have been more profitable if the Wrights had not insisted that no contracts be made to include flights on Sunday.) But inevitably the exhibition part of the business began to taper off—and such profits as might still have come from it were reduced by the persistent illegal competition of patent infringers. More and more, the company's dealings were with the United States Army and Navy and with private buyers of planes. The first private plane sold had gone to Robert J. Collier, and others seeking the excitement or prestige of owning a plane had been making inquiries. The retail price of a plane was $5,000.

With aviation thus becoming more practical, the Wrights were receiving from their invention a form of reward they had never expected. They would now have wealth, not vast, but enough to enable them to look forward to the time when they might retire and work happily together on scientific research. They were making plans, too, for their new home on a seventeen-acre wooded tract they had named Hawthorn Hill, in the Dayton suburb of Oakwood. But tragic days were ahead. Early in May, shortly after visiting the new home site with other members of the family, Wilbur was taken ill. What at first was assumed to be a minor indisposition proved to be typhoid fever. Worn out from worries over protecting in patent litigation the rights he knew were his and his brother's, he was not in condition to combat the disease. After an illness of three weeks, despite the best efforts of eminent specialists, early in the morning of Thursday, May 30, 1912, Wilbur Wright died. He was aged only forty-five years and forty-four days.

Messages of condolence and expressions of the world's loss poured in from two hemispheres, among them those from heads of governments.

Orville Wright succeeded his brother as president of The Wright Co.

In June, 1913, Grover Loening, a young man who had become acquainted with Wilbur at the time of the Hudson-Fulton exhibition flights, came to The Wright Co. as engineer, and then became factory manager. Loening had the distinction of being the first person in the United States to study aeronautical science in a university.

Business affairs had been complicated earlier that year by the fact that Dayton had the worst flood in its history. The Wright factory was not under water but not many of the employees could reach the building. Among the hundreds of houses under water was the Wright home on Hawthorne Street. To Orville a serious part of the loss there was the damage to photographic negatives showing his and Wilbur's progress toward flight. But the negative of the famous picture of the first power flight was not much harmed.

Accompanied by his sister, Orville made his last trip to Europe in 1913, on business relating to a patent suit in Germany. At about the same time he sanctioned the forming of a Wright company in England. Before Wilbur's death, there had been opportunities for a company in England, but the brothers had held back because all the offers appeared to be purely stock promotions in which the names of members of the English nobility would appear as sponsors. The British company as finally organized did not make planes itself, but issued licenses for use of the patents. Within a year after it was formed the English company accepted from the British Government a flat payment for all claims against the government, for use of the Wright patents up to that time and during the remainder of the life of the basic patents. Though the amount paid was no trifling sum, the settlement was widely applauded by prominent Englishmen, among them Lord Northcliffe, as showing a generous attitude on the part of the patent owner—about as little as could have been compatible with full recognition of the priority of the Wrights' invention.

By this time, The Wright Co. had more applications to train student pilots than they could handle. Even a few young women wished to become pilots.

Two capable students, of a somewhat earlier period, destined to go far in aviation, were Thomas D. Milling, later General Milling, of the United States Army Air Corps; and Henry H. Arnold, who during the Second World War was Lieutenant General Arnold, Com-

manding General of the Army Air Forces and Deputy
Chief of Staff for Air.

One unfortunate student pilot, who had begun his
training at the Wright School in 1912, later got himself
into much trouble. This man became one of the best
flyers in the United States. As he had plenty of money
he bought a plane of his own, and he used to give free
exhibitions at his estate near Philadelphia. In one way
or another he did much for aviation. But in 1917, when
the United States entered the First World War, that
young pilot refused to register in the draft and became
notorious as a draft evader. His name? Grover Cleveland Bergdoll. The early Wright plane he had bought
is today on exhibition at the Franklin Institute in Philadelphia. It is believed to be the only authentic Model B
—the first model built by The Wright Co.—in existence.

In 1914, Orville Wright had bought the stock of all
other shareholders in The Wright Co., except that of
his friend, Robert J. Collier, who, for sentimental reason, wished to retain his interest. Orville's motive in acquiring almost complete ownership of the company had
been as a step toward getting entirely out of business.
Both he and Wilbur Wright had agreed to stay with
the company for a period of years, not yet expired, and
he could not honorably dispose of his own holdings so
long as those with whom he had made the agreement
were still in the company. But almost immediately after
buying the shares of the others, he let it be known that
he might be willing to sell his entire interest. To this,
Collier, the only other shareholder, agreed. In 1915,
Orville received an offer and gave an option to a small

group of eastern capitalists that included William Boyce Thompson and Frank Manville, the latter president of the Johns-Manville Co. The deal was closed in October, 1915.

Just after Orville had given his option to the eastern syndicate, Robert J. Collier came to tell him an important piece of news, and to urge him not to sell just yet.

Collier had been having some talks with his friend, the wealthy Harry Payne Whitney, and had urged upon him the idea of doing what Collier thought would be a wonderful piece of philanthropy that would mean much for the future of aviation in the United States. What Collier wanted him to do was to buy the stock of The Wright Co., thus gaining ownership of the Wright patents, and then immediately make the patents free to anyone in the United States who wished to manufacture airplanes.

Whitney was willing to carry out the Collier suggestion. To do so he was also ready to pay more for the stock of The Wright Co. than the syndicate had offered.

But Orville explained to Collier that the option already given was legally drawn and the holders presumably wished to exercise it.

Collier's daring idea and Whitney's generous acceptance of it had come just a little too late.

XVIII

PATENT SUITS

THE Wrights had found that patents covering the basic features of their invention were not enough protection against infringers. Indeed, having the technical details on file in the Patent Office, where anyone who desired might see them, was, in a way, to the advantage of those who would help themselves to an inventor's work and ideas. Only a decision in the courts could determine the justice of an inventor's claims. But the courts work slowly and legal procedure is expensive. Except for their good fortune—never contemplated when they started—in realizing substantial sums from their invention, the brothers might not have been financially able to carry on the fight that finally gave them world-wide recognition as the first to contrive a successful flying-machine.

Altogether the brothers had active part in a dozen different suits in the United States against infringers—and there were suits in France and Germany in each of which about a dozen infringers were involved. Most of the suits in the United States did not go beyond the early stages, as the infringers were not disposed to continue after a preliminary injunction had been issued. But three suits were of special importance. One of these was against Louis Paulhan, French aviator, who was about to give exhibitions in the United States, using planes made in France. Another was against Claude Grahame-White, English aviator, also about to give exhibitions in the United States with planes that infringed the Wright patents. The most important suit of all was against the Herring-Curtiss Co. and Glenn H. Curtiss. This case was bitterly contested and was carried up to the U. S. Court of Appeals. It was brought by the Wright brothers, late in 1909, but The Wright Co., formed shortly afterward, succeeded the brothers as complainants.

Because of the importance of this suit in aviation history, it is worth while to examine the background of the relations between the Wrights and Glenn Curtiss. The Wrights' personal acquaintance with Curtiss began in May, 1906, when he wrote to them in regard to the light motors of which he was a manufacturer. Then in early September, 1906, Curtiss visited the Wright office and workshop. He was brought there by his friend, Captain Thomas S. Baldwin, a well-known aeronaut, who was giving exhibition flights in Dayton with his dirigible balloon on which he used a motor he had persuaded Curtiss to build for him. It was to make repairs on that motor that Curtiss had come to Dayton.

After that meeting, the four men, Curtiss, Baldwin, and the Wrights, were together much of the time for several days. When in response to questions about their work, the Wrights showed a number of photographs of their flights made at the Huffman pasture during the two previous years, Curtiss seemed much astonished. He remarked that it was the first time he had been able

to believe anyone had actually been in the air with a
flying-machine.

Long afterward, in an interview in the New York
Times (February 28, 1914), Baldwin recalled the many
talks he and Glenn Curtiss had with the Wrights in that
fall of 1906. "I sometimes suggested to Curtiss," Baldwin told the interviewer, "that he was asking too many
questions, but he kept right on. The Wrights had the
frankness of schoolboys in it all and had a rare confidence in us. I am sure Curtiss at that time never thought
of taking up flying."

A year after the Wrights' first meetings with Curtiss,
in October, 1907, the Aerial Experiment Association
was formed by Alexander Graham Bell and others, with
headquarters first in Nova Scotia and later at Hammondsport, N. Y., where Curtiss lived. He became "Director of Experiments." This was the first time Curtiss
had been directly connected with aviation except as a
manufacturer of motors, and three months later, a letter
he wrote to the Wrights indicated that motors rather
than aviation were still his chief interest. "I just wish to
keep in touch with you," he wrote, "and let you know
that we have been making considerable progress in
engine construction." After listing and describing the
various engines he was building, he proposed to furnish
to the Wrights "gratis" one of his fifty-horsepower
engines. But the offer was not accepted. The letter mentioned that Captain Baldwin was a "permanent fixture
in this establishment"—a fact not without importance,
considering information that Baldwin was later to reveal.
Further on in the letter, Curtiss told of Dr. Bell's reading

to the members of the Aerial Experiment Association the United States Government's specifications for the purchase of a flying-machine, and added: "You, of course, are the only persons who could come anywhere near doing what is required."

About a fortnight after receipt of that letter from Curtiss, the Wrights got another letter dated January 15, 1908, written on Aerial Experiment Association stationery, and signed by Lieutenant T. Selfridge, whose name appeared on the letterhead as secretary of the association. (This was the same Selfridge who was killed a few months later in the tragic airplane accident at Fort Myer.) In that letter, Selfridge, on behalf of the Experiment Association, said:

I am taking the liberty of writing you and asking your advice on certain points connected with gliding experiments, or rather glider construction, which we started here last Monday.

Will you kindly tell me what results you obtained on the travel of the center of pressure both on aerocurves and aeroplanes?

Also, what is a good, efficient method of constructing the ribs of the surfaces so that they will be light and yet strong enough to maintain their curvature under ordinary conditions, and a good means of fastening them to the cloth and upper lateral cords of the frame?

I hope I am not imposing too much by asking you these questions.

Supposing the information would be used only for scientific purposes, the Wrights obligingly replied at once as follows:

You will find much of the information you desire in the addresses of our Mr. Wilbur Wright before the Western Society of Engineers, published in the Journals of the Society of December, 1901, and August, 1903.

The travel of the center of pressure on aeroplanes is from the center at 90 degrees, toward the front edge as the angle becomes smaller. The center of pressure on a curved surface is approximately at its center at 90 degrees, moves forward as the angle is decreased until a critical angle is reached, after which it reverses, and moves toward the rear edge. The critical angle varies for different shaped curves, but is generally reached at some angle between 12 and 18 degrees. With the angles used in gliding flight the travel will be between the center of the surface and a point one-third back from the front edge.

The methods of construction used in our gliders are fully described in an article by Mr. Chanute in the *Revue des Sciences* in 1903 (we do not remember the month) and in the specifications of our United States patent, No. 821,393.

The ribs of our gliders were made of second growth ash, steamed and bent to shape.

Selfridge replied in a few days saying he had been able to obtain a copy of the patent and would endeavor to get the other references the Wrights had supplied.

The data must have been useful to the Aerial Experiment Association for early the following summer, Glenn Curtiss, "Director of Experiments" had a power-driven airplane, called the "June Bug," in which he made a flight on July 4, 1908, at Hammondsport. That flight created the belief in the minds of many who were not fully informed that the Aerial Experiment Association must have done an amazing job of original research. This belief was encouraged by the fact that after the Aerial

Experiment Association began building and experimenting with flying-machines, using much information they had obtained from the Wrights, they neglected, in public statements about their work, to so much as mention the Wright brothers.

Soon after the report of the flight of the "June Bug," there appeared in the press a statement that the Aerial Experiment Association was disbanding, and that Glenn H. Curtiss was going to engage in exhibition flying. That news led Orville Wright to send to Curtiss the following letter:

I learn from the *Scientific American* that your "June Bug" has movable surfaces at the tips of the wings, adjustable to different angles on the right and left sides for maintaining the lateral balance. In our letter to Lieutenant Selfridge of January 18th, replying to his of the 15th, in which he asked for information on the construction of flyers, we referred him to several publications containing descriptions of the structural features of our machines, and to our U. S. patent No. 821,393. We did not intend, of course, to give permission to use the patented features of our machine for exhibitions or in a commercial way.

This patent broadly covers the combination of sustaining surfaces to the right and left of the center of a flying-machine adjustable to different angles, with vertical surfaces adjustable to correct inequalities in the horizontal resistances of the differently adjusted wings. Claim 14 of our patent No. 821,393 specifically covers the combination which we are informed you are using. We believe it will be very difficult to develop a successful machine without the use of some of the features covered in this patent.

The commercial part of our business is taking so much

of our time that we have not been able to undertake public exhibitions. If it is your desire to enter the exhibition business, we would be glad to take up the matter of a license to operate under our patents for that purpose.

Curtiss replied that, contrary to newspaper reports, he did not expect to do anything in the way of exhibitions; that his flights had been in connection with the Aerial Experiment Association's work. The matter of the patents he had referred, he said, to the Secretary of the Association.

A few weeks later, when Orville went to Washington in preparation for the Fort Myer tests of the Wright machine, Captain Baldwin was there teaching Army officers to operate a new dirigible balloon for which Curtiss had furnished the motor. In speaking of the experiments in aviation being carried on by Curtiss and other members of the Aerial Experiment Association at Hammondsport, Baldwin said warningly to Orville: "I hear them talking." He went on to caution Orville that the work those men were doing would infringe the Wright patents.

By the following year, Curtiss had formed a commercial company, The Herring-Curtiss Co., to make or exhibit airplanes.

On January 3, 1910, Judge John R. Hazel, of the Federal Circuit Court, at Buffalo, New York, granted a temporary restraining order against The Herring-Curtiss Co. and Glenn H. Curtiss to prevent them from infringement of the Wright patents. In handing down his decision, Judge Hazel said:

It appears that the defendant Curtiss had notice of the success of the Wright machine, and that a patent had been issued in 1906. Indeed, no one interfered with the rights of the patentees by constructing machines similar to theirs until in July, 1908, when Curtiss exhibited a flying-machine which he called "The June Bug." He was immediately notified by the patentees that such machine, with its movable surfaces at the tips, or wings, infringed the patent in suit, and he replied that he did not intend to publicly exhibit the machine for profit, but merely was engaged in exhibiting it for scientific purposes as a member of the Aerial Experiment Association. To this the patentees did not object. Subsequently, however, the machine, with supplementary planes placed midway between the upper and lower aeroplanes, was publicly exhibited by the defendant corporation, and used by Curtiss in aerial flights for prizes and emoluments. It further appears that the defendants now threaten to continue such use for gain and profit, and to engage in the manufacture and sale of such infringing machine, thereby becoming an active rival of complainant in the business of constructing flying-machines embodying the claims in suit, but such use of the infringing machine it is the duty of this Court on the papers presented to enjoin.

Then, in February, 1910, Judge Learned Hand, in the Federal Circuit Court, at New York, issued an injunction to prevent the French aviator, Louis Paulhan, from making exhibitions in the United States unless he would put up an indemnity to the amount of $25,000. The Court declared that both the Bleriot and Farman planes that the defendant was planning to use were infringements of the Wright patents.

Not until January 13, 1914, did the U. S. Circuit Court of Appeals hand down its decision in the Wright suit against Curtiss. The decision was in favor of The Wright Co.

In his interview in the New York *Times,* already quoted from, published in the New York *Times,* February 28, 1914, Captain Thomas S. Baldwin, though a close associate of Curtiss, heartily endorsed the final decision in the Wright *vs.* Curtiss case. Referring to that decision he told the interviewer:

"It is high time for all the rest of us to step up and admit that not a one of us ever would have got off the ground in flight if the Wrights had not unlocked the secret for us.

"I want to go on record as saying that the Wrights are fully entitled to the decision they have at last received. . . .

"Mr. Curtiss is a friend of mine today," said Baldwin, "and I have served in his companies as a director. But it is due to the Wrights as a simple matter of justice to have the story of the actual genesis of flight fully established."

By that time, Captain Baldwin had abandoned the dirigible balloon for the airplane, and thus he, too, had been an infringer of the Wright patent. But as his public statements indicated, he showed an attitude quite different from that of most other infringers. Glenn Martin was another, like Baldwin, who acknowledged indebtedness to the Wrights.

After the Wrights had won their important suit against Curtiss in the Circuit Court of Appeals, Curtiss made no secret of the fact that he still hoped to find a possible loophole to get around the Wright patent. Since the decision of the Court enjoined him from using two ailerons operating simultaneously in opposite directions, he thought perhaps he could escape penalty by using just one aileron at a time, while the other remained in-operative. This, however, was covered by Claim 1 of the Wright patent, if the claim were given a liberal in-terpretation, as the Court had said the Wright Patent was entitled to, on account of the Wrights being the pioneers in the art of flying. But Claim 1 had not been cited in the former suits, and so had not as yet been adjudicated. If Curtiss could just show, or seem to show, in some way that the Wrights were not exactly pioneers, that some other machine capable of flight antedated the Wright machine, then he would be in a stronger posi-tion to defend himself against Claim 1 if it should be cited against him. Anticipating a suit, Curtiss took astounding means to prepare for combating it—as will appear.

But after all the evidence was taken in that case and just before the case was to come to trial, Orville Wright sold his interest in The Wright Co. to New York capi-talists. Curtiss then contrived to gain delay after delay by approaching the new owners with proposals of settle-ment. These negotiations dragged on until the United States entered the First World War, and the Manu-facturers Aircraft Association was organized for cross-licensing manufacturers who were building machines for the United States Government. Through this cross-licensing agreement, The Wright Co. received royalty on all planes manufactured for the Government. Conse-quently, this last case against Curtiss never came to trial.

The Wrights won their patent suits, too, in the highest courts of both Germany and France. The court in Germany made the comment in its oral decision that their discovery that a rear rudder was a balancing device rather than a steering device should entitle them to a basic patent.

Without going into too much detail about the various patent suits, the important point is that the priority of the Wright patents was sustained by the courts in both the United States and Europe. Every airplane that flies, in any part of the world, even today, does so by use of devices and discoveries first made by the Wright brothers.

These patent suits were a terrible ordeal for the attorneys and judges concerned, for aviation was so new that many of the technical terms were beyond the knowledge of nearly everyone. It was as if lawyers and judges had to learn a new language and take a course in the theoretical side of aeronautical engineering as they went along.

In a case against a foreign aviator, Wilbur Wright was called upon in Court to explain the function and operation of a rudder when an aeroplane is making a circle. Wilbur got hold of a piece of string and a fragment of chalk and went to a blackboard, where he made it clear to the Judge that when a machine is making a turn the pressure is on the opposite side of an aeroplane rudder from what it is on a ship's or a dirigible's rudder when they are making the same turn.

After the Judge had issued a temporary restraining order, at the end of the day's proceedings, Clarence J.

Shearn, attorney for the defendant, gloomily remarked: "If it hadn't been for Wright and that damned piece of string, we would have won."

One bit of testimony in another case was in regard to the accuracy of observations of men who fly airplanes. To show the inaccuracy of most people's observations on phenomena having to do with physical laws, Wilbur used for illustration what a man thinks happens when riding a bicycle.

"I have asked dozens of bicycle riders," said Wilbur, "how they turn a bicycle to the left. I have never found a single person who stated all the facts correctly when first asked. They almost invariably said that, to turn to the left, they turned the handlebar to the left and as a result made a turn to the left. But on further questioning them, some would agree that they first turned the handlebar a little to the right, and then as the machine became inclined to the left, they turned the handlebar to the left and made the circle, inclining inwardly. To a scientific student it is very clear that without the preliminary movement of the handlebar to the right, a movement of the handlebar to the left would cause the bicycle to run out from under the man, who would continue headlong in his original direction. Yet I have found many people who would deny having ever noticed the preliminary movement of the handlebar to the right. I have never found a non-scientific bicycle rider who had particularly noticed it and spoke of it from his own conscious observation and initiative. I found the same condition among aviators with whom I have flown. Some have almost no consciousness of whether the machine is rising a little or descending a little, or whether it is sliding somewhat to the right or to the left. The ability to notice these things, even in small degrees, is the main quality which distinguishes skilled aviators from novices and born flyers from men who will never be able to handle flying-machines competently."

Even though the Wrights won all their patent suits, collecting royalties proved to be something else!

XIX

WHY THE WRIGHT PLANE WAS EXILED

WHY was the original Wright airplane, the first flying-machine in the world capable of flight, deposited in the Science Museum at South Kensington, London, England, rather than in the United States National Museum, administered by the Smithsonian Institution, at Washington? Why should Exhibit A of one of the greatest of all American scientific achievements be in exile?

For the answer to these questions, puzzling to a vast number of patriotic Americans, we must trace events back a number of years.

It will be remembered that Dr. Samuel P. Langley, while Director and Secretary of the Smithsonian, with a $50,000 government fund at his disposal for experiments (besides $20,000 from the Hodgkins fund), had failed in his attempts to build a successful man-carrying flying-machine. At each trial, in 1903, his machine promptly fell from its launching platform into the Potomac. Doubtless Langley's failure was a bitter disappointment to him—all the more so because he was derided in the public press for having even tried what was commonly believed to be impossible. But when the Wrights flew, only nine days after Langley's final unsuccessful trial, they in a measure saved the Langley reputation. No one could any longer say that he was a "crank." The Wrights had vindicated his belief that man could fly.

Langley uttered no word to minimize the importance of the Wrights' feat. Nor was anything unfriendly toward Langley ever said by either of the Wrights. On the contrary, the Wrights more than once gave Langley credit for having been a source of inspiration to them, from the simple fact that he, an eminent scientist, considered human flight possible. Indeed, the Wrights took advantage of an opportunity to save the Langley name from being made ridiculous. After Dr. Langley's death, the Smithsonian Regents ordered the erection in the Smithsonian building of a tablet in his memory. The plan was to inscribe on the tablet the "Langley Law," as Langley's chief contribution to aeronautical science. Dr. Charles D. Walcott, who succeeded Dr. Langley as Secretary of the Smithsonian, sent the proposed inscription to the Wrights for their opinion of it. Wilbur Wright replied that it would be both unwise and unfair to Langley to rest his reputation in aerodynamics especially on that so-called Langley Law or upon the computations which gave rise to it. The Wrights knew at that time, as all aeronautical engineers know today, that the Langley Law was simply a mistake and not true. Because of what Wilbur Wright pointed out in his letter, the Langley Law was omitted from the memorial tablet. But, having eliminated the discredited Law that *was* Langley's, Dr. Walcott then put in its place on the tablet an inscription crediting Langley for a discovery that *was not* his! The inscription claimed for Langley that he had "discovered the relations of speed and angle of inclination to the lifting power of surfaces moving in the air." (His tables of air pressures had been antedated by both Duchemin and Lilienthal.)

This tendency to claim for Langley what was not his was destined to show itself in a more pernicious form in later acts of Dr. Walcott. If Langley had lived, the relations between the Smithsonian and the Wrights would doubtless have continued to be marked by mutual respect and consideration. But after Dr. Langley's death, the attitude of the Smithsonian began to change. The Institution started a subtle campaign to belittle the Wrights, to try to take from them much of the credit for having both produced and demonstrated the first machine capable of flight, and for having done the original research that made the machine possible. Indeed, the Institution even went so far as to issue false and misleading statements.

One of these was in connection with the first award of a Langley medal, publicly presented to the Wrights in February, 1910. In referring to that presentation, the Annual Report for the year 1910 (page 23), by the Secretary of the Institution, quoted Wilbur Wright as making a statement not made by him on that occasion at all, but used in a different connection at another time. The improper use of that quotation helped to create a false impression over the world that the Wrights had acknowledged indebtedness to Langley's scientific work. The truth was that Wilbur Wright had in a private letter mentioned indebtedness to Langley, not for scientific data but for the fact that it was encouraging to know that the head of a scientific institution believed human flight to be possible. (Langley's published work in the field of aerodynamics dealt with measurements of air pressures on flat surfaces only—and later experiments proved even that to be incorrect.)

The Smithsonian has more than once mentioned the award of the Langley medal to the Wrights as a proof of the Institution's disposition to honor them. But the truth is that the Langley medal was established to honor Langley, not the Wrights. Neither in the award nor in the presentation of the medal to the Wright Brothers was there any suggestion that the Wrights were the first to fly.

In 1910, Dr. Walcott made it evident that the Institution actually did not want the original Wright plane of 1903 as an exhibit. This could be seen in letters he sent to Wilbur Wright in the spring of 1910. The first of these, dated March 7, said: [1]

The National Museum is endeavoring to enlarge its collections illustrating the progress of aviation and, in this connection, it has been suggested that you might be willing to deposit one of your machines, or a model thereof, for exhibition purposes.

The great public interest manifested in this science and the numerous inquiries from visitors for the Wright machine make it manifest that if one were placed on exhibition here it would form *one of the most interesting* specimens in the national collections. It is sincerely hoped that you may find it possible to accede to this request.

[1] The italics in all letters quoted in this chapter are supplied.

Wilbur Wright replied as follows:

My Dear Dr. Walcott: . . . If you will inform us just what your preference would be in the matter of a flier for the National Museum we will see what would be possible in the way of meeting your wishes. At present nothing is in condition for such use. But there are three possibilities. We might construct a small model showing the general construction of the aeroplane, but with a dummy power plant. Or we can reconstruct the 1903 machine with which the first flights were made at Kitty Hawk. Most of the parts are still in existence. This machine would occupy a space 40 feet by 20 feet by 8 feet. Or a model showing the general design of the latter machine could be constructed.

The peculiar attitude of the Smithsonian then began to appear. In his next letter to Wilbur Wright, dated April 11, 1910, Dr. Walcott wrote:

. . . The matter of the representation of the Wright airplane has been very carefully considered by Mr. George C. Maynard, who has charge of the Division of Technology in the National Museum. I told him to indicate what he would like for the exhibit, in order that the matter might be placed clearly before you and your brother. In his report he says:

"The following objects illustrating the Wright inventions would make a very valuable addition to the aeronautical exhibits in the Museum:

"1. A quarter-size model of the aeroplane used by Orville Wright at Fort Myer, Virginia, in September, 1908. Such a model equipped with a dummy power plant, as suggested by the Wrights, would be quite suitable.

"2. If there are any radical differences between the machine referred to and the one used at Kitty Hawk, a second model of the latter machine would be very appropriate.

"3. A full-sized Wright aeroplane. Inasmuch as the machine used at Fort Myer [1] has attracted such world-wide interest, that machine, if it can be repaired or reconstructed, would seem most suitable. If, however, the Wright brothers think the Kitty Hawk machine would answer the purpose better, their judgment *might* decide the question.

"4. If the Wright brothers have an engine of an early type used by them which could be placed in a floor case for close inspection that will be desirable."

The engine of the Langley Aerodrome is now on exhibition in a glass case and the original full-size machine is soon to be hung in one of the large halls. The three Langley quarter-size models are on exhibition. The natural plan would be to install the different Wright machines along with the Langley machines, making the exhibit illustrate two very important steps in the history of the aeronautical art.

The request of Mr. Maynard is rather a large one, but we will have to leave it to your discretion as to what you think it is practicable for you to do.

Sincerely yours,
CHARLES D. WALCOTT,
Secretary.

If Dr. Walcott's suggestions, that the Wrights provide a reproduction in model size of their 1908 plane and the 1908 plane itself, had been accepted, then the proposed exhibits in the National Museum of models and full-size machines by Langley and the Wrights could easily have been of a nature to give a wrong impression. Surely a good many uninformed visitors to the museum would hardly have known, or stopped to

---

[1] A still later plane, the one sold by the Wrights to the United States Government in 1909, was afterward given to the Smithsonian by the War Department, and it was placed on exhibition. It was wrongly labeled as the 1908 plane.

think, that it is one thing to build and fly a small model plane, but an altogether different problem to build and fly a plane, of the same design, large enough to carry a man. Small models of flying-machines were flown by the Frenchman, Pénaud, as early as 1871. But a larger machine of the same design could not be flown—as the Wrights themselves in early boyhood had found out. Likewise, the fact that Langley flew a steam-driven model in 1896, and a gas-driven model in 1903, would not indicate to anyone who understands such matters that a full-size machine of the same design as either of the models could support itself in the air. Langley's own experiments had proved how great is the gap between success with a model and with a larger machine. His full-size machine of 1903, of the same design as the model flown earlier that year, collapsed the moment it was launched. But suppose an uninformed visitor noticed, side by side, a Langley model plane of 1903, and a reproduction in model size of the Wright machine flown with a pilot in 1908. If he hadn't read the labels carefully, or if the labels didn't go into enough detail to make the facts clear, couldn't he easily have received the false impression that Langley had been at least five years ahead of the Wrights? And if the visitor didn't know that the Langley full-size machine of 1903 never flew, wouldn't the sight of it, alongside the Wright machine flown in 1908, have seemed to confirm the wrong impression? Perhaps, however, that was the impression Dr. Walcott wanted museum visitors to receive!

The Walcott letter said, it may be noted, that if there were "any radical differences" between the first Wright machine and the one flown in 1908, then a "model" of the first machine might be appropriate. But since there were no radical differences between the 1903 and 1908 machines, not even a small-sized model of the first machine ever to be flown was being asked for. The Wrights took the letter to mean that the Smithsonian did not want an exhibit that would emphasize the fact of their having flown a successful, man-carrying machine as early as 1903. They thought it was significant that the letter did not say that the Wrights' own opinion would decide which machine was more suitable, but only that their judgment "might" decide the question. Because of their strong belief that the Smithsonian was showing a prejudiced attitude, they made no reply to the Walcott letter.

There was no further correspondence on this subject between the Smithsonian and the Wrights until six years later. In 1916, the original Wright plane was exhibited at the dedication of the new buildings of the Massachusetts Institute of Technology. Dr. Alexander Graham Bell, a Regent of the Smithsonian Institution, saw the plane and expressed astonishment. It was the first he knew that it was still in existence. Shortly afterward, in a conversation with Orville Wright, he asked why the plane was not being exhibited by the Smithsonian.

"Because," replied Orville, "the Smithsonian does not want it."

"Indeed the Smithsonian does want it!" exclaimed Dr. Bell. He was sincere in thinking so and requested Dr. Walcott to get in touch with Orville Wright.

Walcott on December 23, 1916, wrote what Orville

considered a perfunctory letter saying: ". . . the importance of securing for the National Museum the Wright aeroplane which was exhibited at the opening of the new buildings of the Massachusetts Institute of Technology *has been suggested to me*."

Orville Wright replied that he would be glad to take up the question with Dr. Walcott in a personal interview. A few days later the two met in Washington, but it was soon evident to Orville that Dr. Walcott's attitude had not changed; that he did not want that original Wright machine which had flown exhibited beside the Langley machine which had failed to fly.

When Orville found that Walcott's attitude had not changed in the six years since the former correspondence, he gave the question no further consideration.

Meanwhile, in 1914, after the Federal courts had upheld the Wright patents in the suits against Glenn H. Curtiss and others, and recognized the Wrights as "pioneers" in the practical art of flying with heavier-than-air machines, an astounding thing happened.

A few days after the final court decision had been delivered, Lincoln Beachey, a Curtiss stockholder, telegraphed to Secretary Walcott, of the Smithsonian, asking permission to attempt a flight with the original Langley machine. That proposal was not accepted; but two months later, when Glenn H. Curtiss himself said he would like to test the Langley machine, his request was granted. The Smithsonian entered into a deal with Curtiss in which he was to receive a payment of $2,000, and was permitted to take the original Langley plane from the Smithsonian to his shop at Hammondsport, New

York. There he made numerous vital changes in the machine, using knowledge of aerodynamics discovered by the Wrights but never possessed by Langley. No information is available to indicate that the Smithsonian offered any objection to these alterations being made. The Smithsonian's official observer, in connection with the tests of the machine, was Dr. A. F. Zahm, who had been technical expert for Curtiss in the recent lawsuits and was to serve again in that capacity in another suit soon to follow. No one officially representing any disinterested scientific body was present during the time the changes in the machine were made nor during the time it was tested.

It seems highly improbable that Dr. Walcott could have been so unintelligent or so uninformed as not to know about the recent decision of the U. S. Court of Appeals against Curtiss; and equally improbable that he could have been unaware of Zahm's relations with Curtiss as expert witness and adviser. One may well wonder, too, if Dr. Walcott could have failed to understand why Curtiss had recently become interested in testing the Langley plane. In hundreds of pages of direct testimony in the lawsuits, neither Curtiss nor Zahm had mentioned Langley's name, though they had more than once referred to Chanute, Maxim, Henson, Marriott, Boulton, Pilcher, Harte, and other pioneers. One may further wonder if Walcott could have been unaware when, in 1913, the Smithsonian awarded the Langley medal to Curtiss, that he had already been pronounced an infringer of the Wright patents by a Federal court, and that another decision in a higher court was pending. It almost looked as if there might have been an intent to try to influence that decision.

Curtiss had a strong motive for wanting to make it appear that the Langley plane could have flown. The United States Court of Appeals had held that the Wrights were pioneers in the field of heavier-than-air flying-machines, and that therefore their patent claims were entitled to a "liberal interpretation." If Curtiss could demonstrate, or seem to demonstrate, that a machine capable of flight had been built before the Wright machine, then he could weaken their claims, to his financial advantage, in a patent suit he expected to have to defend. In consequence of the important changes that were made, Curtiss finally was able to make several short hops, of less than five seconds, with the reconstructed machine, in May and June, 1914, over Lake Keuka, at Hammondsport, N. Y. Then the Smithsonian, in its annual report of the U. S. National Museum for that year, falsely stated that the original Langley plane had been flown "without modification"! And the annual report of the Smithsonian Institution for 1914, with equally glaring falsity, said: "It [the Langley machine] has demonstrated that *with its original structure and power*, it is capable of flying with a pilot and *several hundred pounds of useful load*. It is the *first aeroplane* in the history of the world of which this can truthfully be said"! (Italics supplied.)

The Institution's annual report for 1915 continued to repeat such untruths. "The tests thus far made have shown that former Secretary Langley had succeeded in building the first aeroplane capable of sustained free flight with a man."

Similar misstatements were made in the Institution's reports for 1916, 1917, 1918, and afterward.

Altogether here had been something probably unique in scientific procedure. A test was made purporting to determine if the original Langley plane was capable of flight; but the test was not made with the machine as designed and built by Langley, nor with an exact copy of it. No disinterested official observer was present. Misstatements were published about the results, and no information was furnished, regarding the changes made, to enable anyone to learn the truth. To have made one more honest test of the Langley plane that had immediately crashed each time it was launched over the Potomac would have been permissible. But for a scientific institution officially to distort scientific facts, and in collaboration with a man who stood to gain financially by what he was doing, has been called worse than scandalous.

After the Langley machine had been restored as nearly as possible to its original state, it was placed on exhibition by the Smithsonian. Soon afterward it bore a label that falsely proclaimed it to be "the first man-carrying aeroplane in the history of the world capable of sustained free flight."

But neither in connection with the exhibit of the Langley plane nor in any report of the Smithsonian Institution was there any hint of the fundamental changes made at Hammondsport, without which the plane could not possibly have carried its weight. One of these changes had to do with the supporting posts on the

wings. Professor Langley had not known—indeed, no
one knew until the Wrights' wind-tunnel experiments
established the facts—where the center of the air pressure would be on a curved surface, and consequently
he had failed to place his wing-trussing posts where
they were most needed. In the attempts to fly the machine over the Potomac, in 1903, the wing that bore
the greater part of the weight had each time collapsed
at the moment the apparatus left the starting platform.
(Lacking the knowledge about curved surfaces that
later was available, those in charge of the 1903 trials
had blamed the trouble on the launching apparatus.)
At the Hammondsport tests, the trussing posts were
moved thirty inches rearward. This brought the guy
posts almost exactly in the same plane with the center
of pressure on the wings and thus eliminated the backward pull that had wrecked the machine in the 1903
tests.

Three fundamental changes were made in the design
of the wings themselves: (1) The camber was greatly
changed; (2) the shape of the leading edge was entirely
different; (3) the aspect ratio—the ratio of span to chord
—was increased. These three features are the most important characteristics in determining the efficiency of
a wing. The change of the camber of itself may increase
the efficiency of a wing by thirty per cent. And not
only were the wings changed as to design, but they were
strengthened by various means of reinforcing and trussing not used by Langley. Even the cloth on the wings
was improved by varnishing, to make the wings more
efficient. Langley had not used varnish on the cloth.

Numerous changes were made in other parts of the machine. The large fixed vertical keel surface, situated below the main frame in 1903, was entirely omitted in 1914. This omission improved the machine's stability. A different kind of rudder was used. The position of the "Pénaud tail" used by Langley was raised about ten inches to increase the stability of the machine, and was connected to a modern steering post, to give better control. The forward corners of the original Langley propellers were cut off in the manner of the early Wright propellers to increase their efficiency. As the system of control Langley had used was not adequate, the aileron system, covered by Wright patents, a system unknown to Langley, was added.

How did all these changes become known? Orville Wright called attention to them in an affidavit in 1915 in the Wright-Curtiss lawsuit. One way to learn most of the facts is astonishingly simple. All that is necessary to any observer who knows what to look for is to make careful comparisons of the Smithsonian photographs of the original Langley machine with Smithsonian photographs of the machine tested at Hammondsport.

It was learned, too, that even the engine used by Langley was changed in several respects. A modern type carburetor, a new intake manifold, a magneto ignition, and a modern radiator were installed.

Though all these changes and many others were made in the machine at Hammondsport, the Smithsonian published only a few of them—the less important. It did not tell of the fundamental changes. And the Institution made statements that, by implication, practically amounted to a denial that any changes of importance had been made.

By omitting from its published reports at the time and for many years afterward, the facts about the changes in the Langley machine, the Smithsonian Institution succeeded in deluding the public. If the stories about these fake tests had been issued by Curtiss, who conducted them, or by an organization less well known than the Smithsonian, they might not have been taken seriously. But when false and misleading announcements were backed by the prestige of a famous scientific institution, it was possible to have the fraudulent character of the experiments pass generally unsuspected. When the reports of Secretary Walcott of the Smithsonian Institution said the *"original"* Langley machine had made "flights," and when the report of the National Museum said the Langley machine had been flown "without modification," such statements, untrue though they were, naturally carried weight. Indeed, the misstatements were so widely accepted as fact that they began to find their way into school text-books and into encyclopedias.

Griffith Brewer, the English aeronaut, delivered a lecture before the Royal Aeronautical Society in London, in October, 1921, and exposed the fraudulent nature of the Hammondsport tests. In this lecture he mentioned many of the vital changes made in the Langley plane before any attempt was made to fly it. Dr. Walcott made a statement in reply to Brewer. Up to this time Orville Wright had thought that Walcott could have been ignorant of those changes; but after reading the Walcott statement he was convinced that there was nothing accidental or unintentional about the misstatements published by the Smithsonian regarding the tests at Hammondsport.

While the Kitty Hawk plane rested in its storage place, subject to possible fire hazards, officials of the Science Museum at South Kensington, London, England, had made requests to have the machine for exhibition there. After Orville Wright became convinced that none of the Members or Regents of the Smithsonian Institution or any other influential persons were enough interested in establishing the facts in controversy to go to the trouble of making an investigation, he reluctantly decided, in 1923, to accede to the requests from London. In reply to letters deploring this decision, he has expressed his reasons as follows:

I believe my course in sending our Kitty Hawk machine to a foreign museum is the only way of correcting the history of the flying-machine, which by false and misleading statements has been perverted by the Smithsonian Institution.

In its campaign to discredit others in the flying art, the Smithsonian has issued scores of these false and misleading statements. They can be proved to be false and misleading from documents. But the people of today do not take the trouble to examine this evidence.

With this machine in any American museum the national pride would be satisfied; nothing further would be done and the Smithsonian would continue its propaganda. In a foreign museum this machine will be a constant reminder of the reason of its being there, and after the people and petty jealousies of this day are gone, the historians of the future may examine impartially the evidence and make history accord with it.

Your regret that this old machine must leave our country can hardly be so great as my own.

Reluctant to carry out his intention to send the Kitty Hawk plane out of the country, Orville Wright in 1925 proposed that the controversy be settled through the investigations of an impartial committee. But the suggestion got no response. He wrote a letter, on May 14, 1925, to Chief Justice William Howard Taft, as Chancellor of the Smithsonian Institution, in the hope that it might yet be possible to have an impartial hearing. In this letter, after reviewing the relations of the Wrights and the Smithsonian, he said:

It was not until 1921 that I became convinced that the officials of the Smithsonian, at least Dr. Walcott, were fully acquainted with the character of the tests at Hammonds-port. I had thought up to that time that they might have been ignorant of the fundamental changes which had been incorporated in the machine before these tests were made, and that when these changes were pointed out to them they would hasten to correct their erroneous reports. They did not do this, but have continued to repeat their early state-ments. By these the public has been led to think that flights were made in 1914 with the original Langley machine, with no changes, excepting such as were necessary to attach floats for the new system of launching.

When the proofs on both sides concerning these changes are shown, I do not think it will take you five minutes to make up your mind whether the changes were made and whether they were of importance.

It seems to me possible that you as Chancellor of the

Smithsonian Institution may wish me to present personally to you my evidence on these points and to have Dr. Walcott present at the same time to give his proofs to the contrary. It may be a way of cutting short a long and bitter controversy.

Chief Justice Taft replied that his position as Chancellor and head of the Smithsonian was purely nominal; that his other duties were such that he did not have the time to give any real attention to questions that have to be settled by the Institution's Secretary.

A similar preference to stand aside was shown by others nominally in a position to exercise authority over the acts of the Smithsonian. That Institution has as its members the President of the United States, the Vice President, the Chief Justice of the Supreme Court, and members of the President's cabinet. Its Board of Regents is made up of the Chief Justice, the Vice President, three members of the Senate, three members of the House of Representatives, and six citizens appointed by joint resolution of Congress. Any one of these members of the Board of Regents could doubtless have forced an investigation of any reported injustice committed by the Smithsonian. But all had other duties to occupy their time and, like Chief Justice Taft, they were willing to let the Secretary of the Smithsonian act as he saw fit. Thus the Secretary of the Smithsonian, which administers several important government bureaus besides the National Museum, could exercise great influence. That is how it came about that the attempt to mislead the public regarding the epochal achievements of the Wrights went so long unchecked by official action. And as

Orville Wright once said he had discovered, "Silent truth cannot withstand error aided by continued propaganda."

After the exchange of letters with Chief Justice Taft, Orville Wright still delayed sending the Kitty Hawk plane to England. There was nothing impetuous about what he did. Not until early in 1928, or fourteen years after the fraudulent tests at Hammondsport, with the Smithsonian still showing no intention to correct its false record of those flights, did he send the machine to the Science Museum at South Kensington. The arrangement he made with the Science Museum was that the plane should stay there for not less than five years, and permanently unless brought back to the United States within his lifetime.

Early in 1928, a bill was introduced in Congress to ascertain which was the first heavier-than-air flying-machine. Shortly afterward the Smithsonian adopted a resolution declaring that "to the Wrights belongs the credit of making the first successful flight with a power-propelled heavier-than-air machine carrying a man."

That resolution was, of course, superfluous, for there had never been any question, even by the Smithsonian, as to the first machine to make a sustained flight. But the Smithsonian continued to claim for Professor Langley credit for the *invention* of the first machine *capable* of flight.

Dr. Charles G. Abbot became the Secretary and Director of the Smithsonian Institution in 1928, succeeding Dr. Walcott, who had died in 1927. Soon after he became the head of the Institution, Dr. Abbot invited Orville Wright to go to lunch with him at the Carlton Hotel in Washington. In the course of their talk Dr. Abbot expressed the wish that they might come to an agreement by which the Kitty Hawk plane could be returned to America and placed under the care of the Smithsonian in the National Museum. Orville Wright said that this could easily be done. All that he asked for, he said, was a correction in the Smithsonian publications of the false and misleading statements previously made in those publications. Dr. Abbot expressed a willingness to do so, provided this could be accomplished without injuring the reputation of his predecessor or the prestige of the Institution.

But the painful fact was that the Smithsonian, however spotless its previous reputation, had committed a reprehensible act, and its reputation and prestige were bound to suffer when its guilt became known. Having committed a serious offense, one or the other of two courses were open to it: (1) to confess its guilt and make a full, frank correction; or (2) to try to keep the misdeed concealed. Unfortunately, the Institution adopted, at the beginning, the latter course, evidently in the belief that its great prestige, acquired through an honorable past, could crush any imputation against it. Indeed, that course did prove successful up to the time Orville Wright sent the Kitty Hawk plane abroad.

Dr. Abbot had not been responsible for the disgraceful situation he inherited when he became Secretary of the Smithsonian and found himself in the unenviable position of having to make an embarrassing decision. But it seemed as if he could not quite muster the courage to break away from the course the Institution had been following. Instead, he at first tried to justify the Institution's previous attitude, though he did concede that it was not true that the Langley plane had been flown at Hammondsport "without modification" as the Smithsonian had published. There were "many differences," he admitted. "Some of the changes were favorable, some unfavorable, to success," he declared. "Just what effects, favorable or unfavorable, the sum total of these changes produced can never be precisely known." Orville Wright, on the other hand, insisted that the "effects, favorable or unfavorable" could easily be determined by experts if only the changes were made known to them.

But Dr. Abbot still failed to publish the changes.

Since then Orville Wright more than once let the Smithsonian know what he thought should be done to settle the controversy. In a letter he sent to Dr. Abbot on December 23, 1933, he wrote:

The points involved in the straightening of the record are not on matters of mere opinion. They are on matters of fact, which at this time can be easily and definitely established. All that I have demanded in the past has been that there be an impartial investigation of the matters in controversy and that the record then be made to agree with the facts.

The suggestion made by me in 1925, three years before the plane left this country, that a committee be appointed to make an impartial investigation and settle the controversy, received from the Smithsonian no response. Nevertheless, I shall be most happy now to join with you in the selection of such a committee, with the understanding that the committee will fully investigate the matters in controversy and will make a full report of its findings.

In a letter a few weeks later, Dr. Abbot suggested that, if it were agreeable to Orville Wright, he would ask three public officials each to name an expert to serve on "an impartial committee" of three to investigate and report on the experiments at Hammondsport in 1914, and their bearing on the capacity of the Langley machine for flight in 1903. But all three of the Government officials that he mentioned were members of the Smithsonian. If the suggested plan had been followed, presumably Dr. Abbot himself would have had the naming of the investigating committee, for in organizations, such as the Smithsonian, appointing of committees by members is usually referred to the Secretary. (Chief Justice Taft, Chancellor of the Smithsonian, had written that because he did not have the time, he let questions regarding the Institution be settled by the Secretary.) It appeared to Orville Wright that Dr. Abbot did not have too much confidence in the findings of a committee, even if wholly appointed by the Smithsonian, for Abbot specified just what questions the committee was to investigate. And most of these were wholly irrelevant.

A little later, Orville Wright, in reply to a letter from Dr. Abbot, made this suggestion: That the Smithsonian publish a paper presenting a list of specifications in parallel columns of those features of the Langley machine of 1903 and of the Hammondsport machine of 1914 in which there were differences, along with an introduction stating that the Smithsonian now finds it was misled by the Zahm report of 1914; that through the Zahm report the Institution was led to believe that the aeroplane tested at Hammondsport was "as nearly as possible in its original condition"; that as a result of this misinformation the Smithsonian had published erroneous statements from time to time alleging that the original Langley machine, without modification, or with only such modifications as were necessary for the addition of floats, had been successfully flown at Hammondsport in 1914; that it ask its readers to disregard all of its former statements and expressions of opinion regarding the flights at Hammondsport in 1914, because these were based upon misinformation as the accompanying list of changes would show. (The accuracy of the list of changes was to be settled before publication by the Smithsonian, Orville Wright and a mediator.)

But the suggestion was not followed.

It will be noted that Orville Wright did not even ask that the Smithsonian should say it did not believe the original Langley machine could fly. All he asked was that the facts regarding the Hammondsport trials be made public by the Smithsonian. It has been his contention that if this information had not been withheld, then anyone having a knowledge of the science of aviation could form for himself an opinion regarding the importance of the differences between the original Langley machine of 1903 and the Zahm-Curtiss-Langley machine of 1914. He has been willing to stake his and his brother's reputation on the conclusion that a committee of competent disinterested scientists would reach if they had all the facts.

Dr. Abbot, in the years 1933 to 1942, proposed a number of times to issue a statement by the Smithsonian for the declared purpose of correcting the record. All these statements, however, except the final one, would have left the record as confusing as it was before. The first statement proposed was to contain: (1) A history of Langley's work up to December, 1903, which was entirely irrelevant to the controversy and would have filled hundreds, if not thousands, of pages of print; (2) a history of the Langley machine from 1903 to 1914, which, likewise, had no part in the controversy; (3) A. F. Zahm's report of the tests of the Langley machine at Hammondsport in 1914, with no correction by the Institution of its many misrepresentations of fact about those tests; (4) Orville Wright's list of changes made in the Langley machine at Hammondsport in 1914, without any acknowledgement by the Smithsonian of its accuracy. (The accuracy of the list was later acknowledged by the Institution.) (5) A long list of "amendments" by A. F. Zahm to Orville Wright's list of changes. (These "amendments," or comments, had the appearance of being corrections of errors in Orville Wright's list, though a careful reading will disclose that they were not corrections.)

Dr. Abbot's proposed statement thus would have dealt almost entirely with matters not involved in the controversy. About all that did touch on questions in the controversy would have been contradictory statements by Zahm and Wright. The reader, having no way of knowing which one was telling the truth, would have been more confused than ever.

All the publications proposed later, except the final one, were similar to the first, though less voluminous. None of them would have clarified the situation any more than the first. Not until September, 1942, did Dr. Abbot submit a statement which, with some amendments, was satisfactory to Orville Wright. That statement, published by the Smithsonian on October 24, 1942, is given here verbatim, as follows:

THE 1914 TESTS OF THE LANGLEY "AERODROME" [1]

By C. G. ABBOT
Secretary, Smithsonian Institution

NOTE—This paper has been submitted to Dr. Orville Wright, and under date of October 8, 1942, he states that the paper as now prepared will be acceptable to him if given adequate publication.

It is everywhere acknowledged that the Wright brothers were the first to make sustained flights in a heavier-than-air machine at Kitty Hawk, North Carolina, on December 17, 1903.

Mainly because of acts and statements of former officers of the Smithsonian Institution, arising from tests made with the reconditioned Langley plane of 1903 at Hammondsport, New York, in 1914, Dr. Orville Wright feels that the Institution adopted an unfair and injurious attitude. He therefore sent the original Wright Kitty Hawk plane to England in 1928. The nature of the acts and statements referred to are as follows:

[1] For an account of early Langley and Wright aeronautical investigations, see Smithsonian Report for 1900 and The Century Magazine of September 1908.

In March 1914, Secretary Walcott contracted with Glenn H. Curtiss to attempt a flight with the Langley machine. This action seems ill considered and open to criticism. For in January 1914, the United States Court of Appeals, Second Circuit, had handed down a decision recognizing the Wrights as "pioneers in the practical art of flying with heavier-than-air machines" and pronouncing Glenn H. Curtiss an infringer of their patent. Hence, in view of probable further litigation, the Wrights stood to lose in fame and revenue and Curtiss stood to gain pecuniarily, should the experiments at Hammondsport indicate that Langley's plane was capable of sustained flight in 1903, previous to the successful flights made December 17, 1903, by the Wrights at Kitty Hawk, N. C.

The machine was shipped to Curtiss at Hammondsport, N. Y., in April. Dr. Zahm, the Recorder of the Langley Aerodynamical Laboratory and expert witness for Curtiss in the patent litigation, was at Hammondsport as official representative of the Smithsonian Institution during the time the machine was being reconstructed and tested. In the reconstruction the machine was changed from what it was in 1903 in a number of particulars as given in Dr. Wright's list of differences which appears later in this paper. On the 28th of May and the 2d of June, 1914, attempts to fly were made. After acquiring speed by running on hydroplane floats on the surface of Lake Keuka the machine lifted into the air several different times. The longest time off the water with the Langley motor was approximately five seconds. Dr. Zahm stated that "it was apparent that owing to the great weight which had been given to the structure by adding the floats it was necessary to increase the propeller thrust." So no further attempts were made to fly with the Langley 52 HP engine.

It is to be regretted that the Institution published statements repeatedly [1] to the effect that these experiments of 1914 demonstrated that Langley's plane of 1903 without essential modification was the first heavier-than-air machine capable of maintaining sustained human flight.

As first exhibited in the United States National Museum, January 15, 1918, the restored Langley plane of 1903 bore the following label:

THE ORIGINAL, FULL-SIZE
LANGLEY FLYING MACHINE, 1903

For this simple label others were later substituted containing the claim that Langley's machine "was the first man-carrying aeroplane in the history of the world capable of sustained free flight."

Though the matter of the label is not now an issue, it seems only fair to the Institution to say that in September 1928, Secretary Abbot finally caused the label of the Langley machine to be changed to read simply as follows:

LANGLEY AERODROME

THE ORIGINAL SAMUEL PIERPONT LANGLEY
FLYING MACHINE OF 1903, RESTORED.

Deposited by
The Smithsonian Institution

301,613

This change has frequently been overlooked by writers on the controversy.

In January 1942, Mr. Fred C. Kelly, of Peninsula, Ohio, communicated to me a list of differences between the Langley plane as tested in 1914 and as tested in 1903, which he had received from Dr. Wright. This list is given

[1] Smithsonian Reports: 1914, pp. 9, 219, 221, 222; 1915, pp. 14, 121; 1917, p. 4; 1918, pp. 3, 28, 114, 166. Report of U. S. National Museum, 1914, pp. 46 and 47.

verbatim below. The Institution accepts Dr. Wright's statement as correct in point of facts. Inferences from the comparisons are primarily the province of interested experts and are not discussed here.

COMPARISON OF THE LANGLEY MACHINE OF 1903 WITH THE HAMMONDSPORT MACHINE OF MAY-JUNE, 1914.

LANGLEY, 1903.   HAMMONDSPORT, 1914.

WINGS.

1 SIZE: 11'6" x 22'6" (L.M.* p. 206)

SIZE: 10'11¾" x 22'6"

2 AREA: 1040 sq. ft. (L.M. p. 206)

AREA: 988 sq. ft.

3 ASPECT RATIO: 1.96

ASPECT RATIO: 2.05

4 CAMBER: 1/12 (L.M. p. 205)

CAMBER: 1/18

5 LEADING EDGE: Wire 1/16" diameter (L.M. Pl.66)

LEADING EDGE: Cylindrical spar 1½" dia. at inner end, tapering to 1" dia. at outer end.

6 COVERING: Cotton fabric, not varnished.

COVERING: Cotton fabric, varnished.

7 CENTER SPAR: Cylindrical wooden spar, measuring 1½" dia. for half its length and tapering to 1" at its tip. (L.M. p. 204.) Located on upper side of wing.

CENTER SPAR: Cylindrical spar about 1½" dia. at inner end, tapering to about 1" dia. at outer end. Located on upper side of wing. This center spar was reinforced (1) by an extra wooden member on the underside of the wing, which measured 1" x 1½" and extended to the 7th rib from the center of the machine; and (2) by another wooden reinforcement on the underside extending out about one-fourth of the length of the wing.

8 RIBS: Hollow box construction. (L.M. Plates 66, 67.)

RIBS: Most of the original Langley box ribs were replaced with others made at Hammondsport. (Manly letter, 1914.) The Hammondsport ribs were of solid construction and made of laminated wood. That part of the rib in front of the forward spar was entirely omitted.

* The letters L.M. in first column refer to Langley Memoir.

LANGLEY WING TRUSSING 1903.

HAMMONDSPORT WING TRUSSING 1914.

LANGLEY, 1903.	HAMMONDSPORT, 1914.

LANGLEY, 1903.

9 LOWER GUY-POSTS: A single round wooden post for each pair of wings (see Fig. 3), 1¼" in dia. 6½' long. (L.M. Plate 62, p. 184.)

10 The front wing guy-post was located 28½" in front of the main center spar. (L.M. Plate 53.)

11 The rear wing guy-post was located 31½" in front of the main center spar. (L.M. Plate 53.)

12 UPPER GUY-POSTS: For each pair of wings a single steel tube ¾" dia., 43" long. (L.M. p. 184, pl. 62.)

13 Front wing upper guy-post located 28½" in front of the main center spar. (L.M. pl. 53.)

14 The rear wing upper guy-post was located 31½" in front of the main center spar. (L.M. pl. 53.)

HAMMONDSPORT, 1914.

LOWER GUY-POSTS: Four for each pair of wings (see Fig. 4), two of which were of streamline form measuring 1¼" x 3½" x 54" long; and two measuring 2" x 2" with rounded corners, 3'9" long.
The front-wing guy-posts were located directly underneath the main center spar, 28½" further rearward than in 1903.
The rear wing guy-posts were located directly under the main center spar, 31½" further rearward than in 1903.
UPPER GUY-POSTS: For each pair of wings, two streamline wooden posts each 1¼" x 3½", 76" long, forming an inverted V. (See Fig. 4.)
Front wing upper guy-posts located directly over main spar, 28½" further rearward than in 1903.
The rear wing guy-posts were located directly over the main center spar, 31½" further rearward than in 1903.

LANGLEY, 1903.

HAMMONDSPORT, 1914.

15 TRUSSING: The wing trussing wires were attached to the spars at the 5th, 7th and 9th ribs out from the center (L.M. pl. 54.) The angles between these wires and the spars to which they were attached are shown in Fig. 3.

TRUSSING: A different system of wing trussing was used, and the wing trussing wires were attached to the spars at the 3rd, 6th and 9th ribs from the center. The angles between these wires and the spars to which they were attached were all different from those in the original Langley machine. (See Fig. 4.)

CONTROL SURFACES.

16 VANE RUDDER: A split vane composed of two surfaces united at their leading edges and separated 15″ at their trailing edges, thus forming a wedge. Each surface measured 2′3″ x 4′6″, with aspect ratio .5. (L.M. p. 214, pls. 53, 54.)

VERTICAL RUDDER: The Langley vane rudder was replaced by a single plane vertical rudder which measured 3′6″ x 5′, with aspect ratio of .7.

17 Operated by means of a wheel located slightly in front of the pilot at his right side and at the height of his shoulder (L.M. p. 216, pls. 53, 54.)

Operated at Hammondsport through the Curtiss steering wheel in some tests (Zahm affidavit pp. 5, 6), through the Curtiss shoulder yoke in some others (Manly letter, 1914), and fixed so as not to be operable at all in still others (Zahm affidavit p. 7).

18 Used for steering only. (L.M. p. 214.)

Used "as a vertical aileron to control the lateral poise of the machine" (Zahm affidavit p. 6), as well as for steering (Zahm affidavit p. 7).

19 PENAUD TAIL: This was a dart-shaped tail having a vertical and a horizontal surface (Penaud tail), each measuring 95 sq. ft. It was located in the rear of the main frame.

TAIL RUDDER: Same size and construction as in 1903.

20 Attached to a bracket extending below the main frame.

Attached to same bracket at a point about 8″ higher than in 1903.

21 "Normally inactive," (L.M. p. 216) but adjustable about a transverse horizontal axis by means of a self-locking wheel located at the right side of the pilot, even with his back, and at the height of his shoulder. (L.M. pls. 51, 53.)

Operable about a transverse horizontal axis and connected to a regular Curtiss elevator control post directly in front of the pilot (Zahm affidavit p. 5).

LANGLEY, 1903.

HAMMONDSPORT, 1914.

22 Immovable about a vertical axis. (L.M. p. 214, pl. 56, Fig. 1.) No means were provided for adjusting this rudder about a vertical axis in flight. "Although it was necessary that the large aerodrome should be capable of being steered in a horizontal direction, it was felt to be unwise to give the Penaud tail and rudder motion in the horizontal plane in order to attain this end." (L.M. p. 214.)

Immovable about a vertical axis on May 28, 1914, only. Thereafter it was made movable about a vertical axis and was connected through cables to a Curtiss steering wheel mounted on a Curtiss control post directly in front of the pilot.

23 KEEL: A fixed vertical surface underneath the main frame measuring 3'2" in height by 6' average length. Area 19 sq. ft. (L.M. pl. 53.)

KEEL: Entirely omitted.

SYSTEM OF CONTROL.

24 LATERAL STABILITY: The dihedral only was used for maintaining lateral balance. (L.M. p. 45.)

LATERAL STABILITY: Three means were used for securing lateral balance at Hammondsport: The dihedral angle as used by Langley, a rudder which "serves as a vertical aileron" (Zahm affidavit p. 6), and the Penaud tail rudder. The last two constituted a system "identical in principle with that of Complainant's [Wright] combined warping of the wings and the use of the vertical rudder." (Zahm affidavit p. 6.)

25 LONGITUDINAL STABILITY: Langley relied upon the Penaud system of inherent stability for maintaining the longitudinal equilibrium. "For the preservation of the equilibrium [longitudinal] of the aerodrome, though the aviator might assist by such slight movements as he was able to make in the limited space of the aviator's car, the main reliance was upon the Penaud tail." (L.M. p. 215.)

LONGITUDINAL STABILITY: At Hammondsport the Penaud inherent longitudinal stability was supplemented with an elevator system of control.

26 STEERING: Steering in the horizontal plane was done entirely by the split-vane steering rudder located underneath the main frame. (L.M. p. 214.)

STEERING: On one day, May 28, 1914, steering in the horizontal plane was done with the vertical rudder which had been substituted for the original Langley

LANGLEY, 1903.	HAMMONDSPORT, 1914.
	split-vane steering rudder. After May 28th the steering was done by the vertical surface of the tail rudder (Zahm affidavit p. 7), which in 1903 was immovable about a vertical axis (L.M. p. 214.)

POWER PLANT.

27 MOTOR: Langley 5 cylinder radial.	MOTOR: Langley motor modified.
28 IGNITION: Jump spark with dry cell batteries. (L.M. p. 262.)	IGNITION: Jump spark with magneto.
29 CARBURETOR: Balzer carburetor consisting of a chamber filled with lumps of porous cellular wood saturated with gasoline. The air was drawn through this wood. There was no float feed. (L.M. p. 225.)	CARBURETOR: Automobile type with float feed.
30 RADIATOR: Tubes with radiating fins.	RADIATOR: Automobile radiator of honeycomb type.
31 PROPELLERS: Langley propellers (L.M. pl. 53, pp. 178-182).	PROPELLERS: Langley propellers modified "after fashion of early Wright blades."

LAUNCHING AND FLOATS.

32 LAUNCHING: Catapult mounted on a houseboat.	LAUNCHING: Hydroplanes, developed 1909-1914, attached to the machine.
33 FLOATS: Five cylindrical tin floats, with conical ends, attached to underside of main frame at appropriate points, and about six feet above lowest part of machine.	FLOATS: Two wooden hydroplane floats, mounted beneath and about 6 feet to either side of the center of the machine at the lateral extremities of the Pratt system of trussing used for bracing the wing spars of the forward wings; and one (part of the time two) tin cylindrical floats with conical ends, similar to but larger than the Langley floats, mounted at the center of the Pratt system of trussing used for bracing the rear wings. All of the floats were mounted from four to five feet lower than the floats of the original Langley, thus keeping the entire machine above the water.

LANGLEY, 1903.　　　　HAMMONDSPORT, 1914.

WEIGHT.

	LANGLEY, 1903.	HAMMONDSPORT, 1914.
34	TOTAL WEIGHT: With pilot 850 pounds (L.M. p. 256).	TOTAL WEIGHT: With pilot, 1170 pounds.
35	CENTER GRAVITY: ⅜″ above line of thrust.	CENTER GRAVITY: About one foot below line of thrust.

Since I became Secretary, in 1928, I have made many efforts to compose the Smithsonian-Wright controversy, which I inherited. I will now, speaking for the Smithsonian Institution, make the following statement in an attempt to correct as far as now possible acts and assertions of former Smithsonian officials that may have been misleading or are held to be detrimental to the Wrights.

1. I sincerely regret that the Institution employed to make the tests of 1914 an agent who had been an unsuccessful defendant in patent litigation brought against him by the Wrights.

2. I sincerely regret that statements were repeatedly made by officers of the Institution that the Langley machine was flown in 1914 "with certain changes of the machine necessary to use pontoons," without mentioning the other changes included in Dr. Wright's list.

3. I point out that Assistant Secretary Rathbun was misinformed when he stated that the Langley machine "without modification" made "successful flights."

4. I sincerely regret the public statement by officers of the Institution that "The tests" (of 1914) showed "that the late Secretary Langley had succeeded in building the first aeroplane capable of sustained free flight with a man."

5. Leaving to experts to formulate the conclusions arising from the 1914 tests as a whole, in view of all the facts, I repeat in substance, but with amendments, what I have already published in Smithsonian Scientific Series, Vol. 12. 1932, page 227:

The flights of the Langley aerodrome at Hammondsport in 1914, having been made long after flying had become a common art, and with changes of the machine indicated by Dr. Wright's comparison, as given above, did not warrant the statements published by the Smithsonian Institution that these tests proved that the large Langley machine of 1903 was capable of sustained flight carrying a man.

6. If the publication of this paper should clear the way for Dr. Wright to bring back to America the Kitty Hawk machine to which all the world awards first place, it will be a source of profound and enduring gratification to his countrymen everywhere. Should he decide to deposit the plane in the United States National Museum, it would be given the highest place of honor, which is its due.

Publication of this statement in the Smithsonian Annual Report presumably should mark the end of the long controversy.

INDEX

Abbot, Dr. Charles G., 318-21, 323-33
accidents and mishaps, 91, 97, 127, 129, 131-32, 161, 221, 229-31, 234, 250, 265
Ader, Clement, 47, 187
Aerial Experiment Assn., 289-94
Aero Club of America, 145, 146, 157, 158, 171, 194, 258
Aéro Club of France, 166, 167, 170, 174, 175, 177, 180, 182, 191, 236, 239, 248-49
Aéro Club of the Sarthe, 244-45, 249, 250, 257
Aero Club of the United Kingdom, 258
Aeronautical Annual, 46
Aeronautical Society of Great Britain, 147, 173, 243, 246, 247, 258
Aérophile, 166, 168, 170, 174, 179
air pressure, 53-54, 67, 71, 73-76, 80, 291
Alexander, Patrick Y., 147, 173, 191, 217
Alfonso of Spain, 252
Algeciras conference, 188
Alger, Russell A. and Frederick M., 268, 270, 271
Allen, Genl. James, 208, 211, 212, 259
American Assn. for the Advancement of Science, 109-10
American Magazine of Aeronautics, 210
angle of incidence, 67-68, 82
AP, 106, 108, 109, 110
Archdeacon, Ernest, 167-68, 170, 237
Arnold (Lt. Genl.), Henry H., 284
Auto, 174, 179, 182
Auvours flying field, 234, 241, 243, 247, 248, 250

Baden-Powell, Maj. B. F. S., 246, 247
balance—*see* equilibrium
Baldwin, Capt. Thomas S., 288-89, 293, 295
Balfour, Arthur, 253
Barnum & Bailey, 203
Barriquand & Marre, 206
Barthou, Louis, 248
Bates, Maj. Genl. J. C., 153
Beacham, Thomas, 95
Beachey, Lincoln, 308
Beard, David, 146
Beard family, 136, 142, 178
Beard, Luther, 139-41
Beck, Mabel, 273
Bell, Dr. Alexander Graham, 3, 289, 307
Belmont, August, 270

Belmont Park Aviation Tournament, 281
Benham, Catharine—*see* Thompson, Mrs. Samuel
Bennett, James Gordon, 191-92, 219, 222, 251
Bennett balloon race, 207
Berg, Hart O., 195, 196, 197, 201, 204, 233, 234, 236, 238, 246-47
Berg, Mrs. Hart O., 246-47, 248
Bergdoll, Grover C., 285
Berlin *B. Z. Mittag*, 217; *Lokal Anzeiger*, 254, 261
Berry, Walter V. R., 187
Bertrand, Col. Charles A., 172, 223
Berwind, E. J., 270
Besançon, Georges, 170-71, 174-75, 179, 180, 181
bicycle shop, the Wrights'—*see* Wright Cycle Co.
bidders on plane for U. S. War Dept., 211
Bierce, Nelson, 174
Billman, C. S., 145, 177
Bleriot, Louis, 239-40, 294
blinkers, 130-31
"bluffeur," 234, 238
Bollée, Léon, 233, 235-36, 241, 245
Bollée, Mme., 248
Bond, Miss, 24
Bonel, Comdt., 187-200, 203
Boulton, 309
Brewer, Griffith, 244, 247, 258, 3.4
Brinkley, W. C., 98
British government, 147-48, 151-52
British War Office, 151, 156-57
British Wright company, 284
Brookins, Walter, 274, 279
Burkhardt, J. C., 224
Butler, F. H., 247

Cabot, Samuel and Godfrey L., 115-16, 157, 158
Calderara, Lt., 255-56
Camber, 69-70, 121, 130
Capper, Lt. Col. J. E., 147-48
Carvin, Louis, 257
catapult—*see* derrick catapult
Celleri, Count and Countess di, 255
center of gravity, 47-48, 121 n., 127
Chandler, Capt. Charles DeF., 212
Chanute, Octave, 47, 48, 52, 68-69, 72-73, 78, 92, 106, 110, 126, 148, 152,

335

155, 157, 166, 169, 171, 224, 291, 309;
Progress in Flying Machines, 46, 52
Chicago—Orville Wright's speech at, 73-
75; aviation meet at, 279
Chicago *Daily News*, 109; *Record-
Herald*, 105, 109, 278-79; *Tribune*,
224, 278
Cie. Gén. de Nav. Aérienne, 213
Cincinnati *Enquirer*, 105-107, 123, 125;
Post, 145
Claudy, C. H., 231
Cleveland *Leader*, 218-19
Coffyn, Frank T., 275
Collier, Robert J., 270, 282, 285, 286
Collier's Weekly, 146, 220, 223, 225, 270
Coquelle, Robert, 179-81
Cordley, F. R., 195, 197
commercial express, plane first used for,
280
Cox, James M., 134, 135
Crane, Spencer C., 274
Crozier, Brig. Genl. William, 158, 159,
208
Curtiss, Glenn H., 288-96; tests Langley
machine, 308-15, 318; his alterations,
327-32

Daniels, John T., 95, 98, 102
Dargent, M., 168
Dayton (O.) celebration for Wrights,
258-59; flood (1913), 283; *Daily News*,
107, 123, 134-35, 145; *Journal*, 105-
107, 123, 139, 140, 145; first flight
over, 280
Dayton, Genl. Jonathan, 21
Delagrange, Léon, 217-18, 240
derrick catapult, 128, 236, 249
Deutsch de la Meurthe, Henri, 170, 198,
199, 213
Dewey, Orville, 23
Dickin, Mr., 245
Dickson, Capt. T. C., 155
Dienstbach, Carl, 169
Dosher, Joseph J., 56, 103, 217
Dough, W. S., 95, 98
Doumer, Paul, 248
Duchemin, 302
Dunbar, Paul Laurence, 37

Eddy, U. S., 194
Edison, Thomas A., 3
Edward VII, King, 252
Eiffel Tower, 141, 266
elevator, 51, 53-55, 63, 65-67, 82, 127,
131-34
Ellis, E. W., 145, 258-59
engines, 84-86, 121-22, 194
Englehardt, Capt. Paul, 263
equilibrium, 47-49, 50-55, 64, 70-71, 81-
83
Esnault-Pelterie, Robert, 170
Estournelles, Baron d', 245
Etheridge, A. D., 98
Etienne, M., 186
Evening Item (Dayton), 38

exhibition flights, 277-79, 282; charges
for, 277

Farman, Henri, 217-18, 240
Fédération Aéronautique Internationale,
171
Feight, John G., 114
Ferber, Capt. Louis F., 167-73, 181-85,
189
Fiske, Wilbur, 23
flight, the Wrights' first, 90-119; Or-
ville's narrative, 96-102; telegram,
103-104, 106, 107; press treatment,
103-11; cost, 112-14; public's reception
of story, 114-17
Flint, Charles R., 194, 195, 261
Flint & Co., 194-96, 203, 233
flying-fields, 122, 226-32, 234, 255, 261,
263 (*see also* Huffman field, Fort
Myer, Auvours)
Fordyce, Arnold, 183-91, 198, 200-203,
245
Fort Myer (Va.) tests, 215, 226-32,
260, 293
Foster, Col. H., 152, 156-57
Foulois, Lt. Benj. D., 260, 266
Fournier, Capt., 187
Fouts, William, 145, 178
France, aeronautics in, 166-93, 198-203,
213, 233-53
Frederick William, Crown Prince, 262-64
Freedman, Andrew, 270
French War Ministry, 198-203, 234, 266
French Wright company, 213, 248, 251,
255, 281
Fuller, Maj. Samson M., 162, 165, 208
Furnas, Charles W., 215, 221, 226, 231

Gardner, Gilson, 224
Gary, Judge Elbert H., 269
gasoline motors—see engines
German War Dept., 204-206
German Wright company, 256, 257, 263
Gillespie, Maj. Genl. G. L., 150
Girardville, Capt. Lucas de, 248
Gleanings in Bee Culture, 118, 143
Gleichen, Col., 157
gliders, 49-55, 57-75, 79-83, 168-70
Gould, Howard, 270
Grahame-White, Claude, 288
"Great W. J. & M. Circus," 15-18
"Great Truxell Bros. & LaRue Show,"
33-34
Greater Dayton Assn., 280
Greensboro (N. C.) *News*, 217
Griscom, Lloyd, 256
Gross, Der, 262-63

Hamburger, Frank, 145
Hand, Judge Learned, 294
Hare, James H., 220-25
Harmon, Gov. Judson, 259
Harrison, Pres. Benjamin, 36
Harte, 309
Hawthorn Hill, 282

Hazel, Judge John R., 293-94
helicopter, 8-9, 45
Henson, W .S., 309
Herring, A. M., 211, 212
Herring-Curtiss Co., 288, 293
Hildebrandt, Capt. Alfred, 254, 261, 263
Hill, James J., 256
hobble skirt, 247
Hobbs, Capt., 104
horseless buggy, 43-44
Hoster, William, 220-25
Hoxsey, Arch, 274, 275
Hudson-Fulton Celebration, 265, 283
Huffaker, E. C., 69
Huffman field, 122-23, 126 ff., 134-38, 139, 142, 144-45, 157, 214, 274-76, 280, 288
Huffman, Torrence, 122-23, 145
Humphreys, Lt. Frederic E., 266
Hunaudières track, 234, 236, 241

Illustrierte Aeron. Mitteilungen, 167, 169
Independent, 116
infringers—*see* lawsuits and Wright patents
Internat'l Aviation Tournament, 281
Italy, aeronautics in, 254-56

Jamestown Exposition, 160
Jamieson, O. F., 145
Jennings, Alice, 25, 32
Johnston, "Corky," 17
Johnston, Gansey, 14
Johnston, Griswold, 17
Johnstone, Ralph, 275
"June Bug," Glenn Curtiss's, 291-92, 294

Kehler, Capt. von, 256, 257
Keidel, Herr, 263
Kelly, Fred C., 141, 326
kite-flying, 12, 50
kite, man-carrying, 52
Kitty Hawk (N. C.), 55-66, 68-72, 79-83, 90-111, 215-25
Kitty Hawk plane, disposition of, 300-33
Knabenshue, Roy, 272-74, 279-80
Koerner, John G., 19-20
Koerner, Mrs. John G. (Catherine Fry), 20
Koerner, Susan Catherine—*see* Wright, Mrs. Milton
Kohlsaat, H. H., 278-79
Krupp Co., 256
Kumler, Dan, 134-35

LaChapelle, Duval, 275
Lahm, Lt. Frank P., 207-208, 212, 228-29, 266
Lahm, Frank S., 173-77, 179, 180-82, 192-93, 207, 248
Lake, Simon, 195
Lambers, Bernard H., 145
Lambert, Count Charles de, 248, 251, 266
Lambert, Comtesse Charles de, 251-52

"Langley Law," 138, 301
Langley medal, 302, 303, 309
Langley, Samuel P., 46, 76, 90, 117, 137, 211, 300-303, 305, 306, 309, 310, 312, 313, 318, 323, 330, 332; *Experiments in Aerodynamics*, 46; *Experiments in Mechanical Flight*, 46
Langley's flying-machine, 92, 300-333; borrowed by Curtiss for test, 308; how altered, 309-13, 322, 324-33
LaRue, Fred, 33
Lassence, Mayor de, 251
lathe, 12-13
launching—*see* derrick catapult
lawsuits, 287-99, 308, 309, 313, 325
letter-press, 29
Le Mans, 233-50
Letellier, M., 183-86, 198, 200
Lilienthal, Otto, 45-48, 281, 302; *Problem of Flying*, 46-47
Lodge, Sen. Henry Cabot, 158
Loening, Grover, 283
London *Daily Mail*, 220, 222, 223, 252

McCormick, Harold, 277-79
McGowan, P. H., 220-25
Mansfield *News*, 180
Manufacturers Aircraft Assn., 296
Manville, Frank, 286
Margherita of Italy, 247
Marriott, 309
Martin, Glenn, 295
Mass. Institute of Technology, 307, 308
material used—cloth in gliders, 66; wood in planes, 122
Maxim, Sir Hiram S., 47, 90, 309
Maxwell Field, 274
Maynard, George C., 304
Means, James, 46
Melville, Rear Admiral G. W., 117
Midget, 31
Michelin Cup, 250
Milling (Genl.) Thomas D., 284
Moore, H. P., 104, 105, 106, 109
Moore, Johnny, 98, 100
Moore, Willis, 51
Morehouse-Martin Co., 280
Morgan, J. P., 256, 269, 270-71
Morgan & Co., 184-85, 187, 189, 268
Morgan, Harjes & Co., 185, 186, 187
Morrow, Harry, 14, 15, 16
Morse, Sherman, 191-92
Mouillard, *Empire of the Air*, 46
Myers, Howard M., 145

Nevin, R. M., 149, 150
New York *American*, 105; *Globe*, 209; *Herald*, 111, 182, 190, 192, 217, 218, 219, 222, 224; *Times*, 227, 289, 295; *World*, 228
Newcomb, Simon, 116-17, 228
newspapers—*see* press
Newton, Byron R., 219-25
Nicolai, M., 234
Nicoll, DeLancey, 269

Night and Day Bank Bldg., 271
Nolte, George H., 195
Norfolk (Va.) *Virginian-Pilot*, 104-106, 108, 216
North American Review, 117
Northcliffe, Lord, 252, 253, 284

Ogilvie, Alec, 281
O'Neal, "Uncle Benny," 95

Packard Automobile Co., 268
Painlevé, Paul, 247-48
Paris *Figaro*, 239, 245; *Herald*, 192, 197, 217-18, 222, 238-39, 245, 246; *Journal*, 183, 185, 186, 198, 200, 201, 239; *Matin*, 198, 240
Parmalee, Phil O., 275
Parseval, Maj. von, 257
Parsons, Herbert, 161-62
Patterson Field, 275 n.
Pau, 250-53
Paulhan, Louis, 287-88, 294
Payne, Capt. S. J., 104
Pénaud, Alphonse, 8, 45, 48, 306; helicopter, 8-9, 45
Perry, Israel, 58-59
Peterkin, Clinton R., 268-69, 271
Phila. *Record*, 105
Picquart, Genl. M. G., 199, 200, 266
Pilcher, Percy, 47, 309
pilot, position of, 214-15
pilots, training of, 255-56, 274, 275, 284-85
Pirelli, Dr., 248, 254
Plant, Mortimer F., 270
Popular Science Monthly, 110, 118
press, its treatment of Kitty Hawk flight, 103-11; of later developments, 123-26, 134-35, 139-41, 145, 190-91; of (1908) experiments, 216-25; of Fort Myer tests, 227-28 (*see also* Paris and N. Y. C. papers)
Press, J. C., 146
printing press, the Wrights', 30-38
propellers, 86-90, 133, 231; shafts, 92-94
public's reaction to Wright experiments, 114-17, 135-42
Puck, 141-42

Rathbun, Asst. Secy., 332
Reeder, Catharine—*see* Wright, Mrs. Dan
Reeder, Mr. and Mrs. George, 21
Reichel, Franz, 245
Religious Telescope, 23
Revue des Sciences, 166, 291
Richmond (Ind.) *Evening Item*, 15
Rodgers, Cal P., 281-82
Rolls, Charles S., 244, 247
Roosevelt, Pres. Theodore, 160, 161-62, 212, 227
Roosevelt, Theodore, Jr., 227
Root, A. I., 117-19, 142-43
rudder—*see* elevator

Ruhl, Arthur, 220-25
Ruse, Cordy, 43
Russell, Frank, 271
Ryan, Allan A., 270
Ryan, Thomas F., 270

Salley, D. Bruce, 218-19
Santos-Dumont, Alberto, 107, 115, 141, 166, 170, 192
Savoia, Lt., 256
Scherl, Herr, 254
Schindler, Reuben, 145
Scientific American, 143-44, 146, 161, 169, 292
Scott, J. F., 211
Selfridge, Lt. Thomas, 229-30, 245, 290-91, 292
Shaffer, Bert, 9
Shank, W. H., 145
Shearn, Clarence J., 297-98
Shonts, Theodore P., 270
Simms station—*see* Huffman field
Sines, Edwin Henry, 6, 30, 33, 36, 39, 258-59
Sines & Wright, 30-37
Smithsonian Institution, 46, 137, 300-333
Snapshots, 38
Sonnino, Baron Sidney, 256
South Kensington Science Museum, 300, 315, 318
Sports, 179, 182
Spratt, Dr. George A., 68-69, 92
Squier, Maj. George O., 229
Stauffer, Amos, 144, 146, 178
Steinmetz, C. P., 4
Studien Gesellschaft, 256-57
Surcouf, Edouard, 238

Taft, William Howard, 150, 152, 153, 158, 162, 211-12, 258, 316-17, 318, 321
tail, 79-83, 86
tail-spin, 81, 128-29, 131
Tate, "Dan," 80
Tate, William J., 56-57, 59-61, 62, 65, 66, 80, 102
Tattler, 37
Taylor, Charlie, 86, 121, 127, 136, 202, 226, 231
telegram reporting Kitty Hawk flight, 103-104, 106, 107
Tempelhof field, 261
Thompson, Samuel, 20
Thompson, Mrs. Samuel, 20-21
Thompson, William Boyce, 286
Thorne, Tom, 41-42
tires, 41
Tissandier, Paul, 248, 250
Tomlinson, John, 145
Tono-Bungay, 216
transcontinental plane flight, first, 281-82
Truxell boys, 33
Tunison, Frank, 106, 140
Turpin, C. O., 275

U. S. Board of Ordnance, 150, 153, 154, 155, 158-60, 162-65, 208, 211
U. S. Signal Corps, 208, 211, 212-13, 265
U. S. War Dept., 147-65, 207-209, 213, 226, 305 n.

Vanderbilt, Cornelius, 270
Veblen, Thorstein, 5
Victor Emmanuel of Italy, 256
Voisin, Gabriel, 168-69

Waddell, Theodore, 146
Wainwright, L. M., 90
Walcott, Dr. Charles D., 301-309, 314-15, 318, 325
warping mechanism, 63-66, 79, 81, 132-33
Washington (D. C.) *Post*, 105, 109
Weaver, Henry M., 175, 207
Weaver, Henry, Jr., 175-79, 180, 182, 192
Webbert brothers, 145
Webbert, Mr., 115
Weber, William, 145
Weiller, Lazare, 213, 255
Weiller, Mme., 248
"well-digging," 81
Welsh, A. L., 275
West Side News, 36
Westcott, Robert, 95
Western Society of Engineers, 73, 291; *Journal*, 75, 291
Whitfield, Forrest, 32
Whitney, Harry Payne, 286
Wilhelm, Kaiser, 204, 256-57, 262, 264
Wilson, Mary, 25
wind-tunnel, 74-78
woodcuts, 29
Wright brothers:
  NOTE: This entry covers joint activities only. For individual activities, *see below*—Wright, Orville, and Wright, Wilbur. *See also* Wright Co., W. medals, W. monuments, W. patents, W. planes, W. records, etc., below.
  Ancestors and parents, 19-22; boyhood, 5-18, 23-28; early interest in mechanics, 5-9, 25; lathe, 12-13; circuses, 15-18, 33-34; reading, 26-27; weekly paper, 38; start bicycle business, 38-39; begin manufacture and repair work, 39-44
  Early interest in aeronautics, 45; reading on it, 46-47; experiments in building gliders, 48-55; first Kitty Hawk experiments (1901), 55-72; make wind-tunnels, 74-78; at K. H. (1902), 79; meet tail-spin problem, 81-83
  Develop engine, 84-90; transmission and propeller problems, 89-90; power flights at K. H. (1903), 90-95; first successful flight, 95-103; get

flying field near Dayton, 122-23; early public trials, 124-26; track and launching problems, 127-29; improve records, 130, 137-38; first complete circular flight, 130, 142; their first three planes described, 84-94, 112-13, 121-22, 130-34
  Early relations with public and press, 103-11, 134-46; first eye-witness story printed, 142-43; early dealings with U. S. and British govts., 147-65; abandon project to demonstrate at Jamestown, 160-61
  Their work discussed in France, 166-71; asked for information and prices, 171-73; their letter shown at Aéro Club, 174-75; visited by Weaver, and demonstrate for him, 175-79; investigated by Coquelle, 179-80; approached by Ferber for French govt., 182-83; visited by Fordyce, 183-85; visited by French Commission, 187-91; by Alexander, 191; by *Herald* reporter, 191-92; meet Flint in N. Y., 194-96; go to Paris, 202-204; to Berlin, 204-206
  Negotiations with U. S. War Dept., 208-14; their bid accepted, 211-12; add improvements to 1905 plane, 214-15; go to K. H., 215-25; publicity begins, 216-25; in France (1909), 250-53; to Rome, 255; plan formation of German Wright company, 257; to Le Mans for gift bronze, 257-58; to London for medals, etc., 258; to Washington for Aero Club medals, 258
  Return to Dayton celebrated, 258-59; get Govt. bonus after Fort Meyer tests, 260; organize The Wright Company, 268-71; their only joint flight, 276; build house at Hawthorn Hill, 282
Wright, "Buster," 281
Wright Company, 268-71, 278, 279, 281, 283, 285, 286, 288, 295, 296 (*see also* French—German—British Wright Co.)
Wright Cycle Co., 39-44, 77, 114, 120-21, 148, 176, 271
Wright, Dan, 21-22
Wright, Mrs. Dan, 21
Wright exhibition flights, charges for, 277
Wright, Katharine, 13, 23, 37, 47, 106, 113, 217, 250-53, 261, 262, 266, 280, 284
Wright, Lorin, 22, 25, 31, 81, 106, 281
Wright medals, prizes, etc., 248-49, 250, 257-58, 259, 264
Wright, Mrs. Milton, 5, 6, 7, 11, 20, 22, 26, 34, 91
Wright, Rev. Milton, 5-8, 11, 21-23, 26, 27, 103, 106, 107, 115, 259, 276-77, 278

Wright monuments—Kitty Hawk, 221; Pau, 250; Dayton, 275 n.

Wright, Orville
  NOTE: For joint activities with Wilbur, *see above,* Wright brothers.
  Birth, 23; boyhood enterprises, 7, 9-12, 13-15; schooling, 24-25, 37; letter-press, 29; printing work, 30-38; builds press, 34-36; interest in bicycle racing, 38; starts bicycle business, 38-44; illness, 46; first trip to Kitty Hawk, 61-72; makes wind-tunnel, 74; his story of first successful power flight, 96-102; telegram announcing it, 103-104
  Goes to Europe, 202-206; orders engines in Paris, 206; to K. H. for practice (1908), 216-25; to Fort Myer for tests (1908), 226-32; establishes new records, 229; to France, 250; in train accident, 250
  Govt. trials at Fort Myer (1910), 260; goes to Germany, 261-64; in Paris, investigates French Wright company, 266-67; trains pilots in Alabama, 274; opens flying school at Dayton, 275; further experiments at K. H., 281; succeeds W. as pres. of The Wright Co., 283; last trip to Europe (1913), 284; acquires almost complete ownership of Company, 285; and sells entire interest, 285-86, 296
  Relations and correspondence with Glenn Curtiss, 288-96, 308-33 (*see also* lawsuits and Wright patents); dealings with Smithsonian in regard to Langley machine, 307-33
  Style of flying, 276; flying dress, 275-76; memory, 202; effective demonstration at a patent-suit trial, 297-98; comment on cyclists' notions about steering, 298-99

Wright patents, 49, 83, 112, 130, 271, 273, 281, 284, 287-99

Wright planes: Kitty Hawk (1903), 84-94, 112-13, 300, 315, 318; 1904 model, 121-22, 170; 1905 model, 130-34, 214-15; 1907 model, 202, 204, 206, 233, 234-53; plane sold to U. S. Signal Corps, 208-13, 226-32; planes built in Europe from parts sent over, 255; Model B, 285

Wright planes, prices of, 172-73, 184-85, 208, 211-12, 282

Wright records, 228-29, 238, 240, 263, 264, 281

Wright, Reuchlin, 22, 113

Wright, Wilbur
  NOTE: For joint activities with Orville, *see above,* Wright brothers.
  Birth, 22; boyhood enterprises, 7, 8-9, 12-13, 15; schooling, 23-24; illness, 26; joins O. in printing newspaper, 37-38; in bicycle business, 38-44; makes warping device for glider, 49-50; goes to Kitty Hawk, 58-72; makes Chicago address, 73-75
  Goes to England, 196-97; Paris, 197-204; Berlin, 204-206; appears before U. S. Ordnance Board, and bids, 208; to K. H. (1908), 215-25; to France for demonstrations, 226, 227, 233-53; his records, 238, 240; at Le Mans, 234-44; guest of Aéro Club (Sarthe), 244-45; wins altitude prizes, 248-49, 250; at Pau, 250-53; to Rome, 255; trains Italian flyers, 255-56
  Flies at Hudson-Fulton Celebration, 265; begins training U. S. pilots, 265-66; last flight as pilot, 276; dealings with Smithsonian in regard to Langley machine, 301-307; illness and death, 282-83
  Character, 235, 236, 241-43; memory, 204; athletic activities, 38

Zahm, Dr. A. F., 309, 322-25
Zens, Ernest, 245
Zeppelin airships, 228
Zeppelin, Count Ferdinand von, 262

A CATALOG OF SELECTED
DOVER BOOKS
IN ALL FIELDS OF INTEREST

A CATALOG OF SELECTED DOVER
BOOKS IN ALL FIELDS OF INTEREST

DRAWINGS OF REMBRANDT, edited by Seymour Slive. Updated Lippmann, Hofstede de Groot edition, with definitive scholarly apparatus. All portraits, biblical sketches, landscapes, nudes. Oriental figures, classical studies, together with selection of work by followers. 550 illustrations. Total of 630pp. 9⅛ × 12¼.
21485-0, 21486-9 Pa., Two-vol. set $25.00

GHOST AND HORROR STORIES OF AMBROSE BIERCE, Ambrose Bierce. 24 tales vividly imagined, strangely prophetic, and decades ahead of their time in technical skill: "The Damned Thing," "An Inhabitant of Carcosa," "The Eyes of the Panther," "Moxon's Master," and 20 more. 199pp. 5⅜ × 8½.   20767-6 Pa. $3.95

ETHICAL WRITINGS OF MAIMONIDES, Maimonides. Most significant ethical works of great medieval sage, newly translated for utmost precision, readability. Laws Concerning Character Traits, Eight Chapters, more. 192pp. 5⅜ × 8½.
24522-5 Pa. $4.50

THE EXPLORATION OF THE COLORADO RIVER AND ITS CANYONS, J. W. Powell. Full text of Powell's 1,000-mile expedition down the fabled Colorado in 1869. Superb account of terrain, geology, vegetation, Indians, famine, mutiny, treacherous rapids, mighty canyons, during exploration of last unknown part of continental U.S. 400pp. 5⅜ × 8½.   20094-9 Pa. $6.95

HISTORY OF PHILOSOPHY, Julián Marías. Clearest one-volume history on the market. Every major philosopher and dozens of others, to Existentialism and later. 505pp. 5⅜ × 8½.   21739-6 Pa. $8.50

ALL ABOUT LIGHTNING, Martin A. Uman. Highly readable non-technical survey of nature and causes of lightning, thunderstorms, ball lightning, St. Elmo's Fire, much more. Illustrated. 192pp. 5⅜ × 8½.   25237-X Pa. $5.95

SAILING ALONE AROUND THE WORLD, Captain Joshua Slocum. First man to sail around the world, alone, in small boat. One of great feats of seamanship told in delightful manner. 67 illustrations. 294pp. 5⅜ × 8½.   20326-3 Pa. $4.95

LETTERS AND NOTES ON THE MANNERS, CUSTOMS AND CONDITIONS OF THE NORTH AMERICAN INDIANS, George Catlin. Classic account of life among Plains Indians: ceremonies, hunt, warfare, etc. 312 plates. 572pp. of text. 6⅛ × 9¼.   22118-0, 22119-9 Pa. Two-vol. set $15.90

ALASKA: The Harriman Expedition, 1899, John Burroughs, John Muir, et al. Informative, engrossing accounts of two-month, 9,000-mile expedition. Native peoples, wildlife, forests, geography, salmon industry, glaciers, more. Profusely illustrated. 240 black-and-white line drawings. 124 black-and-white photographs. 3 maps. Index. 576pp. 5⅜ × 8½.   25109-8 Pa. $11.95

CATALOG OF DOVER BOOKS

THE BOOK OF BEASTS: Being a Translation from a Latin Bestiary of the Twelfth Century, T. H. White. Wonderful catalog real and fanciful beasts: manticore, griffin, phoenix, amphivius, jaculus, many more. White's witty erudite commentary on scientific, historical aspects. Fascinating glimpse of medieval mind. Illustrated. 296pp. 5⅜ × 8¼. (Available in U.S. only)   24609-4 Pa. $5.95

FRANK LLOYD WRIGHT: ARCHITECTURE AND NATURE With 160 Illustrations, Donald Hoffmann. Profusely illustrated study of influence of nature—especially prairie—on Wright's designs for Fallingwater, Robie House, Guggenheim Museum, other masterpieces. 96pp. 9¼ × 10¾.   25098-9 Pa. $7.95

FRANK LLOYD WRIGHT'S FALLINGWATER, Donald Hoffmann. Wright's famous waterfall house: planning and construction of organic idea. History of site, owners, Wright's personal involvement. Photographs of various stages of building. Preface by Edgar Kaufmann, Jr. 100 illustrations. 112pp. 9¼ × 10.

23671-4 Pa. $7.95

YEARS WITH FRANK LLOYD WRIGHT: Apprentice to Genius, Edgar Tafel. Insightful memoir by a former apprentice presents a revealing portrait of Wright the man, the inspired teacher, the greatest American architect. 372 black-and-white illustrations. Preface. Index. vi + 228pp. 8¼ × 11.   24801-1 Pa. $9.95

THE STORY OF KING ARTHUR AND HIS KNIGHTS, Howard Pyle. Enchanting version of King Arthur fable has delighted generations with imaginative narratives of exciting adventures and unforgettable illustrations by the author. 41 illustrations. xviii + 313pp. 6⅛ × 9¼.   21445-1 Pa. $5.95

THE GODS OF THE EGYPTIANS, E. A. Wallis Budge. Thorough coverage of numerous gods of ancient Egypt by foremost Egyptologist. Information on evolution of cults, rites and gods; the cult of Osiris; the Book of the Dead and its rites; the sacred animals and birds; Heaven and Hell; and more. 956pp. 6⅛ × 9¼.
22055-9, 22056-7 Pa., Two-vol. set $21.90

A THEOLOGICO-POLITICAL TREATISE, Benedict Spinoza. Also contains unfinished *Political Treatise*. Great classic on religious liberty, theory of government on common consent. R. Elwes translation. Total of 421pp. 5⅜ × 8½.
20249-6 Pa. $6.95

INCIDENTS OF TRAVEL IN CENTRAL AMERICA, CHIAPAS, AND YUCATAN, John L. Stephens. Almost single-handed discovery of Maya culture; exploration of ruined cities, monuments, temples; customs of Indians. 115 drawings. 892pp. 5⅜ × 8½.   22404-X, 22405-8 Pa., Two-vol. set $15.90

LOS CAPRICHOS, Francisco Goya. 80 plates of wild, grotesque monsters and caricatures. Prado manuscript included. 183pp. 6⅜ × 9⅜.   22384-1 Pa. $4.95

AUTOBIOGRAPHY: The Story of My Experiments with Truth, Mohandas K. Gandhi. Not hagiography, but Gandhi in his own words. Boyhood, legal studies, purification, the growth of the Satyagraha (nonviolent protest) movement. Critical, inspiring work of the man who freed India. 480pp. 5⅜ × 8½. (Available in U.S. only)
24593-4 Pa. $6.95

ILLUSTRATED DICTIONARY OF HISTORIC ARCHITECTURE, edited by
Cyril M. Harris. Extraordinary compendium of clear, concise definitions for over
5,000 important architectural terms complemented by over 2,000 line drawings.
Covers full spectrum of architecture from ancient ruins to 20th-century Modernism.
Preface. 592pp. 7½ × 9⅜.   24444-X Pa. $14.95

THE NIGHT BEFORE CHRISTMAS, Clement Moore. Full text, and woodcuts
from original 1848 book. Also critical, historical material. 19 illustrations. 40pp.
4⅝ × 6.   22797-9 Pa. $2.50

THE LESSON OF JAPANESE ARCHITECTURE: 165 Photographs, Jiro
Harada. Memorable gallery of 165 photographs taken in the 1930's of exquisite
Japanese homes of the well-to-do and historic buildings. 13 line diagrams. 192pp.
8⅜ × 11¼.   24778-3 Pa. $8.95

THE AUTOBIOGRAPHY OF CHARLES DARWIN AND SELECTED LET-
TERS, edited by Francis Darwin. The fascinating life of eccentric genius composed
of an intimate memoir by Darwin (intended for his children); commentary by his
son, Francis; hundreds of fragments from notebooks, journals, papers; and letters to
and from Lyell, Hooker, Huxley, Wallace and Henslow. xi + 365pp. 5⅜ × 8.
                                                            20479-0 Pa. $5.95

WONDERS OF THE SKY: Observing Rainbows, Comets, Eclipses, the Stars and
Other Phenomena, Fred Schaaf. Charming, easy-to-read poetic guide to all manner
of celestial events visible to the naked eye. Mock suns, glories, Belt of Venus, more.
Illustrated. 299pp. 5¼ × 8¼.   24402-4 Pa. $7.95

BURNHAM'S CELESTIAL HANDBOOK, Robert Burnham, Jr. Thorough guide
to the stars beyond our solar system. Exhaustive treatment. Alphabetical by
constellation: Andromeda to Cetus in Vol. 1; Chamaeleon to Orion in Vol. 2; and
Pavo to Vulpecula in Vol. 3. Hundreds of illustrations. Index in Vol. 3. 2,000pp.
6⅛ × 9¼.   23567-X, 23568-8, 23673-0 Pa., Three-vol. set $37.85

STAR NAMES: Their Lore and Meaning, Richard Hinckley Allen. Fascinating
history of names various cultures have given to constellations and literary and
folkloristic uses that have been made of stars. Indexes to subjects. Arabic and Greek
names. Biblical references. Bibliography. 563pp. 5⅜ × 8½.   21079-0 Pa. $7.95

THIRTY YEARS THAT SHOOK PHYSICS: The Story of Quantum Theory,
George Gamow. Lucid, accessible introduction to influential theory of energy and
matter. Careful explanations of Dirac's anti-particles, Bohr's model of the atom,
much more. 12 plates. Numerous drawings. 240pp. 5⅜ × 8½.   24895-X Pa. $4.95

CHINESE DOMESTIC FURNITURE IN PHOTOGRAPHS AND MEASURED
DRAWINGS, Gustav Ecke. A rare volume, now affordably priced for antique
collectors, furniture buffs and art historians. Detailed review of styles ranging from
early Shang to late Ming. Unabridged republication. 161 black-and-white drawings, photos. Total of 224pp. 8⅝ × 11¼. (Available in U.S. only) 25171-3 Pa. $12.95

VINCENT VAN GOGH: A Biography, Julius Meier-Graefe. Dynamic, penetrat-
ing study of artist's life, relationship with brother, Theo, painting techniques,
travels, more. Readable, engrossing. 160pp. 5⅜ × 8½. (Available in U.S. only)
                                                            25253-1 Pa. $3.95

HOW TO WRITE, Gertrude Stein. Gertrude Stein claimed anyone could understand her unconventional writing—here are clues to help. Fascinating improvisations, language experiments, explanations illuminate Stein's craft and the art of writing. Total of 414pp. 4⅝ × 6⅜. 23144-5 Pa. $5.95

ADVENTURES AT SEA IN THE GREAT AGE OF SAIL: Five Firsthand Narratives, edited by Elliot Snow. Rare true accounts of exploration, whaling, shipwreck, fierce natives, trade, shipboard life, more. 33 illustrations. Introduction. 353pp. 5⅜ × 8½. 25177-2 Pa. $7.95

THE HERBAL OR GENERAL HISTORY OF PLANTS, John Gerard. Classic descriptions of about 2,850 plants—with over 2,700 illustrations—includes Latin and English names, physical descriptions, varieties, time and place of growth, more. 2,706 illustrations. xlv + 1,678pp. 8½ × 12¼. 23147-X Cloth. $75.00

DOROTHY AND THE WIZARD IN OZ, L. Frank Baum. Dorothy and the Wizard visit the center of the Earth, where people are vegetables, glass houses grow and Oz characters reappear. Classic sequel to *Wizard of Oz*. 256pp. 5⅜ × 8. 24714-7 Pa. $4.95

SONGS OF EXPERIENCE: Facsimile Reproduction with 26 Plates in Full Color, William Blake. This facsimile of Blake's original "Illuminated Book" reproduces 26 full-color plates from a rare 1826 edition. Includes "The Tyger," "London," "Holy Thursday," and other immortal poems. 26 color plates. Printed text of poems. 48pp. 5¼ × 7. 24636-1 Pa. $3.50

SONGS OF INNOCENCE, William Blake. The first and most popular of Blake's famous "Illuminated Books," in a facsimile edition reproducing all 31 brightly colored plates. Additional printed text of each poem. 64pp. 5¼ × 7. 22764-2 Pa. $3.50

PRECIOUS STONES, Max Bauer. Classic, thorough study of diamonds, rubies, emeralds, garnets, etc.: physical character, occurrence, properties, use, similar topics. 20 plates, 8 in color. 94 figures. 659pp. 6⅛ × 9¼. 21910-0, 21911-9 Pa., Two-vol. set $15.90

ENCYCLOPEDIA OF VICTORIAN NEEDLEWORK, S. F. A. Caulfeild and Blanche Saward. Full, precise descriptions of stitches, techniques for dozens of needlecrafts—most exhaustive reference of its kind. Over 800 figures. Total of 679pp. 8⅜ × 11. Two volumes. Vol. 1 22800-2 Pa. $11.95
Vol. 2 22801-0 Pa. $11.95

THE MARVELOUS LAND OF OZ, L. Frank Baum. Second Oz book, the Scarecrow and Tin Woodman are back with hero named Tip, Oz magic. 136 illustrations. 287pp. 5⅜ × 8½. 20692-0 Pa. $5.95

WILD FOWL DECOYS, Joel Barber. Basic book on the subject, by foremost authority and collector. Reveals history of decoy making and rigging, place in American culture, different kinds of decoys, how to make them, and how to use them. 140 plates. 156pp. 7⅞ × 10¾. 20011-6 Pa. $8.95

HISTORY OF LACE, Mrs. Bury Palliser. Definitive, profusely illustrated chronicle of lace from earliest times to late 19th century. Laces of Italy, Greece, England, France, Belgium, etc. Landmark of needlework scholarship. 266 illustrations. 672pp. 6⅛ × 9¼. 24742-2 Pa. $14.95

ILLUSTRATED GUIDE TO SHAKER FURNITURE, Robert Meader. All furniture and appurtenances, with much on unknown local styles. 235 photos. 146pp. 9 × 12.   22819-3 Pa. $7.95

WHALE SHIPS AND WHALING: A Pictorial Survey, George Francis Dow. Over 200 vintage engravings, drawings, photographs of barks, brigs, cutters, other vessels. Also harpoons, lances, whaling guns, many other artifacts. Comprehensive text by foremost authority. 207 black-and-white illustrations. 288pp. 6 × 9.
24808-9 Pa. $8.95

THE BERTRAMS, Anthony Trollope. Powerful portrayal of blind self-will and thwarted ambition includes one of Trollope's most heartrending love stories. 497pp. 5⅜ × 8½.   25119-5 Pa. $8.95

ADVENTURES WITH A HAND LENS, Richard Headstrom. Clearly written guide to observing and studying flowers and grasses, fish scales, moth and insect wings, egg cases, buds, feathers, seeds, leaf scars, moss, molds, ferns, common crystals, etc.—all with an ordinary, inexpensive magnifying glass. 209 exact line drawings aid in your discoveries. 220pp. 5⅜ × 8½.   23330-8 Pa. $4.50

RODIN ON ART AND ARTISTS, Auguste Rodin. Great sculptor's candid, wide-ranging comments on meaning of art; great artists; relation of sculpture to poetry, painting, music; philosophy of life, more. 76 superb black-and-white illustrations of Rodin's sculpture, drawings and prints. 119pp. 8⅜ × 11¼.   24487-3 Pa. $6.95

FIFTY CLASSIC FRENCH FILMS, 1912–1982: A Pictorial Record, Anthony Slide. Memorable stills from Grand Illusion, Beauty and the Beast, Hiroshima, Mon Amour, many more. Credits, plot synopses, reviews, etc. 160pp. 8¼ × 11.
25256-6 Pa. $11.95

THE PRINCIPLES OF PSYCHOLOGY, William James. Famous long course complete, unabridged. Stream of thought, time perception, memory, experimental methods; great work decades ahead of its time. 94 figures. 1,391pp. 5⅜ × 8½.
20381-6, 20382-4 Pa., Two-vol. set $19.90

BODIES IN A BOOKSHOP, R. T. Campbell. Challenging mystery of blackmail and murder with ingenious plot and superbly drawn characters. In the best tradition of British suspense fiction. 192pp. 5⅜ × 8½.   24720-1 Pa. $3.95

CALLAS: PORTRAIT OF A PRIMA DONNA, George Jellinek. Renowned commentator on the musical scene chronicles incredible career and life of the most controversial, fascinating, influential operatic personality of our time. 64 black-and-white photographs. 416pp. 5⅜ × 8¼.   25047-4 Pa. $7.95

GEOMETRY, RELATIVITY AND THE FOURTH DIMENSION, Rudolph Rucker. Exposition of fourth dimension, concepts of relativity as Flatland characters continue adventures. Popular, easily followed yet accurate, profound. 141 illustrations. 133pp. 5⅜ × 8½.   23400-2 Pa. $3.50

HOUSEHOLD STORIES BY THE BROTHERS GRIMM, with pictures by Walter Crane. 53 classic stories—Rumpelstiltskin, Rapunzel, Hansel and Gretel, the Fisherman and his Wife, Snow White, Tom Thumb, Sleeping Beauty, Cinderella, and so much more—lavishly illustrated with original 19th century drawings. 114 illustrations. x + 269pp. 5⅜ × 8½.   21080-4 Pa. $4.50

SUNDIALS, Albert Waugh. Far and away the best, most thorough coverage of ideas, mathematics concerned, types, construction, adjusting anywhere. Over 100 illustrations. 230pp. 5⅜ × 8½. 22947-5 Pa. $4.50

PICTURE HISTORY OF THE NORMANDIE: With 190 Illustrations, Frank O. Braynard. Full story of legendary French ocean liner: Art Deco interiors, design innovations, furnishings, celebrities, maiden voyage, tragic fire, much more. Extensive text. 144pp. 8⅞ × 11¾. 25257-4 Pa. $9.95

THE FIRST AMERICAN COOKBOOK: A Facsimile of "American Cookery," 1796, Amelia Simmons. Facsimile of the first American-written cookbook published in the United States contains authentic recipes for colonial favorites— pumpkin pudding, winter squash pudding, spruce beer, Indian slapjacks, and more. Introductory Essay and Glossary of colonial cooking terms. 80pp. 5⅜ × 8½. 24710-4 Pa. $3.50

101 PUZZLES IN THOUGHT AND LOGIC, C. R. Wylie, Jr. Solve murders and robberies, find out which fishermen are liars, how a blind man could possibly identify a color—purely by your own reasoning! 107pp. 5⅜ × 8½. 20367-0 Pa. $2.50

THE BOOK OF WORLD-FAMOUS MUSIC—CLASSICAL, POPULAR AND FOLK, James J. Fuld. Revised and enlarged republication of landmark work in musico-bibliography. Full information about nearly 1,000 songs and compositions including first lines of music and lyrics. New supplement. Index. 800pp. 5⅜ × 8¼. 24857-7 Pa. $14.95

ANTHROPOLOGY AND MODERN LIFE, Franz Boas. Great anthropologist's classic treatise on race and culture. Introduction by Ruth Bunzel. Only inexpensive paperback edition. 255pp. 5⅜ × 8½. 25245-0 Pa. $5.95

THE TALE OF PETER RABBIT, Beatrix Potter. The inimitable Peter's terrifying adventure in Mr. McGregor's garden, with all 27 wonderful, full-color Potter illustrations. 55pp. 4¼ × 5½. (Available in U.S. only) 22827-4 Pa. $1.75

THREE PROPHETIC SCIENCE FICTION NOVELS, H. G. Wells. *When the Sleeper Wakes, A Story of the Days to Come* and *The Time Machine* (full version). 335pp. 5⅜ × 8½. (Available in U.S. only) 20605-X Pa. $5.95

APICIUS COOKERY AND DINING IN IMPERIAL ROME, edited and translated by Joseph Dommers Vehling. Oldest known cookbook in existence offers readers a clear picture of what foods Romans ate, how they prepared them, etc. 49 illustrations. 301pp. 6⅛ × 9¼. 23563-7 Pa. $6.50

SHAKESPEARE LEXICON AND QUOTATION DICTIONARY, Alexander Schmidt. Full definitions, locations, shades of meaning of every word in plays and poems. More than 50,000 exact quotations. 1,485pp. 6½ × 9¼. 22726-X, 22727-8 Pa., Two-vol. set $27.90

THE WORLD'S GREAT SPEECHES, edited by Lewis Copeland and Lawrence W. Lamm. Vast collection of 278 speeches from Greeks to 1970. Powerful and effective models; unique look at history. 842pp. 5⅜ × 8½. 20468-5 Pa. $11.95

CATALOG OF DOVER BOOKS

PLANTS OF THE BIBLE, Harold N. Moldenke and Alma L. Moldenke. Standard reference to all 230 plants mentioned in Scriptures. Latin name, biblical reference, uses, modern identity, much more. Unsurpassed encyclopedic resource for scholars, botanists, nature lovers, students of Bible. Bibliography. Indexes. 123 black-and-white illustrations. 384pp. 6 × 9.
25069-5 Pa. $8.95

FAMOUS AMERICAN WOMEN: A Biographical Dictionary from Colonial Times to the Present, Robert McHenry, ed. From Pocahontas to Rosa Parks, 1,035 distinguished American women documented in separate biographical entries. Accurate, up-to-date data, numerous categories, spans 400 years. Indices. 493pp. 6½ × 9¼.
24523-3 Pa. $9.95

THE FABULOUS INTERIORS OF THE GREAT OCEAN LINERS IN HIS-TORIC PHOTOGRAPHS, William H. Miller, Jr. Some 200 superb photographs capture exquisite interiors of world's great "floating palaces"—1890's to 1980's: Titanic, Ile de France, Queen Elizabeth, United States, Europa, more. Approx. 200 black-and-white photographs. Captions. Text. Introduction. 160pp. 8⅜ × 11¼.
24756-2 Pa. $9.95

THE GREAT LUXURY LINERS, 1927–1954: A Photographic Record, William H. Miller, Jr. Nostalgic tribute to heyday of ocean liners. 186 photos of Ile de France, Normandie, Leviathan, Queen Elizabeth, United States, many others. Interior and exterior views. Introduction. Captions. 160pp. 9 × 12.
24056-8 Pa. $9.95

A NATURAL HISTORY OF THE DUCKS, John Charles Phillips. Great landmark of ornithology offers complete detailed coverage of nearly 200 species and subspecies of ducks: gadwall, sheldrake, merganser, pintail, many more. 74 full-color plates, 102 black-and-white. Bibliography. Total of 1,920pp. 8⅜ × 11¼.
25141-1, 25142-X Cloth. Two-vol. set $100.00

THE SEAWEED HANDBOOK: An Illustrated Guide to Seaweeds from North Carolina to Canada, Thomas F. Lee. Concise reference covers 78 species. Scientific and common names, habitat, distribution, more. Finding keys for easy identifica-tion. 224pp. 5⅜ × 8½.
25215-9 Pa. $5.95

THE TEN BOOKS OF ARCHITECTURE: The 1755 Leoni Edition, Leon Battista Alberti. Rare classic helped introduce the glories of ancient architecture to the Renaissance. 68 black-and-white plates. 336pp. 8⅜ × 11¼.
25239-6 Pa. $14.95

MISS MACKENZIE, Anthony Trollope. Minor masterpieces by Victorian master unmasks many truths about life in 19th-century England. First inexpensive edition in years. 392pp. 5⅜ × 8½.
25201-9 Pa. $7.95

THE RIME OF THE ANCIENT MARINER, Gustave Doré, Samuel Taylor Coleridge. Dramatic engravings considered by many to be his greatest work. The terrifying space of the open sea, the storms and whirlpools of an unknown ocean, the ice of Antarctica, more—all rendered in a powerful, chilling manner. Full text. 38 plates. 77pp. 9¼ × 12.
22305-1 Pa. $4.95

THE EXPEDITIONS OF ZEBULON MONTGOMERY PIKE, Zebulon Mont-gomery Pike. Fascinating first-hand accounts (1805–6) of exploration of Missis-sippi River, Indian wars, capture by Spanish dragoons, much more. 1,088pp. 5⅜ × 8½.
25254-X, 25255-8 Pa. Two-vol. set $23.90

A CONCISE HISTORY OF PHOTOGRAPHY: Third Revised Edition, Helmut Gernsheim. Best one-volume history—camera obscura, photochemistry, daguerreotypes, evolution of cameras, film, more. Also artistic aspects—landscape, portraits, fine art, etc. 281 black-and-white photographs. 26 in color. 176pp. 8⅜ × 11¼. 25128-4 Pa. $12.95

THE DORÉ BIBLE ILLUSTRATIONS, Gustave Doré. 241 detailed plates from the Bible: the Creation scenes, Adam and Eve, Flood, Babylon, battle sequences, life of Jesus, etc. Each plate is accompanied by the verses from the King James version of the Bible. 241pp. 9 × 12. 23004-X Pa. $8.95

HUGGER-MUGGER IN THE LOUVRE, Elliot Paul. Second Homer Evans mystery-comedy. Theft at the Louvre involves sleuth in hilarious, madcap caper. "A knockout."—Books. 336pp. 5⅜ × 8½. 25185-3 Pa. $5.95

FLATLAND, E. A. Abbott. Intriguing and enormously popular science-fiction classic explores the complexities of trying to survive as a two-dimensional being in a three-dimensional world. Amusingly illustrated by the author. 16 illustrations. 103pp. 5⅜ × 8½. 20001-9 Pa. $2.25

THE HISTORY OF THE LEWIS AND CLARK EXPEDITION, Meriwether Lewis and William Clark, edited by Elliott Coues. Classic edition of Lewis and Clark's day-by-day journals that later became the basis for U.S. claims to Oregon and the West. Accurate and invaluable geographical, botanical, biological, meteorological and anthropological material. Total of 1,508pp. 5⅜ × 8½. 21268-8, 21269-6, 21270-X Pa. Three-vol. set $25.50

LANGUAGE, TRUTH AND LOGIC, Alfred J. Ayer. Famous, clear introduction to Vienna, Cambridge schools of Logical Positivism. Role of philosophy, elimination of metaphysics, nature of analysis, etc. 160pp. 5⅜ × 8½. (Available in U.S. and Canada only) 20010-8 Pa. $2.95

MATHEMATICS FOR THE NONMATHEMATICIAN, Morris Kline. Detailed, college-level treatment of mathematics in cultural and historical context, with numerous exercises. For liberal arts students. Preface. Recommended Reading Lists. Tables. Index. Numerous black-and-white figures. xvi + 641pp. 5⅜ × 8½. 24823-2 Pa. $11.95

28 SCIENCE FICTION STORIES, H. G. Wells. Novels, *Star Begotten* and *Men Like Gods*, plus 26 short stories: "Empire of the Ants," "A Story of the Stone Age," "The Stolen Bacillus," "In the Abyss," etc. 915pp. 5⅜ × 8½. (Available in U.S. only) 20265-8 Cloth. $10.95

HANDBOOK OF PICTORIAL SYMBOLS, Rudolph Modley. 3,250 signs and symbols, many systems in full; official or heavy commercial use. Arranged by subject. Most in Pictorial Archive series. 143pp. 8⅜ × 11. 23357-X Pa. $5.95

INCIDENTS OF TRAVEL IN YUCATAN, John L. Stephens. Classic (1843) exploration of jungles of Yucatan, looking for evidences of Maya civilization. Travel adventures, Mexican and Indian culture, etc. Total of 669pp. 5⅜ × 8½. 20926-1, 20927-X Pa., Two-vol. set $9.90

CHRISTMAS CUSTOMS AND TRADITIONS, Clement A. Miles. Origin, evolution, significance of religious, secular practices. Caroling, gifts, yule logs, much more. Full, scholarly yet fascinating; non-sectarian. 400pp. 5⅜ × 8½.
23354-5 Pa. $6.50

THE HUMAN FIGURE IN MOTION, Eadweard Muybridge. More than 4,500 stopped-action photos, in action series, showing undraped men, women, children jumping, lying down, throwing, sitting, wrestling, carrying, etc. 390pp. 7⅞ × 10⅝.
20204-6 Cloth. $19.95

THE MAN WHO WAS THURSDAY, Gilbert Keith Chesterton. Witty, fast-paced novel about a club of anarchists in turn-of-the-century London. Brilliant social, religious, philosophical speculations. 128pp. 5⅜ × 8½.
25121-7 Pa. $3.95

A CEZANNE SKETCHBOOK: Figures, Portraits, Landscapes and Still Lifes, Paul Cezanne. Great artist experiments with tonal effects, light, mass, other qualities in over 100 drawings. A revealing view of developing master painter, precursor of Cubism. 102 black-and-white illustrations. 144pp. 8¾ × 6⅜.
24790-2 Pa. $5.95

AN ENCYCLOPEDIA OF BATTLES: Accounts of Over 1,560 Battles from 1479 B.C. to the Present, David Eggenberger. Presents essential details of every major battle in recorded history, from the first battle of Megiddo in 1479 B.C. to Grenada in 1984. List of Battle Maps. New Appendix covering the years 1967–1984. Index. 99 illustrations. 544pp. 6½ × 9¼.
24913-1 Pa. $14.95

AN ETYMOLOGICAL DICTIONARY OF MODERN ENGLISH, Ernest Weekley. Richest, fullest work, by foremost British lexicographer. Detailed word histories. Inexhaustible. Total of 856pp. 6½ × 9¼.
21873-2, 21874-0 Pa., Two-vol. set $17.00

WEBSTER'S AMERICAN MILITARY BIOGRAPHIES, edited by Robert McHenry. Over 1,000 figures who shaped 3 centuries of American military history. Detailed biographies of Nathan Hale, Douglas MacArthur, Mary Hallaren, others. Chronologies of engagements, more. Introduction. Addenda. 1,033 entries in alphabetical order. xi + 548pp. 6½ × 9¼. (Available in U.S. only)
24758-9 Pa. $11.95

LIFE IN ANCIENT EGYPT, Adolf Erman. Detailed older account, with much not in more recent books: domestic life, religion, magic, medicine, commerce, and whatever else needed for complete picture. Many illustrations. 597pp. 5⅜ × 8½.
22632-8 Pa. $8.95

HISTORIC COSTUME IN PICTURES, Braun & Schneider. Over 1,450 costumed figures shown, covering a wide variety of peoples: kings, emperors, nobles, priests, servants, soldiers, scholars, townsfolk, peasants, merchants, courtiers, cavaliers, and more. 256pp. 8⅜ × 11¼.
23150-X Pa. $7.95

THE NOTEBOOKS OF LEONARDO DA VINCI, edited by J. P. Richter. Extracts from manuscripts reveal great genius; on painting, sculpture, anatomy, sciences, geography, etc. Both Italian and English. 186 ms. pages reproduced, plus 500 additional drawings, including studies for *Last Supper, Sforza* monument, etc. 860pp. 7⅞ × 10¾. (Available in U.S. only) 22572-0, 22573-9 Pa., Two-vol. set $25.90

THE ART NOUVEAU STYLE BOOK OF ALPHONSE MUCHA: All 72 Plates from "Documents Decoratifs" in Original Color, Alphonse Mucha. Rare copyright-free design portfolio by high priest of Art Nouveau. Jewelry, wallpaper, stained glass, furniture, figure studies, plant and animal motifs, etc. Only complete one-volume edition. 80pp. 9⅜ × 12¼. 24044-4 Pa. $8.95

ANIMALS: 1,419 COPYRIGHT-FREE ILLUSTRATIONS OF MAMMALS, BIRDS, FISH, INSECTS, ETC., edited by Jim Harter. Clear wood engravings present, in extremely lifelike poses, over 1,000 species of animals. One of the most extensive pictorial sourcebooks of its kind. Captions. Index. 284pp. 9 × 12. 23766-4 Pa. $9.95

OBELISTS FLY HIGH, C. Daly King. Masterpiece of American detective fiction, long out of print, involves murder on a 1935 transcontinental flight—"a very thrilling story"—NY Times. Unabridged and unaltered republication of the edition published by William Collins Sons & Co. Ltd., London, 1935. 288pp. 5⅜ × 8½. (Available in U.S. only) 25036-9 Pa. $4.95

VICTORIAN AND EDWARDIAN FASHION: A Photographic Survey, Alison Gernsheim. First fashion history completely illustrated by contemporary photographs. Full text plus 235 photos, 1840–1914, in which many celebrities appear. 240pp. 6½ × 9¼. 24205-6 Pa. $6.00

THE ART OF THE FRENCH ILLUSTRATED BOOK, 1700–1914, Gordon N. Ray. Over 630 superb book illustrations by Fragonard, Delacroix, Daumier, Doré, Grandville, Manet, Mucha, Steinlen, Toulouse-Lautrec and many others. Preface. Introduction. 633 halftones. Indices of artists, authors & titles, binders and provenances. Appendices. Bibliography. 608pp. 8⅜ × 11¼. 25086-5 Pa. $24.95

THE WONDERFUL WIZARD OF OZ, L. Frank Baum. Facsimile in full color of America's finest children's classic. 143 illustrations by W. W. Denslow. 267pp. 5⅜ × 8½. 20691-2 Pa. $5.95

FRONTIERS OF MODERN PHYSICS: New Perspectives on Cosmology, Relativity, Black Holes and Extraterrestrial Intelligence, Tony Rothman, et al. For the intelligent layman. Subjects include: cosmological models of the universe; black holes; the neutrino; the search for extraterrestrial intelligence. Introduction. 46 black-and-white illustrations. 192pp. 5⅜ × 8½. 24587-X Pa. $6.95

THE FRIENDLY STARS, Martha Evans Martin & Donald Howard Menzel. Classic text marshalls the stars together in an engaging, non-technical survey, presenting them as sources of beauty in night sky. 23 illustrations. Foreword. 2 star charts. Index. 147pp. 5⅜ × 8½. 21099-5 Pa. $3.50

FADS AND FALLACIES IN THE NAME OF SCIENCE, Martin Gardner. Fair, witty appraisal of cranks, quacks, and quackeries of science and pseudoscience: hollow earth, Velikovsky, orgone energy, Dianetics, flying saucers, Bridey Murphy, food and medical fads, etc. Revised, expanded In the Name of Science. "A very able and even-tempered presentation."—The New Yorker. 363pp. 5⅜ × 8. 20394-8 Pa. $6.50

ANCIENT EGYPT: ITS CULTURE AND HISTORY, J. E Manchip White. From pre-dynastics through Ptolemies: society, history, political structure, religion, daily life, literature, cultural heritage. 48 plates. 217pp. 5⅜ × 8½. 22548-8 Pa. $4.95

CATALOG OF DOVER BOOKS

SIR HARRY HOTSPUR OF HUMBLETHWAITE, Anthony Trollope. Incisive, unconventional psychological study of a conflict between a wealthy baronet, his idealistic daughter, and their scapegrace cousin. The 1870 novel in its first inexpensive edition in years. 250pp. 5⅜ × 8½. 24953-0 Pa. $5.95

LASERS AND HOLOGRAPHY, Winston E. Kock. Sound introduction to burgeoning field, expanded (1981) for second edition. Wave patterns, coherence, lasers, diffraction, zone plates, properties of holograms, recent advances. 84 illustrations. 160pp. 5⅜ × 8¼. (Except in United Kingdom) 24041-X Pa. $3.50

INTRODUCTION TO ARTIFICIAL INTELLIGENCE: SECOND, ENLARGED EDITION, Philip C. Jackson, Jr. Comprehensive survey of artificial intelligence—the study of how machines (computers) can be made to act intelligently. Includes introductory and advanced material. Extensive notes updating the main text. 132 black-and-white illustrations. 512pp. 5⅜ × 8½. 24864-X Pa. $8.95

HISTORY OF INDIAN AND INDONESIAN ART, Ananda K. Coomaraswamy. Over 400 illustrations illuminate classic study of Indian art from earliest Harappa finds to early 20th century. Provides philosophical, religious and social insights. 304pp. 6⅛ × 9⅜. 25005-9 Pa. $8.95

THE GOLEM, Gustav Meyrink. Most famous supernatural novel in modern European literature, set in Ghetto of Old Prague around 1890. Compelling story of mystical experiences, strange transformations, profound terror. 13 black-and-white illustrations. 224pp. 5⅜ × 8½. (Available in U.S. only) 25025-3 Pa. $5.95

ARMADALE, Wilkie Collins. Third great mystery novel by the author of *The Woman in White* and *The Moonstone*. Original magazine version with 40 illustrations. 597pp. 5⅜ × 8½. 23429-0 Pa. $9.95

PICTORIAL ENCYCLOPEDIA OF HISTORIC ARCHITECTURAL PLANS, DETAILS AND ELEMENTS: With 1,880 Line Drawings of Arches, Domes, Doorways, Facades, Gables, Windows, etc., John Theodore Haneman. Sourcebook of inspiration for architects, designers, others. Bibliography. Captions. 141pp. 9 × 12. 24605-1 Pa. $6.95

BENCHLEY LOST AND FOUND, Robert Benchley. Finest humor from early 30's, about pet peeves, child psychologists, post office and others. Mostly unavailable elsewhere. 73 illustrations by Peter Arno and others. 183pp. 5⅜ × 8½. 22410-4 Pa. $3.95

ERTÉ GRAPHICS, Erté. Collection of striking color graphics: *Seasons, Alphabet, Numerals, Aces* and *Precious Stones*. 50 plates, including 4 on covers. 48pp. 9⅜ × 12¼. 23580-7 Pa. $6.95

THE JOURNAL OF HENRY D. THOREAU, edited by Bradford Torrey, F. H. Allen. Complete reprinting of 14 volumes, 1837-61, over two million words; the sourcebooks for *Walden*, etc. Definitive. All original sketches, plus 75 photographs. 1,804pp. 8½ × 12¼. 20312-3, 20313-1 Cloth., Two-vol. set $80.00

CASTLES: THEIR CONSTRUCTION AND HISTORY, Sidney Toy. Traces castle development from ancient roots. Nearly 200 photographs and drawings illustrate moats, keeps, baileys, many other features. Caernarvon, Dover Castles, Hadrian's Wall, Tower of London, dozens more. 256pp. 5⅜ × 8¼. 24898-4 Pa. $5.95

CATALOG OF DOVER BOOKS

AMERICAN CLIPPER SHIPS: 1833–1858, Octavius T. Howe & Frederick C. Matthews. Fully-illustrated, encyclopedic review of 352 clipper ships from the period of America's greatest maritime supremacy. Introduction. 109 halftones. 5 black-and-white line illustrations. Index. Total of 928pp. 5⅜ × 8½.
25115-2, 25116-0 Pa., Two-vol. set $17.90

TOWARDS A NEW ARCHITECTURE, Le Corbusier. Pioneering manifesto by great architect, near legendary founder of "International School." Technical and aesthetic theories, views on industry, economics, relation of form to function, "mass-production spirit," much more. Profusely illustrated. Unabridged translation of 13th French edition. Introduction by Frederick Etchells. 320pp. 6⅛ × 9¼. (Available in U.S. only)
25023-7 Pa. $8.95

THE BOOK OF KELLS, edited by Blanche Cirker. Inexpensive collection of 32 full-color, full-page plates from the greatest illuminated manuscript of the Middle Ages, painstakingly reproduced from rare facsimile edition. Publisher's Note. Captions. 32pp. 9⅜ × 12¼.
24345-1 $4.95

BEST SCIENCE FICTION STORIES OF H. G. WELLS, H. G. Wells. Full novel *The Invisible Man*, plus 17 short stories: "The Crystal Egg," "Aepyornis Island," "The Strange Orchid," etc. 303pp. 5⅜ × 8½. (Available in U.S. only)
21531-8 Pa. $4.95

AMERICAN SAILING SHIPS: Their Plans and History, Charles G. Davis. Photos, construction details of schooners, frigates, clippers, other sailcraft of 18th to early 20th centuries—plus entertaining discourse on design, rigging, nautical lore, much more. 137 black-and-white illustrations. 240pp. 6⅛ × 9¼.
24658-2 Pa. $5.95

ENTERTAINING MATHEMATICAL PUZZLES, Martin Gardner. Selection of author's favorite conundrums involving arithmetic, money, speed, etc., with lively commentary. Complete solutions. 112pp. 5⅜ × 8½.
25211-6 Pa. $2.95

THE WILL TO BELIEVE, HUMAN IMMORTALITY, William James. Two books bound together. Effect of irrational on logical, and arguments for human immortality. 402pp. 5⅜ × 8½.
20291-7 Pa. $7.50

THE HAUNTED MONASTERY and THE CHINESE MAZE MURDERS, Robert Van Gulik. 2 full novels by Van Gulik continue adventures of Judge Dee and his companions. An evil Taoist monastery, seemingly supernatural events; overgrown topiary maze that hides strange crimes. Set in 7th-century China. 27 illustrations. 328pp. 5⅜ × 8½.
23502-5 Pa. $5.95

CELEBRATED CASES OF JUDGE DEE (DEE GOONG AN), translated by Robert Van Gulik. Authentic 18th-century Chinese detective novel; Dee and associates solve three interlocked cases. Led to Van Gulik's own stories with same characters. Extensive introduction. 9 illustrations. 237pp. 5⅜ × 8½.
23337-5 Pa. $4.95

Prices subject to change without notice.

Available at your book dealer or write for free catalog to Dept. GI, Dover Publications, Inc., 31 East 2nd St., Mineola, N.Y. 11501. Dover publishes more than 175 books each year on science, elementary and advanced mathematics, biology, music, art, literary history, social sciences and other areas.